F I R E P O W E R
SEA WARFARE

FIREPOWER
SEA WARFARE

EDITOR
CHRIS BISHOP

**CHARTWELL
BOOKS, INC.**

Published by
CHARTWELL BOOKS, INC.
A Division of **BOOK SALES, INC.**
114 Northfield Avenue
Edison, New Jersey 08837

Copyright ©1999 Orbis Publishing Ltd
Copyright ©1999 Aerospace Publishing Ltd

Some of this material has previously appeared in the Orbis reference set **'Firepower'**.

ISBN 0-7858-1087-0

Editorial and design by Brown Packaging Books Ltd
Bradley's Close
74-77 White Lion Street
London N1 9PF

Editor: Chris Bishop

Printed in Singapore

Contents

Introduction

Since the end of the Second World War the destructive power of warships has risen dramatically. The big gun has been replaced by the carrier-launched aircraft armed with bombs and torpedoes, although the 16-inch guns of the US Navy's battleships Iowa and Missouri were fired in anger in the Gulf War of 1991. The apparent dominance of the long-range anti-ship missile, particularly when launched from small fast attack craft, has proved to be something of a mirage. Far from being driven from the oceans by these 'mosquito craft', the big frigate and anti-air warfare destroyer have continued to flourish. The air crews of the US Navy's giant nuclear-powered carriers describe the launch of the full air group as 'doing the Big Godzilla' with good reason. The December 1998, Operation Desert Fox, strike against Iraq involved the launch of over 300 Tomahawk cruise missiles most launched by surface ships.

The firepower of naval aircraft includes long-range air-to-air missiles like the AIM-120 AMRAAM, laser-guided bombs, rockets and cluster-bombs. Most frigates and larger ships now have anti-ship missiles, in addition to any specialised weaponry for their mission, and the ship-launched helicopter provides mid-course guidance for long-range missile strikes as well as light missiles to attack 'soft' targets such as small craft. Since the end of the Cold War, major navies are adapting to the very different demands of littoral warfare, with greater emphasis on land-attack. At the same time, such operations are at risk from short-range ballistic weapons like the 'Scud', so a new generation of Theatre Ballistic Missile Defence weapons is being created. Naval warfare in the future promises to be much more destructive than anything yet seen.

Firepower: Sea Warfare gives detailed profiles of current vessels in service wsith the world's navies and documents first-hand accounts of missions from the officers who were in the thick of the action.

Left: The **John C. Stenis** *carries a Carrier Air Wing made up of nine squadron of aircraft – attack, electronic and anti-submarine – and has a total complement of 6,054 officers and men.*

A Federal German Navy Type 143A Gepard Fast Attack Craft. Each vessel is equipped with four Aerospatiale MM38 Exocet surface-to-surface missiles.

FAST ATTACK CRAFT

Racing through the sea, the fast missile craft is the quick-stinging raider of naval warfare.

Since the beginning of this century, fast attack craft have combined breathtaking performance with a heavy combat punch. The US Navy's 'Pegasus' class hydrofoil Taurus (PHM 3), seen here banking into a turn off Seattle, Washington, is one of the most advanced in the world. Armed with a 76-mm gun and eight Harpoon anti-ship missiles, it has a firepower that would not look out of place in a vessel five times its size.

The islands, some crowned with trees, others little more than rocky crags breaking the surface of the sea, are scattered across the water as if thrown down by a giant hand. Between them, narrow channels, treacherously shallow, create a maze of hidden waterways.

Several miles offshore, in the deep water, a big cruiser, crammed with the latest electronic detection equipment and bristling with missile launchers, passes confidently on its way. But, effectively hidden among the islands, a tiny vessel, only one hundredth of the cruiser's size, has launched one of its own

SS-N-2 'Styx' missiles.

Low over the water, the 'Styx' is already homing on its target before it is detected and the cruiser's crew can begin to bring their defences to bear on it. And meanwhile, as soon as the missile is fired, the attacker has moved, jinking a course at more than 40 knots

9

The end of the *Eilat*

21 October 1967. The crew of the Israeli
destroyer *Eilat* were confident. Four months
earlier, Israel's armed forces had smashed the
Arabs in the Six Day War, and now the flagship
of Israel's navy was cruising 20 kilometres off Port
Said. That confidence was a mistake. Two odd-
looking small craft were moving about the
harbour. Without warning, they launched missiles
from huge boxes mounted aft. Targetted on the
Israeli ship out in the Mediterranean, they settled
down on course. Minutes later, three out of four
missiles exploded, blowing the *Eilat* out of the
water. The Soviet-built 'Komar' class missile boats
of the Egyptian navy had just mounted the first
successful ship-to-ship missile engagement, and in
the process changed the face of war at sea.

FAST ATTACK CRAFT Reference File

235

FORMER USSR

'Osa' class

The USSR pioneered the small attack
craft armed with powerful anti-ship
missiles, and after early experience
with the 'Komar' class based on the
hull of the 'P6' class motor torpedo
boat, in 1961 moved to a larger type
offering greater seaworthiness as well
as a primary armament of four rather
than two SS-N-2 'Styx' missiles.

This is the **'Osa I'** class, which had
a full-load displacement of 215 tons, a
missile armament of four SS-N-2As in
four large enclosed bins (the two
units of the front pair angled to fire
upwards and 12° and the two units of
the rear pair at 15° to fire over the
front pair), and a powerplant of three
3000-kW (4,025-hp) M503A diesels
powering three shafts for a speed of

38 kt (70.5 km/h; 43.75 mph). The
'Osa II' class had small but significant
improvements, notably the use of
more capable missiles in neater bins,
more fuel and more powerful yet
considerably more reliable and fuel-
economical engines. Locally-produced
variants were Chinese **'Huangfen'**
class, the Finnish **'Tuima'** class and
the North Korean **'Sohu'** class.

Specification
'Osa II' class
Type: coastal guided-missile attack
and patrol craft
Displacement: 230 tons full load
Armament: four 30-mm guns in twin
mountings, four SS-N-2B/C 'Styx' anti-
ship missiles, and (in some craft) one

quadruple launcher for SA-N-5 'Grail' or
SA-N-8 'Gremlin' SAMs
Propulsion: three 3725-kW (4,995-
hp) M504 diesels powering three shafts
Performance: maximum speed 37 kt
(68.5 km/h; 42.5 mph); range 1675 km
(1,040 miles)
Dimensions: length overall 39 m

(127 ft 11 in), beam 7.8 m 125 ft 7 in)
Crew: 30
Users: Algeria, Angola, Bulgaria,
China, Cuba, Egypt, Ethiopia, Finland,
India, Iraq, Libya, North Korea,
Pakistan, Poland, Romania, Somalia,
Syria, USSR, Vietnam, Yemen and
Yugoslavia

through the islands to another hiding place.

For close on 100 years, small, fast vessels, lurking in the coastal shallows, have posed such a threat to larger and far more powerful, but inevitably slower – both in speed and in response – traditional warships. In World War II they operated as MTBs and MGBs, but they had a limited value as they required a clear line of sight to launch their torpedoes or fire their guns, which rendered them vulnerable to counter-attack. Moreover, an MGB is a notoriously unstable gun platform, which means that it must approach close to its target.

Since 1945, the performance of these fast attack craft has been greatly improved by the adoption of gas-turbine and lighter-weight diesel engines. And electronic target detection, ECM, fire control systems and guided missiles have made them a formidable threat to larger vessels. With their present sophisticated equipment they are by no means inexpensive, but at only a fraction of the cost of a conventional warship they present a very attractive alternative, particularly to smaller navies.

Eilat destroyed

The Israeli navy learned the value of fast attack craft to its cost on 21 October 1967, when the destroyer Eilat was sunk off Port Said by a Soviet-made 'Styx' missile fired from an Egyptian 70-ton 'Komar' class fast attack

---

The Professional's View:

The missile boat threat

"They can be a real danger if you let them. Most of the time, we don't regard them as a threat. After all, we spend our time training for operations out in the North Atlantic, and no small vessel is going to be able to do much out there. But we do have to take them seriously. We might be called on to make a hostage rescue somewhere in Africa, or South America, and that's their backyard. The best of them are equipped with adequate radar and fire control, and their missiles are as good as anything we've got. The one advantage a full-size vessel has is in the number of countermeasures we carry. Most missile boats just don't have the space. Even so, it wouldn't be much fun having to take on half a dozen boats in an archipelago, where they can fire and then dodge behind one of the islands for cover. That is where they do their best work."

**Royal Navy Frigate Captain,
North Atlantic**

236

FORMER USSR

'Nanuchka' class

Developed from the mid-1960s as an advanced guided-missile corvette type for operation in coastal waters, the **'Nanuchka I'** class was built at Leningrad from 1969, with production augmented from 1978 by deliveries from the yard at Petrovsky in the Soviet Far East.

Though comparatively small for its role, the 'Nanuchka' class hull is fairly fast and provides accommodation for a capable offensive and defensive electronic suite as well as a nicely-balanced armament fit including dual-purpose guns, surface-to-air missiles for self-defence, and two three-round launchers for the potent SS-N-9 'Siren' anti-ship missile, which can carry a small nuclear or large HE warhead to a range of 110 km (68 miles). Variants include the **'Nanuchka II'** class for export with older SS-N-2 'Styx' missiles and a downgraded electronic suite, the **'Nanuchka III'** class with the gun armament altered to one 76-mm (3-in) and one 30-mm CIWS mounting, and the **'Nanuchka IV'** class derivative of the 'Nanuchka III' class with two six-round launchers for a new anti-ship missile. The single 'Nanuchka IV' was a trials unit but was not put into production.

Specification
'Nanuchka I' class
Type: coastal guided-missile corvette

and patrol vessel
Displacement: 660 tons full load
Armament: two 57-mm guns in a twin mounting, six SS-N-9 'Siren' anti-ship missiles, and one twin launcher for SA-N-4 'Gecko' SAMs
Propulsion: six 3750-kW (5,030-hp) M504 diesels powering three shafts

Performance: maximum speed 36 kt (67 km/h; 41.5 mph); range 8350 km (5,190 miles)
Dimensions: length overall 59.3 m (194 ft 6 in); beam 13 m (42 ft 8 in)
Crew: 60
Users: Algeria, India, Libya and Russia

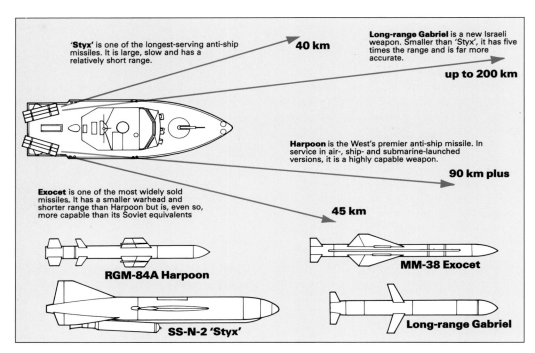

'Styx' is one of the longest-serving anti-ship missiles. It is large, slow and has a relatively short range.

40 km

Long-range Gabriel is a new Israeli weapon. Smaller than 'Styx', it has five times the range and is far more accurate.

up to 200 km

Harpoon is the West's premier anti-ship missile. In service in air-, ship- and submarine-launched versions, it is a highly capable weapon.

90 km plus

Exocet is one of the most widely sold missiles. It has a smaller warhead and shorter range than Harpoon but is, even so, more capable than its Soviet equivalents.

45 km

RGM-84A Harpoon

MM-38 Exocet

SS-N-2 'Styx'

Long-range Gabriel

The development of the surface-to-surface missile has revolutionised warfare at sea. With missiles, the smallest of craft can carry weapons as powerful as the massive shells fired by the battleships of World War II, and targets can be hit with amazing accuracy at ranges beyond the dreams of weapons designers of only a generation ago.

craft that had not even left harbour.

Alone among major powers, the Soviet navy had kept a large number of fast attack craft in commission after World War II. These were intended to defend the long coastline against invasion, particularly in the Baltic, Black and Barents Seas to the west, and the Bering and Okhotsk Seas on the Pacific. From 1952 onwards some 500 P4 and P6 fast attack craft were commissioned, and between 1959 and 1961 a number of P6 boats, now known as the 'Komar' class, were converted to carry 'Styx' missiles. At the same time the Soviets began to build their first fast attack craft specifically designed to carry missiles, the 'Osa' class. Boats of both classes were also sold to many smaller nations.

Missile development

The sinking of the *Eilat* by missile produced consternation among Western navies: the US Navy pushed ahead with development of Harpoon, the French began rapid research on the MM.38 Exocet, the Italians started work – with the French – on Otomat, the Israelis accelerated their Gabriel programme, and Norway produced a similar missile called Penguin. The Royal Navy, with no missiles of

---

237 'Pegasus' class

USA

The US Navy's primary interest is in 'blue water' operations, and virtually the only coastal types to feature in its inventory are minehunters and minesweepers. In the late 1950s, however, it investigated the capabilities of the fast hydrofoil. After trials with the experimental 'Highpoint' in the anti-submarine role, the missile-armed hydrofoil was focussed on as a successor to the conventional 'Asheville' class.

The result was the **'Pegasus'** class, which was planned at 30 units but later cut to six. The craft were each propelled by two diesel-powered waterjets for slow-speed foilborne operation, and two turbine-powered waterjets for high-speed foilborne

operation. The US Navy believed that, despite their capable gun/missile armament and useful fire control system, the craft required too high a level of logistic support for first-line deployment in areas such as the Mediterranean. They were based in Florida, but were scrapped in the early 1990s.

Specification
'Pegasus' class
Type: coastal guided-missile attack and patrol hydrofoil
Displacement: 240 tons full load
Armament: one 76-mm (3-in) gun and eight RGM-84 Harpoon anti-ship missiles

Propulsion: two MTU MB 831 TC81 diesel engines for hullborne propulsion, and one 13240-kW (18,000-shp) General Electric LM2500 gas turbine for foilborne propulsion
Performance: maximum speed 48 kt (89 km/h; 55 mph) foilborne; range 3140 km (1,950 miles)

Dimensions: length overall 44.3 m (145 ft 4 in) with foils retracted and 40.5 m (132 ft 10 in) with foils extended; beam 14.5 m (47 ft 6 in) with foils extended and 8.6 m (28 ft 3 in) with foils retracted
Crew: 24
User: USA

---

238 'Spica' class

SWEDEN

Between 1966 and 1968, Sweden commissioned six **'Spica I'** class attack craft with gas-turbine propulsion. These were originally armed with a single 57-mm gun and six tubes for 533-mm (21-in) wire-guided torpedoes, but are currently fitted with one 57-mm gun, two or four tubes for 533-mm (21-in) wire-guided torpedoes, and four or eight RBS15 anti-ship missiles.

Between 1973 and 1976, the Swedish navy commissioned another 12 craft of the improved **'Spica II'** class variant, which carries the same armament as the revised 'Spica I' class craft but uses the PEAB 9LV200 fire control system (plus Ericsson Sea Giraffe air-search radar) in place of the less capable Hollandse

Signaalapparaten M22.

The **'Spica III'** or **'Stockholm'** class comprises two corvette-type flotilla leaders for the fast attack craft. These have a 320-ton full load displacement, more modern and capable electronics, and a primary armament similar to that of the 'Spica II' class (one 57-mm gun, one 40-mm gun, two 533-mm/21-in tubes and eight RBS15 missiles) but augmented by an anti-submarine suite with variable-depth sonar and two tubes for 400-mm (15.75-in) wire-guided torpedoes.

Specification
'Spica II' class
Type: coastal guided-missile attack and patrol craft

Displacement: 230 tons full load
Armament: one 57-mm gun, up to six tubes for 533-mm (21-in) anti-ship torpedoes or up to eight RBS15 anti-ship missiles, or a mix of anti-ship torpedoes and missiles
Propulsion: three 3205-kW (4,300-hp) Rolls-Royce Proteus gas turbines

powering three shafts
Performance: maximum speed 40.5 kt (46.5 km/h; 75 mph); range not revealed
Dimensions: length overall 43.6 m (143 ft 1 in); beam 7.1 m (23 ft 3 in)
Crew: 27
Users: Malaysia and Sweden

its own, announced that it would buy Exocet as soon as the weapon was proved.

The first Exocet-carrying fast attack craft was the French 'Combattante II' class – actually a modification of a West German design – 20 of which were supplied to the West German Baltic fleet from 1972 to 1975. The building of these boats at Cherbourg was a device to allow the West Germans to sell 12 of their 'Saar' class boats to Israel in 1968-9; these were immediately equipped with Gabriels. At the same time, Israel began building its own 'Reshef' class boats, six of which were commissioned in 1973-5 and armed at first solely with Gabriels, Harpoons being added at a later date.

A shortcoming faced by the Israelis was the fact that the Gabriel has a range of only 21000 metres, compared with nearly 50000 metres for the 'Styx'. The solution was to employ a wide variety of ECM to enable the Israeli boats to close range without being hit.

France has exported many missile boats, known as Patrouilleur Rapide, often building them to modified West German designs. This is the Exocet-armed PR-72P class corvette Herrera, constructed at Villeneuve-la-Garonne for the Peruvian navy.

239

'Type 143' class

The two **'Type 143'** class groups were the most important attack and patrol craft in service with the West German navy, and the same basic **'Lürssen FPB/PG-57'** class is used by many other navies in a number of forms, with a large and interesting variety of armament and electronic fits.

Germany's original batch of 10 'Type 143' class craft was commissioned in 1976 and 1977 as multi-role vessels with an armament of two 76-mm (3-in) guns, four MM.38 Exocet anti-ship missiles and two tubes for 533-mm (21-in) wire-guided torpedoes. The batch has since become the **'Type 143B'** class, with the after gun mounting replaced by an EX-31 launcher for 24 RIM-116 RAM surface-to-air missiles.

This model is fitted with four 4000-kW (5,365-hp) MTU 16V956 TB91 diesels powering four shafts for a maximum speed of 40+ kt (74+ km/h; 46+ mph) and a range of 2400 km (1,490 miles) and, being slightly less automated, it has a crew of 40. The **'Type 143A'** class is another batch of 10 basically similar craft, commissioned between 1982 and 1984, with a slightly different and less powerful propulsion system for marginally reduced performance but greater range.

Specification
'Type 143A' class
Type: coastal missile-armed attack and patrol craft
Displacement: 391 tons full load
Armament: one 76-mm (3-in) gun, four MM.38 Exocet anti-ship missiles, and one EX-31 launcher for RIM-116 RAM surface-to-air missiles
Propulsion: four 3350-kW (4,495-hp) MTU 16V956 SB80 diesel engines powering four shafts
Performance: maximum speed 40 kt (74 km/h; 46 mph); range 4825 km (3,000 miles)
Dimensions: length overall 57.7 m/ (89 ft 4 in); beam 7.6 m (24 ft 11 in)
Crew: 34
Users: Chile, Ghana, Greece, Indonesia, Kuwait, Morocco, Nigeria, Spain, Turkey and West Germany

---

240

'Province' class

The several states of the Persian Gulf are among the world's most significant operators of fast attack craft, which are ideally suited for offensive and defensive roles in this region, with its confined waters and plentiful, as well as economically important, potential targets. Typical of the craft in service is the four-strong **'Province'** class of Oman, which received the first three craft from the UK in 1982, 1983 and 1984, and was sufficiently impressed with the type's operational performance to order the fourth unit for delivery in 1989. In comparison with smaller attack craft, these relatively large vessels have not only a slightly more comprehensive armament but also much improved sensors and

electronics, which include a back-up optronic director and a capable ESM system with an intercept and jamming element backed by chaff/flare launchers.

Kenya ordered two basically similar **'Nyayo'** class craft in 1984 for delivery in 1987. These have a missile fit of four Otomat Mk 2 anti-ship missiles, backed by a gun armament of one 76-mm (3-in) gun, two 40-mm AA guns in a twin mounting and two 20-mm cannon in single mountings. The propulsion arrangement is the same as that on the Omani craft.

Specification
'Province' class
Type: coastal guided-missile attack  and patrol craft
Displacement: 395 tons full load
Armament: one 76-mm (3-in) gun, two 40-mm guns in a twin mounting, and six or eight MM.40 Exocet anti-ship missiles
Propulsion: four 3392-kW (4,450-hp) Paxman Valenta 18RP-200 diesel engines powering four shafts
Performance: maximum speed 40 kt (74 km/h; 46 mph); range 3700 km (2,300 miles)
Dimensions: length overall 56.7 m (186 ft); beam 8.2 m (26 ft 11 in)
Crew: 54
Users: Kenya and Oman

A modern 200-ton fast attack craft has the same firepower as one broadside from a 50,000-ton World War II battleship

The result of two battles in October 1973 was that 13 Israeli fast attack craft of 'Reshef' and 'Sa'ar' classes, mounting between them 63 Gabriels, inflicted heavy losses for no loss of their own on 27 Syrian and Egyptian 'Komar' and 'Osa' craft, with a total armament of 85 'Styxes'. Using a combination of active and passive counter-measures, the Israeli fast attack craft managed to close to under 20000 metres, while avoiding or destroying in all 12 'Styxes', but within Gabriel range they successfully bagged a total of eight enemy vessels.

This action, the first one in which missile-carrying fast attack craft were tested in battle, caused the major Western navies to take an increasing interest in them. In particular, attempts were made to develop hydrofoil craft, in which the Soviets were among the pioneers with their 'Sarancha' class. A plan was drawn up for collaboration between the US, Italy and West Germany in a NATO hydrofoil programme, but costs were found to be too high.

The United States carried on alone, and built six PMHs (Patrol Missile Hydrofoils) of the 'Pegasus' class in service at Key West, Florida. The great advantage of the hydrofoil is that it can move at greater speeds without the danger of break-up in rough water that threatens a conventionally-hulled boat.

Italy subsequently pursued hydrofoil development with the 'Sparviero' class, based on a small, relatively inexpensive Boeing prototype, the *Tucumcari*. These carried two Otomat missiles. In the Middle East, Israel had three Flagstaff 2 hydrofoils to a Grumman design, the 'Shimrit' class. An improved design is now being considered.

Currently there are many more fast attack craft in service with navies throughout the world than any other type of combat warship. At one time the largest number was to be found in the Chinese fleet. The 150-ton 'Shanghai' class was built in quantity, and many were sold to Albania, Romania, Bangladesh, Pakistan and Vietnam. These were not armed with missiles, however, and have been replaced by 'Hai-Daus', which are armed with Chinese versions of the 'Styx'. There is also the 'Huchuan' class of torpedo hydrofoils, which were among the first operational hydrofoils in the world when they entered service in 1966.

Fast attack craft today

Currently the Russian navy has around 100 fast attack craft in service, most being missile carriers, known to the Russians as *raketny kater*. Many have been replaced by larger craft, missile corvettes; the Russians are reported to be building only one type of fast attack craft and smaller patrol vessels.

All missile fast attack craft are jam-packed with electronic equipment, and also carry guns that can be used in both the surface and anti-aircraft roles. In the Baltic, round the North Cape and all the way down the western Pacific coast, they have been an invaluable factor. With the collapse of Russian military power, however, many of the Soviet-supplied craft are worn out and lack spares.

A 'Dabur' class coastal craft of the Israeli navy patrols the eastern Mediterranean. While they form the basis for the missile-armed 'Dvora' class, the 'Daburs' are more often used as auxiliary anti-submarine craft. They are armed with depth charges and a pair of tubes for American Mk 46 lightweight ASW torpedoes.

The development of FAST ATTACK CRAFT

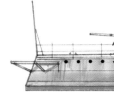

1904 Asashio

Torpedo boats were a product of the late 19th century. Many navies went into panic at the thought of small, agile craft dashing in to sink their lumbering battleships. As a result, they developed torpedo boat destroyers. These were larger vessels, able to catch the torpedo boats and destroy them with guns. Soon, however, it was realised that these new vessels could do the torpedo boat job themselves. The Japanese *Asashio* was a British-built vessel of 365 tons which was armed with a pair of torpedoes. It was craft such as these which administered the *coup de grace* to the Russian battle fleet at Tsushima in 1905, sinking the flagship *Kniaz Suvorov* and several other battleships.

1944 PT boat

The size of American PT boats was dictated by the need to carry four 21-inch torpedoes. The Elco 80-footer was a development of a British design supplied to the US Navy in the 1930s, and served in the Pacific and the Mediterranean. In the Solomon Islands and the Philippines, close-in fighting was brief and bloody, involving large volumes of fire from light automatic weapons. In the later stages of the war in the Pacific, the Japanese were forced to move supplies around in small coasting craft and barges, and as a result many PT boats wore bizarre camouflages and shed some or all of their torpedoes in favour of more cannon, or rockets, or even 81-mm mortars.

Torpedo boats have always had to be fast. Before World War I, the use of steam engines meant that vessels had to weigh 300 tons or so to carry engines powerful enough to be effective. Efficient petrol and diesel engines meant that World War II-era boats could be much smaller and faster, yet have similar armaments. After the war, attack craft began to grow larger again. The rapid development of weapons and weapon systems and the replacement of torpedoes by missiles meant that missile boats needed room for all the various radar and electronic systems essential for high-tech warfare.

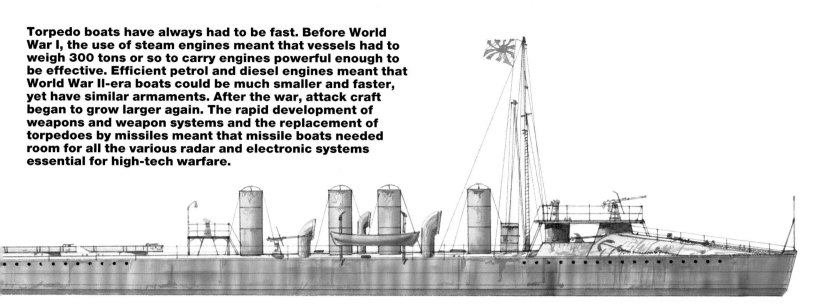

1939 *S-160*

German *Schnellboote* were built of wood on alloy frames, and had a round bilge hull. This yielded lower maximum speed than British hard-chine designs, but the S-boat was able to sustain its top speed in sea states that other boats could not handle. Later S-boats featured an armoured conning tower as a result of the increasingly

powerful gun-armament carried by their British opponents. Even though they had grown to 35 metres in length and displaced more than 100 tons, their triple diesels could power them to 40 knots. The S-boat's quiet engines and low profiles were a considerable advantage to the Germans in the nocturnal melees along the channel coast. Once the Royal Navy boats began to carry radar, however, the balance shifted rapidly to the British.

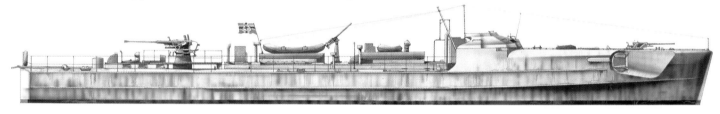

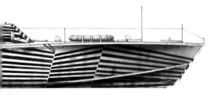

1960 'Komar' class

The 'Komar' class of missile craft was built between 1959 and 1961, and ushered in an entirely new phase of sea warfare. The 80-ton 'Komar' was based on the hull of the P6 torpedo boat. Designated RKA (*raketny kater*, or missile cutter), the 27-metre fast attack craft could make 40 knots. The 'Komar' introduced the SS-N-2 'Styx' anti-ship missile to the world, and it was this combination that sank the Israeli flagship *Eilat* in 1967.

1973 'Reshef' class

The lesson Israel learned in 1967 was applied to their own sophisticated fleet of missile boats. The 450-ton 'Reshef' class vessels were good seaboats, two having been deployed from Haifa to the Red Sea via Gibraltar and the Cape of Good Hope. In addition to eight Harpoon and four Gabriel missiles, they are fitted with a pair of 76-mm guns, although the forward gun was replaced by the American Phalanx 20-mm Gatling gun close-in weapon system.

STING LIKE A BEE

The history of fast attack craft

Since the beginning of the century, one thing about fast attack craft has remained constant. To be successful, no matter what the weapon, you still have to pack as powerful a punch onto as fast and manoeuvrable a platform as you can.

During World War I, the Italians and the British demonstrated the value of coastal craft. Both used their craft singly or in small groups to capitalise on the advantages of agility, surprise and good planning. The Italians were particularly effective in evolving tactics for their small, fast boats to attack the Austrian fleet in its well-defended harbours. The British had to contend with poorer weather in the North and Baltic Seas, and learned the value of larger and stronger designs, accepting a small loss in speed in order to handle heavier seas. From the start, the juggling act between speed, firepower and endurance has remained the main principle of small warship design.

The inter-war years saw interest in coastal craft wane in many navies, but during World War II all the major naval powers developed fast attack craft. These ranged from the small, agile MAS boats of the Italian navy through the fast, hard-hitting PT boats and MTBs of the US and Royal Navies, to the big British Fairmile 'D' boats and the German S-boats.

In the post-war years, the Western nations took little interest in coastal craft. The Soviets, however, developed a huge coastal force, and were to introduce the next major innovation. Fitting anti-ship missiles onto small craft increased their firepower tremendously without a serious reduction in performance, and led to a renewal of interest in fast attack craft in many smaller naval arms.

Few navies can afford new ocean-going warships, but since most countries only require vessels to defend their coasts, a missile destroyer or frigate is often little more than a symbol of national

A Swedish 'Spica' class missile craft fires an RBS15 missile. The development of the naval surface-to-surface missile has given the modern fast attack craft a combat punch unbelievable only a generation ago.

World War I

In the 1870s, the development of the 'locomotive' torpedo — launched from fast, steel-hulled, steam-powered torpedo boats — sent the world's navies into panic. Everyone thought that these new naval mosquitoes could swarm into the line of battle and blow up lumbering battleships with impunity. Although the rapid development of the destroyer (originally the 'torpedo boat destroyer') rendered the small surface craft less effective, they still found a place in combat. British Coastal Motor Boats (CMBs) served with distinction in several theatres during World War I, and one sank the Soviet cruiser *Oleg* in the Baltic during the anti-Bolshevik intervention of 1919. The Italians were even more successful in the Adriatic, with their aggressive use of small craft leading to the sinking of several Austrian warships, including the battleship *Svent Istvan*.

Left: Italian MAS boats bore some resemblance to the British Coastal Motor Boats. The stepped hull was designed to 'plane' the craft over the surface of the water. Since most operations took place in relatively sheltered waters, the boats needed no real rough-sea capabilities. The Italians used them with verve, making daring forays into the heart of Austrian fleet anchorages at the head of the Adriatic and down the Dalmatian coast.

Above: CMBs had a 'vee' bow, leading to a step about halfway along the hull. At speed, the fore-end lifted out of the water and the whole hull skimmed along on the flat section after the step.

World War II

British experience with CMBs was almost totally forgotten during the inter-war years, with coastal forces having to be rapidly brought up to strength with the approach of World War II. The Germans had been experimenting with the *Schnellboot* (fast-boat) concept since 1930, and by 1939 had built up a useful force of potent diesel-powered motor torpedo boats, developed by the Lürssen company. These S-boats (E-boats to the British) clashed with British Motor Torpedo Boats (MTBs) and Motor Gun Boats (MGBs) in the North Sea and the English Channel, but in spite of the frequency of contact the actual amount of shipping sunk by coastal craft was quite low. The same was true in the Pacific, where Japanese torpedo boats achieved little, although the US Navy had more success in the Solomon Islands and the Philippines with its PT boats. Only in the Mediterranean, where an Allied force harried German coastal shipping, were such craft to achieve real success. The Soviets had taken torpedo boats seriously very early, and in the late 1920s the first production boats appeared. Designed by A.N. Tupolev, they were advanced designs, with aluminium hulls and employing many aircraft manufacturing techniques. During World War II, however, they proved to be of limited fighting value.

Above: German Schnellboote, or S-boats, had a round hull section. In perfect conditions this was much slower than a planing hull, but in the rough waters of the North Sea it was much more effective.

pride. Fast attack craft can perform the coastal defence role, using smaller crews. As a result, they are in service around the world, and there has been a thriving export trade.

There are signs, however, that the market is shrinking. In practice fast attack craft lack seaworthiness in the open sea, their weapon systems become useless, and they are vulnerable to air attack. In 1991 three Royal Navy Lynx helicopters armed with Sea Scud missiles crippled virtually the entire Iraqi Navy.

To provide air defence is almost impossible for small hulls, so size is creeping up steadily to accommodate anti-missile systems. Very few small fast attack craft are being built, whereas the market for corvettes is expanding.

Left: US interest in coastal craft in the 1930s grew rapidly after war broke out in Europe. Over 600 PT boats were built, 200 to the Higgins 78-foot design seen here. Although fitted with torpedoes, by the end of the war they were in action most frequently as gunboats, against Japanese coastal shipping.

Right: This **CMB** is in action against the Bolsheviks in 1919. Torpedoes were simply slid out of the trough in the back, with the boat then getting out of the way, fast!

Above: As a result of their great success with torpedo boats in World War I, the Italians continued work on such craft after 1918. The MAS 500 series with which they entered World War II were very fast in good conditions, but left much to be desired in terms of seaworthiness, defensive armament and their ability to withstand punishment.

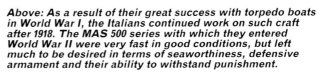

Above: S-boats, known to the British as 'E-boats', were such a menace that the restricted waters of the English Channel and lower North Sea became known as 'E-boat Alley'.

Left: British power boats were instrumental in the revival of Royal Navy interest in coastal craft in the 1930s. Their designs sold well abroad; these 70-foot MGBs were originally built as MA/SBs (motor anti-submarine boats) for the French navy. Undelivered at the fall of France, the boats were taken over by the Royal Navy.

18

Below: The 'Shershen' class, called in Soviet service torpednyy kater, or torpedo cutter, was the last conventional class of torpedo boat built by the Soviets in any numbers. Eighty were completed between 1963 and 1974, most being transferred to other navies. Very fast boats, they are reported to be extremely noisy and hot for their crews.

High-tech missile boats

For all their apparent promise, hydrofoils have proved a disappointment as fast attack craft, proving too complex, expensive and unreliable. The US Navy experimented with various designs in the 1960s and 1970s, but, apart from the six boats of the 'Pegasus' class, the development has come to very little. Italy and Israel are the only other Western nations to operate hydrofoils, the British having experimented between 1979 and 1982 without being convinced. The Soviet Union and China, in contrast, have made extensive use of hydrofoils, although the Chinese craft are really only 'semi-hydrofoils', with foils at the bows but conventional planing hulls. Hydrofoils are not the only advanced craft being considered for the fast attack mission, however. Air Cushion Vessels show some promise, although they too suffer from the problems of complexity, unreliability and high cost. The US Navy has conducted a series of experiments with surface-effect ships — catamaran-type craft, with rigid sidewalls, that ride on a cushion of air. Hovercraft manufacturers have proposed their craft as high-speed coastal defence vessels, with a variety of armaments ranging from machine-guns to missiles. As yet, the high cost has kept any navy from operating such craft.

Left: The Soviet 'Komar' design was the pioneering fast missile craft, and started a revolution in sea warfare. The 'Komars' are simply P6 torpedo boat hulls to which has been added a pair of launchers for SS-N-2 'Styx' missiles. First seen in 1960, the vessels were transferred to a variety of Soviet allies. Few are left in service.

Left: The US Coast Guard operated three SES (Surface Effect Ship) patrol craft. These halfway-houses between hovercraft and catamarans offer a number of advantages, being faster than conventional hulls and more stable than full air-cushion vehicles.

Below: Hydrofoils have not proved successful as missile craft. The Italians had six small 'Sparvieros' in service, while the US Navy operated six Harpoon-armed 'Pegasus' class craft, but both types were discarded (bottom).

Cutting a characteristic dash through the water, the Elco 80-ft PT-333 of the US Navy heads for its patrol area. Allied fast attack craft like these were more successful in the Mediterranean than in any other theatre of war.

MEDITERRANEAN MELEE

World War II in the Mediterranean was one of the most bloody naval campaigns in history, and, in one small corner, coastal craft waged their own private war.

The convoy sneaked through the warm Mediterranean night – half a dozen heavily-armed, shallow-draught barges, loaded with supplies for the armies fighting in the south. To the left, the Italian coast lay in darkness. To the right, a pair of escorting destroyers. Beyond them were the minefields. The German navy crews were fully alert, for they were on a vital and perilous mission. The throb of their own diesel engines was the only thing to break the silence. All seemed well.

Although they did not know it, everything was far from well. A few miles to the south, well-trained American eyes were glued to their radar screens. Already the operators had worked out the course, speed and composition of the convoy. The information had been transmitted to the rest of the powerful Allied force, and the fast attack craft of the Royal and US Navies were about to close the jaws of a trap.

Italy was out of the war. The Allies had landed at Anzio, and German armies were fighting for their lives in the mountains around Monte Cassino. Supplying those armies down the mountainous length of Italy would have been a monumental task, interrupted at regular intervals by partisan attacks and intense British and American bombing raids. Supply by sea was much more effective. By hugging the coast, the convoys could remain under the protection of powerful coastal gun batteries, while minefields along the outer edge of the convoy lane protected the supply vessels from marauding destroyers.

The fast attack craft was the most suitable weapon in the Allied inventory for dealing with the problem. Small, fast, hard-hitting torpedo boats and gunboats were

British Fairmile 'D' MGBs are among the craft tied up at Bastia. This Corsican port, only 80 miles from the Italian coast, was home to the British and American fast craft of the Coastal Forces Battle Squadron.

Above, inset: The Landing Craft Gun was developed to provide fire support to amphibious landings. Armed with a pair of 4.7-inch destroyer guns, these slow boats were the heart of the battle squadron.

A zebra-striped PT boat noses in to its moorings after a mission. These American craft, with their radar and communications gear, were used to co-ordinate the battle squadron's night attacks.

in less danger from the minefields than destroyers, and could wreak havoc among the transports.

The Germans were fast learners, however. They were soon moving their supplies in armed F-lighters, diesel-powered shallow-draught barges that could hug right in to the coast. Soon the American PT boats and British MTBs (Motor Torpedo Boats) and MGBs (Motor Gun Boats) were being outclassed, especially when the Germans introduced the flak-lighters to supplement their regular escort destroyers and S-boats. These were heavily armed F-lighters carrying large numbers of automatic weapons as well as a version of the highly effective 88-mm anti-aircraft and anti-tank gun. A single shell from an 'Acht-Acht' could turn a PT boat to kindling.

Allies strike back

More and more German convoys were getting through. Captain J.F. Stevens, commander of Allied coastal forces in the Mediterranean, commented:

"There can be no question but that the interruption of the enemy's sea communications presents a difficult problem. He has so strengthened his escorts and armed his shipping that our coastal craft find themselves up against considerably heavier metal."

Captain Stevens had seen his 'mosquito' boats reduced from destroyers of the enemy to harassers of the enemy, and he did not like it.

Fortunately, the response to German firepower was not long in coming. In March 1944, Commander Robert Allen of the Royal Navy formed the Coastal Forces Battle Squadron. Based at Bastia in Corsica, this was far and away the most successful small boat unit of the war.

At the heart of the force were to be three Royal Navy LCGs, or Landing Craft Guns. These were standard landing craft fitted with a pair of 4.7-inch destroyer guns, and numerous smaller weapons. Manned by crack Royal Marine gun crews, they outgunned the powerful German flak-lighters by a considerable margin. They were to be protected from German destroyers and S-boats by Royal Navy MTBs and MGBs. Force co-ordination was supplied by the PT boats of the US Navy, which used their radar to scout out the enemy and to keep track of the rest of the squadron.

Right: The German soldiers fighting so desperately at Cassino relied on replenishment by sea. The main aim of the battle group was to get in among the small cargo ships and barges bringing supplies down the coast to Kesselring's armies.

Below: The battle squadron carried such a range of weapons that almost any target could be engaged. Most boats carried a multiplicity of light weapons, such as the 20-mm cannon and 0.5-calibre machine-guns seen here in action aboard a US Navy PT boat.

The battle squadron received its first test at the end of March. Although the LCGs were so slow they could never hope to catch an enemy convoy, they could be placed across the convoy's line of advance. On the evening of 27 March they were in position off San Vincenzo when a message came in from Lieutenant Edwin DuBose in PT-212. Sweeping ahead of the battle group in company with PT-214, the Americans had made radar contact with a south-bound convoy. Six flak-lighters were moving south, escorted by a pair of destroyers. Commander Allen could not open fire without making his slow landing craft into targets for the destroyers, so he had to wait until DuBose made a torpedo attack.

Left: The Royal Navy's Fairmile 'D' MTBs carried four torpedoes, two 6-pdr (50-mm) guns, three 20-mm cannon and eight machine-guns of 0.5 and 0.303 calibre.

Below: Early torpedo boats launched their weapons from tubes, as shown here, but when aircraft torpedoes became available they were launched by simply rolling them over the side.

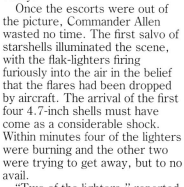

Below: The main opposition to the battle squadron came from German S-boats, whose low silhouettes made them difficult to spot in the confusion of a night battle.

The PT boats closed to within 400 yards of the German escorts, and launched three torpedoes before turning away. PT-214 was hit by a single 37-mm shell, wounding one sailor. One destroyer may have been hit by a torpedo, but the enemy deserted their charges and fled north so fast that this was impossible to verify.

Once the escorts were out of the picture, Commander Allen wasted no time. The first salvo of starshells illuminated the scene, with the flak-lighters firing furiously into the air in the belief that the flares had been dropped by aircraft. The arrival of the first four 4.7-inch shells must have come as a considerable shock. Within minutes four of the lighters were burning and the other two were trying to get away, but to no avail.

"Two of the lighters," reported Commander Allen, "judging from the impressive explosions, were carrying petrol, two ammunition, and one a mixed cargo of both. The sixth sank without exploding."

A month later, many of the same participants were involved in a vicious little fight amid the islands of the Tuscan coast. Once again, Commander Allen had placed his force in the path of the south-bound convoys, and once again the American PT boats had found the enemy. This time, however, they had also made contact with a second force heading north. Commander Allen decided to go for the southbound vessels, but not until the other enemy contacts had moved further north.

Once again, the big guns of the LCGs smashed into the German formation. Two flak-lighters were destroyed almost immediately, along with an ocean-going tug. A third had run for the beach, where it was found and destroyed by MGBs. Three flak-lighters which had been escorting the convoy were now illuminated, and two were hit by the first salvoes fired at them by the LCGs. The third opened fire with everything it had, and 20-mm, 40-mm and 88-mm shells began reaching for the slow-to-manoeuvre LCGs. Before it could do any damage it was hit hard, and retired into the smoke, pursued by Lieutenant Eldredge's PT-209 and several gunboats. One torpedo was enough to finish the crippled flak-lighter.

Success sealed

Away from the battle, the PT boats of the scouting group decided to take out the northbound convoy. Moving slowly and silently, they launched a torpedo attack on what turned out to be an escort group of at least three flak-lighters. One was hit, but the others took the American boats under furious fire as they turned away. The PT boats immediately went to full speed and laid a smokescreen, under which they escaped.

As the battle group returned to Corsica, they received a report of enemy activity around the island of Capraia. The PT boats were sent to investigate, but were quickly spotted by the enemy destroyers and S-boats engaged in minelaying. By firing a captured enemy recognition flare, the PT boats were able to get close enough to the enemy to launch an attack, which damaged a destroyer so badly that she had to be abandoned. Turning away, the small craft came under a storm of German fire, but escaped unscathed.

Amazingly, for all the damage the battle squadron had caused that night, it sustained no damage, nor a single casualty. Over the next two to three months, this model of Allied co-operation was to turn the inshore convoy route into a nightmare for the Germans. Above all, it showed that, in the right circumstances, fast attack craft could be highly effective weapons.

Left: Soviet 'Osa II' class fast missile craft of the Black Sea Fleet maintain a high-speed cruise while on convoy attack exercises. Although the Soviet navy is now more of a 'blue water' fleet than it has ever been, it maintains a significant force of coastal warfare craft.

SOVIET MISSILE ATTACK

From the Kola Peninsula to Vladivostok, the fast missile craft of the Soviet navy were the most important part of the largest force of coastal warfare vessels in the world.

The Soviet navy was for many years little more than a coastal force. It had no real blue-water capabilities, and was content to concentrate on operations in the Baltic and Black Seas and around the major naval bases in the North and the Far East.

The initial expansion of the Soviet navy after World War II concentrated on submarines and on torpedo boat development and tactics. The massive growth seen under the command of Admiral Gorshkov saw a true long-range, deep-water navy emerge, but coastal forces remained important. The Soviets were pioneers in the development of the anti-ship missile, and putting those missiles aboard fast coastal craft was a natural progression. Unlike a gun, a missile has no recoil, and is relatively easy to mount onto the light hull of small attack craft.

When the elderly Israeli destroyer *Eilat* was sunk in 1967 by four 'Styx' missiles fired from a pair of Soviet-supplied 'Komar' class boats of the Egyptian navy, it was clear that David had once again slain Goliath. Small warships now had the ability to challenge more powerful vessels. While they could not maintain patrols for long or at any great distance from home, the Soviets had shown that, in their own domain, coastal forces were a considerable threat.

The Soviet navy's basic coastal unit was the brigade. This normally consisted of three or four squadrons of missile boats. Each squadron has three pairs of craft, which remained together even when withdrawn for refit or repair. Originally, brigades included both torpedo and missile boats, but in the 1980s the use of the torpedo boat declined.

A typical brigade consisted of a squadron of large 'Nanuchka' or 'Tarantul' class missile corvettes, which acted as command and control ships for smaller boats, accompanied by two or three squadrons of 'Osa' or 'Matka' class missile craft. The different missile types carried and the varying capabilities of each type presented a defending force with greater problems than an attack by boats armed with a single type of missile.

Above: The 'Osa' class came into service in the 1960s and was once the world's most numerous attack craft. None remain in service with the Russian fleet; a large number were built in China, and 190 were transferred to other navies.

Above, inset: At nearly 700 tons apiece, 'Nanuchka' class vessels are close to being small frigates, but like the 'Osas' they are designated malyy raketnyy korabl *(small rocket ship) by the Soviet navy.*

Approach to Target

The brigade advances in column of divisions.

The brigade advances at right angles to the direction of the target.

The brigade travels at its maximum cruising speed until the moment comes to attack.

Each division is made up from pairs of fast attack craft, which act as single units.

The division with the longest range missiles are positioned farthest from the target.

Phase One: Covert approach

Missile boats are very powerful for their size, but they lack endurance. They will be tasked for a particular mission while still in port, leaving harbour under cover of darkness to intercept a specific target. This could be an intruding enemy warship or a coastal convoy. Whatever the aim of the mission, the approach will be made as unobtrusively as possible, at maximum cruising speed. Coastal craft are small, and very fragile in comparison with larger ships. Their task is to hit and run, not to slug it out like a flyweight boxer with an Olympic heavyweight. A weapon designed to disable a destroyer will smash a fast attack craft to splinters. The longer a missile boat can escape detection by the enemy, the more likely it is that it is the enemy who will suffer the smashing.

Phase Two: Tactical deployment

Once the target has been located and positively identified, the boats head for the most suitable attack positions, maintaining their maximum cruising speed. In previous years torpedo boats would have led the way, tasked with attacking any merchant ships in a convoy and leaving any escorting warships to the missile boats, whose weapons had four times the range. Nowadays, all ships are targets for missiles. The boats move in squadron column formation, each squadron keeping clear of its neighbour. The attack position is chosen to allow each squadron to deploy and move in without interfering with the others.

Phase Three: Run-in to target

Once at their attack positions, the squadrons turn in towards the target, accelerating to their maximum dash speed. At this point, each squadron moves either into a 'vee' formation to the left or right of the squadron leader, or into line abreast. Control and co-ordination is provided by the brigade commander, who usually travels aboard one of the larger corvette-sized boats. The length of the run-in depends on the range of the missiles carried by the various craft. The boats armed with the old SS-N-2B 'Styx' have to close to within 20 kilometres, while those armed with SS-N-9 or SS-N-22 missiles can mount attacks from over 100 kilometres.

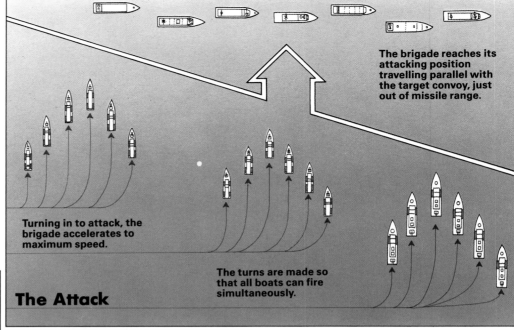

The brigade reaches its attacking position travelling parallel with the target convoy, just out of missile range.

Turning in to attack, the brigade accelerates to maximum speed.

The turns are made so that all boats can fire simultaneously.

The Attack

Left: Soviet missiles tend to be much larger than their Western equivalents. As a result the missile tubes on a fast missile boat such as the 'Osa II' class were much more evident than those on similar boats made elsewhere. Two quadruple Harpoon tubes take up the same space as two SS-N-2 'Styx' launchers. Western missiles are also faster and have better electronics. Where the large Soviet missiles score, however, is in the size of their warheads. An SS-N-2 'Styx' carries twice as much explosive as a Harpoon and three times as much as an Exocet.

Phase Four: The attack

Maintaining their high-speed dash towards their targets, the attack craft launch their missiles. A brigade consisting of one squadron of 'Nanuchka' class corvettes and three squadrons of 'Osa' class missile boats could fire 36 long-range SS-N-9s and 72 of the older SS-N-2 'Styx'. The exact number fired would depend on the target. Soviet doctrine stated that you need to fire seven or eight missiles to disable a large warship. Four were needed for a destroyer, while between two and four missiles are sufficient for an escort vessel or a fast-moving patrol craft. One of two missiles were quite enough for a small transport or a slow-moving, defenceless landing craft. The entire engagement sequence should not last more than 10 or 15 seconds.

Below: A 'Styx' blasts clear of its launch tube aboard an 'Osa I'. In its 30-year operational life, the missile has been upgraded several times.

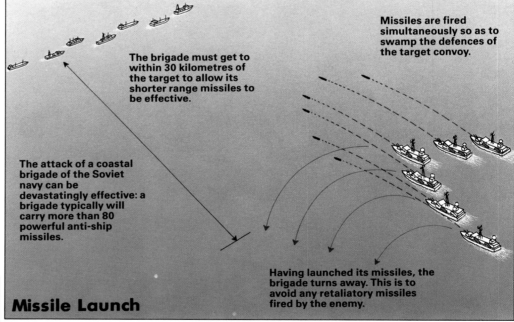

The brigade must get to within 30 kilometres of the target to allow its shorter range missiles to be effective.

Missiles are fired simultaneously so as to swamp the defences of the target convoy.

The attack of a coastal brigade of the Soviet navy can be devastatingly effective: a brigade typically will carry more than 80 powerful anti-ship missiles.

Having launched its missiles, the brigade turns away. This is to avoid any retaliatory missiles fired by the enemy.

Missile Launch

Phase Five: Disengagement

Getting out in a hurry is of the highest priority. Immediately the missiles are launched, the boats disengage. The automatic reaction of any warship to a missile attack is to fire missiles in return, so the attacking boats arrange to be somewhere else, fast. Anything that can interfere with the targetting of return missiles helps, and in this kind of combat the quality of your electronic countermeasures counts for a lot. In 1973 four Syrian 'Osa' class boats were sunk by a pair of Israeli 'Reshef' class boats. The Syrians had fired first, and their missiles had twice the range of the Israeli weapons, yet superior Israeli tactical manoeuvres and better ECM systems were decisive.

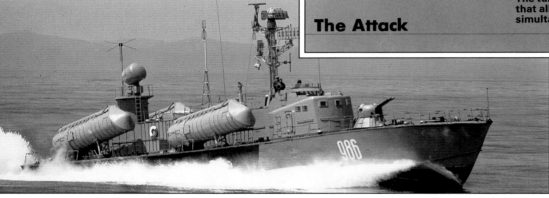

NAVAL FIGHTERS

Naval fighters are the ultimate defenders of the fleet. Patrolling hundreds of miles from their carriers, they are ready for any threat.

You're riding a steel-blue, twin-finned dart of a fighter with the most modern cockpit in the American military, watching three TV screens – all at once. As you fly, those screens change. They continually give you new information – Mach number, bank angle, altitude, course, the works. They manage the aircraft for you so that you can keep your hands on the throttle and control stick throughout the flight.

What aircraft are you flying? No doubt about it – the F/A-18 Hornet.

Monitoring all that information from the display screens is easy once you know how. And today's US Navy 'top gun' is busy. He's a combined fighter and attack pilot if he flies a Hornet, so he has to look out of the window for visual ID on anyone else in the sky, and to make sure he's on the right target – there may be friendlies right in front of his bomb bursts.

Enveloped in steam from the bow catapult of a carrier, a McDonnell Douglas F/A-18 Hornet is prepared for launch. The Hornet is typical of a generation of naval fighters that are at least as good as, and in many cases better than, their land-bound equivalents.

Swarms of big, beefy Hellcats were
launched from the decks of the US Navy's
fast carrier task forces to dominate the
Pacific in the last years of World War II.

Grumman Hellcat

If one weapon could be said to have turned
the tide against the Japanese in World War II,
it would have to be the Grumman F6F Hellcat.
Until its entry into service in mid-1943, the
Japanese had enjoyed air superiority in the
theatre, despite brave Allied attempts to curb it.
Rushed through its design and development
period and hurried into mass production, the
carrier-borne F6Fs of the US Navy immediately
tore into the enemy air fleets, ably assisted by
land-based Hellcats flying with the Marine
Corps. The aircraft did not surrender its mastery
of the air over the Pacific until the war was won,
dominating virtually every battle between its
service entry and the end of the campaign. In
the final tally, its kill-loss ratio was more than a
staggering 19 to one, and it had accounted for
4,947 kills out of the US Navy total of 6,477. At
the heart of the F6F's success were its good
climb performance, hard-hitting six-gun
armament, good speed and, above all, its
immense strength.

*A Grumman F-14 Tomcat from the US Navy's
Fighter Squadron VF-102 'Diamondbacks'
powers into the sky from the deck of a
supercarrier. The Tomcat's combination of
powerful radar and long-range missiles gives it
a lethal reach unmatched by any other fighter
in the world.*

That's why there's a 'head-up' display to
simplify all the data humming out of the TV
screens. It tells the pilot all he needs to know
when the Hornet is zooming in on an air or
ground target.

You can actually ride the F/A-18 down to an
airspeed of zero. It has a HUD airspeed rating
as slow as 48 knots and as fast as Mach 1.8.
That's the kind of speed range that makes it
the ideal low-down attack aircraft for the
Marines, as well as a hot-shot, super-
manoeuvrable high-sky fighter for the Navy.

Today's US carrier force is spearheaded by
the Hornet – a multi-role package of one pilot,

NAVAL FIGHTERS Reference File

363

USA

Grumman F-14 Tomcat

This immensely powerful fleet defence
fighter was designed as an alternative
to the failed F-111B naval version of the
General Dynamics F-111 multi-role
warplane, for which Grumman had
been the prime contractor. The F-14
first flew in December 1970, and drew
heavily on the company's F-111B
experience in features such as the
swing-wing mechanism, engines and
armament system (AWG-9 radar/fire
control system and associated AIM-54
Phoenix long-range AAMs).

The **F-14A Tomcat** began to enter
service in 1972 as the world's first
'look-down/shoot-down' fighter, and is
arguably still the world's most potent
interceptor. The Tomcat was planned
with a useful attack capability, but this

is wholly unused. In addition to its
20-mm cannon for dogfighting combat,
the type's main armament is six
Phoenixes or, more commonly, four
Phoenixes under the fuselage with two
AIM-7 Sparrow medium-range and two
AIM-9 Sidewinder short-range AAMs
on the glove hardpoints.

The type has been upgraded to **F-
14D** standard with 9480-kg (22000-
lb) thrust General Electric F110-
GE4400 turbofans for greater
operational flexibility and reliability,
with considerably more advanced
digital electronics as well as other
improvements. In 1998/9 the
operational inventory is down to 251
aircraft (ten squadrons).

Specification
Grumman F-14A Tomcat
Type: carrier-borne two-seat fleet
defence fighter
Powerplant: two 9840-kg (20,900-lb)
thrust Pratt & Whitney TF30-P-414A
turbofans
Performance: maximum speed
2517 km/h (1,564 mph); range 3220 km
(2,000 miles)

Dimensions: span 19.55 m (64 ft
1.5 in) spread and 11.65 m (38 ft 2.5 in)
swept; length 19.1 m (62 ft 8 in)
Weights: empty 18191 kg (40,104 lb);
maximum take-off 33724 kg (74,349 lb)
Armament: one 20-mm cannon and
up to 6577 kg (14,500 lb) of disposable
stores

The classic carrier fighter of the 1960s was the F-4 Phantom II, an example of which is seen being launched towards Vietnam from the USS Franklin D. Roosevelt.

two engines, electronic circuits, fuel cells and an awesome weapons load. It will remain an integral part of the fleet carrier air wing well into the 21st century, upgraded to F/A-18D and F/A-18F Super Hornet standard.

Hornet and Tomcat team

If the Hornet represents the Navy's newest sting, the F-14 Tomcat is its well-sharpened claws. This mighty swing-wing scrapper has successfully guarded the US fleet since the last days of the Vietnam War.

Designed primarily as a fighter, the Tomcat can range far out to intercept incoming hostiles, or fight close-in.

When the F/A-18 first flew, the manufacturer ran ads with the catchline: "Move over, Phantom". It was a proud boast. A

Phantom successor had to be very good indeed, for the F-4 was a world-beater. The F/A-18 is in a different class to the F-4, but you don't hear many complaints from the people who operate it in today's high-risk carrier aviation environment. Pilots rate it as one of the easiest fighters to fly.

The Hornet and Tomcat are the 1990s successors to a long line of naval fighters, warwinners and peacekeepers alike. The Wildcat, Hellcat and Corsair were the World War II American 'big three'. Then came the Panther, for action in Korea, followed by the Cougar, Skyray, Cutlass, Demon, Tiger and Crusader, the last-named sharing the Vietnam War combat task with Navy Phantoms.

Modern naval fighters come in all shapes and sizes. Most can handle fleet protection, strike force cover and ground attack – the three primary tasks – equally well.

The majority also launch from big carrier decks, propelled by steam catapults. Others, like the British Harrier and Soviet V/STOL Yak-38 'Forger', can fly safely from much smaller decks without using catapults.

Vertical take-off seemed a natural for naval fighters ever since it became possible to provide the lifting power to push a fighter straight up. After many years of research, the Sea Harrier entered service with the Royal Navy in 1979. It didn't seem very likely then that the famous British 'jump jet' would ever fire a shot in anger, but in 1982 came the Falklands war.

With just 20 aircraft, the Royal Navy took

The Professional's View:

The F-14 Tomcat

"Being in an F-14 squadron is unique to the US Navy, and we consider ourselves to be the pinnacle of naval aviation. The Tomcat's primary mission is fleet air defence, which is protecting the carrier and the support ships from the airborne threat. The F-14 was designed to shoot down those incoming missiles but, it turns out, it can hit the platforms they were launched from, too.

"It was, if you like, a curious by-product of the variable-geometry wing that turned the F-14 into a great dogfighter. As good an interceptor as it is, it's equally as good a close-in fighter as the F-16, and far superior to anything in the F-15 series that is currently out on the streets.

"It was always great, even 10 or 15 years ago, but the current F-14D, the Super Tomcat, is as good as anything in the world. We've got a great interceptor, a great fleet air defence fighter and a great close-in dogfighter, with a weapons fit that spans the spectrum.

"We proved that in the Mediterranean, there off the coast of Libya. We were doing round-the-clock combat air patrols. As soon as they'd seen what the Tomcat could do, after that first attack on their boats, the Libyans had a great respect for the aircraft."

F-14 Tomcat pilot, Fighter Squadron 101 'The Grim Reapers', US Navy

---

364

UNITED KINGDOM/USA

McDonnell Douglas AV-8B Harrier II

Entering service with the US Marine Corps in January 1984, the **AV-8B** was the result of a far-reaching Harrier development programme that led concurrently to the GR Mk 5 version for the RAF. A larger wing utilising carbon-fibre composites with leading-edge extensions and more stores pylons, an uprated Pegasus engine and a raised cockpit canopy distinguished the B model from the earlier AV-8A.

The standard AV-8B was further updated in 1984 with a night attack version with nose-mounted FLIR, better head-up/head-down displays and pilot's night vision goggles. The engine performance was again increased, with the result that the Marines now have a true '24-hour' Harrier capability. This

means that while many modern defence systems do not give an attacking pilot much of a second chance to score a hit in daylight, about 70 per cent are useless at night because of their reliance on optical fire control. What they can't see, they can't hit – and that's where a night-capable Harrier comes into its own.

To enable pilots to rapidly convert to the V/STOL Harrier from conventional combat aircraft, the USMC ordered 27 TAV-8B two-seaters. Carrier- or land-based, the AV-8B carries a wide range of ordnance to perform its primary air support mission. These include Sidewinder and Maverick missiles, guided bombs and rocket pods, as well as cannon.

Specification
McDonnell Douglas AV-8B Harrier II
Type: single-seat V/STOL close support fighter
Powerplant: one 24,500-lb st Rolls-Royce F402-RR-48 vectored-thrust turbojet
Performance: maximum speed 1063 km/h (661 mph) at sea level

Dimensions: 9.26 m (30 ft 4 in); length 14.14 m (46 ft 4 in); height 3.59 m (11 ft 7.75 in)
Weights: empty 5935 kg (13,086 lb); loaded 14061 kg (31,000 lb)
Armament: two fuselage weapon packs with a 25-mm cannon (port) and 300 rounds (starboard); up to 8,520 lb of external AAMs, bombs and rocket pods on six hardpoints

on the numerically superior Argentine air forces: it scored heavily against much faster aircraft, and successfully bombed well-defended ground targets. Using the superb AIM-9L Sidewinder missile and guns, this mini force of Sea Harriers proved that it is not always numbers that make the difference in combat.

The Harrier II (AV-88) equips squadrons of the US Marine Corps, and is used to soften up defences before the troops hit the beach. Spain and India are the third and fourth operators of the Harrier in the ship-board role.

British naval fighters

Britain and the USA have pioneered carrier aviation developments since the 1920s, progressively adding new safety and improved capability features. The UK's smaller defence budget has obliged the Royal Navy to take a different path to that of the Americans with their big carriers. The same restrictions have limited the amount of fighters the British fleet can maintain.

The latest Harrier F/A.2 carries on the traditions set by fighters of earlier generations, such as the wartime Seafire and Sea Hurricane and the Sea Fury in Korea.

Left: Britain's Sea Harrier was looked upon as a poor man's naval fighter until the war in the Falklands, where it proved to be a ferocious dogfighter able to take on and defeat conventional high-performance jets.

Right: Naval fighters of the future will continue to display all of the latest aviation technology developed for land-based aircraft. Indeed, in some cases, such as the French Rafale, the same fighter will be built in land- and sea-based versions.

365

USA

McDonnell Douglas F/A-18 Hornet

First flown in November 1978 after radical development from the Northrop YF-17 that lost to the General Dynamics YF-16 in the US Air Force's 1974 Lightweight Fighter competition, the **F/A-18 Hornet** is a very capable successor to the McDonnell Douglas F-4 Phantom II and Vought A-7 Corsair II in the multi-role fighter and attack tasks, as indicated by its unique F/A designation.

The type began to enter service late in 1983, and is optimised aerodynamically for agility and good handling under all flight regimes rather than outright performance, and features very advanced electronics so that the pilot can undertake difficult tasks without the support of a back-seater. In addition to its internal 20-mm cannon and two wingtip missile rails, the Hornet has seven hardpoints for its highly varied load of offensive ordnance.

The original **F/A-18A** was complemented by the **F/A-18B** combat-capable conversion trainer and then followed by the improved **F/A-18C** single-seater and **F/A-18D** two-seater, the latter with the night attack capability that has been common to both production types since 1989. There are also land-based models in service with four other countries, while the **RF-18D** is a naval reconnaissance model under development for the US Navy and Marine Corps.

Specification
McDonnell Douglas F/A-18C Hornet
Type: carrier-borne and land-based single-seat multi-role fighter and attack warplane
Powerplant: two 7257-kg (16,000-lb) thrust General Electric F404-GE-400 turbofans
Performance: maximum speed

1913+ km/h (1,189+ mph); range 3702 km (2,300 miles)
Dimensions: span 11.43 m (37 ft 6 in); length 17.07 m (56 ft)
Weights: empty 10455 kg (23,050 lb); maximum take-off 22328 kg (49,224 lb)
Armament: one 20-mm cannon and up to 7711 kg (17,000 lb) of disposable stores

366

UNITED KINGDOM

Sea Harrier F/A.2

To improve the capability of the **Sea Harrier** to meet fleet air defence requirements in the 1990s and beyond, an initial new-build contract was awarded early in 1990. Running parallel with a mid-life update for the entire Sea Harrier fleet, this order covered 10 **FRS Mk 2**s, the first pre-production example of which made its maiden flight on 19 September 1988.

When the Royal Navy selected the Hughes AIM-120 AMRAAM weapon system, it was obvious that the Sea Harrier needed a far more sophisticated radar than the Blue Fox, which was fitted in the FRS Mk 1. Development led to the Blue Vixen multi-mode pulse Doppler unit which, teamed with AMRAAM, gives the Sea Harrier

beyond-visual-range and multiple-target kill capability. In total, Blue Vixen has 11 operational modes for air-to-air and air-to-surface attack.

Integrating the new radar in a small and already less than spacious airframe meant a number of design revisions, the most obvious being a rear fuselage plug which lengthens the FRS Mk 2 by 350 mm (13.75 in), a more bulbous nose to house the radar scanner, and 'bolt-on' 300-mm (12-in) wingtip extensions to maintain centre-of-lift characteristics. Live AMRAAM firings are scheduled to take place in the US this year. In the meantime, prototype testing continues, helped considerably by a fully duplicated cockpit display built into an HS 125-600B.

Specification
British Aerospace Sea Harrier F/A.2
Type: single-seat air superiority fighter/attack aircraft
Powerplant: one 21,500-lb st Rolls-Royce Pegasus 106
Performance: max speed 640 knots (1185 km/h; 736 mph) at low level; service ceiling 15600 m (51,200 ft); max

combat radius 750 km (460 miles)
Dimensions: span 8.31 m (27 ft 3 in); length 14.1 m (46 ft 3 in); height 3.71 m (12 ft 2 in)
Weights: empty 6374 kg (14,052 lb); maximum take-off 11880 kg (26,200 lb)
Armament: full FRS Mk 1 gun and missile capability with the option of up to four AIM-120A AMRAAM AAMs, or two, plus two cannon pods

Swept wings gave the Scimitar and twin-boomed Sea Vixen higher performance, and the mighty Phantom was the last fighter of the Royal Navy fleet carrier era. This ended when the last British carrier, HMS *Ark Royal,* was scrapped in 1980.

The Harrier ushered in an entirely new approach to air power at sea. The new-generation British small carriers can pack a big punch with a full complement of Sea Harriers, which usually take off with the aid of the unique 'ski-jump' set in the bow.

A 'ski-jump' helps a fully loaded fighter save fuel and carry more stores by giving more lift in the first few seconds of flight. A vertical take-off, though faster, restricts the rocket, bomb or missile load. However, with its mission over, the Sea Harrier routinely lands aboard 'straight down'.

These days, the navies that support a carrier force are few; France does, with Super Etendard attack bombers and Rafar, and the Spanish, Russian, Thai and Indian navies each have a seaborne fighter element. Soviet sea power advanced rapidly in the 1980s with the launch of the supercarrier *Admiral Kutznetsov,* formerly known as the *Tbilisi,* but her sister *Vasyag* was never completed.

367
Sukhoi Su-27K 'Flanker'

FORMER USSR

Similar in configuration to the outstanding land-based **Su-27 'Flanker-B'**, the maritime Su-27 (given the NATO reporting suffix **'K'** after being known as the 'Flanker-B' variant 2) has movable foreplanes, wing-folding capability, twin nosewheel landing gear and arrester gear. The long tailcone seen on land-based aircraft is deleted to prevent tail-scraping during high-angle-of-attack carrier operations.

The ship destined to deploy the initial Soviet maritime squadrons of 'Flankers' is the *Admiral Kuznetsov,* the first of a new generation of Russian 'supercarriers' in the 60,000-ton class. The Su-27 has successfully made a number of trial landings and take-offs from this ship, the exacting art of

carrier operations being enhanced by a new navalised trainer based on the Su-27UB two-seater. This machine features a drastically modified forward fuselage to accommodate side-by-side seating for two crew members. US intelligence sources state that the Air Force trainer is fully combat-capable, but it remains to be confirmed whether the naval version will duplicate this. Trials aircraft have so far been seen only with reduced armament.

The *Admiral Kuznetsov* has a 'ski-jump' bow ramp and this is where the Su-27K's foreplanes come into their own. They enable the pilot to make slow approaches down to 220-240 km/h and to take off from the ramp at speeds as low as 140-60 km/h.

Specification
Sukhoi Su-27K 'Flanker'
Type: single-/two-seat air superiority fighter/attack aircraft
Powerplant: two 27,557-lb st Lyul'ka AL-31F afterburning turbofans
Performance: maximum speed Mach 2.25 at height; Mach 1.1 at sea level; service ceiling 18000 m (59,055 ft); combat radius 1283.46 km

(930 miles)
Dimensions: span 14.72 m (48 ft 2.75 in); length 21.94 m (71 ft 11.5 in); height 5.94 m (19 ft 5.5 in)
Weights: empty 22000 kg (48,500 lb); loaded 30000 kg (66,135 lb)
Armament: one 30-mm gun in starboard wing root extension; up to 10 AAMs, including pairs of AA-9s or AA-10s and four AA-8s or AA-11s

368
Yakovlev Yak-38 'Forger'

FORMER USSR

The **Yak-38 'Forger'** first flew in the early 1970s, and began to enter service with the Soviet navy in 1976 as the world's second operational STOVL warplane. The type used a composite powerplant with one Lyul'ka turbojet (exhausting via twin thrust-vectoring nozzles under the rear fuselage) and two Koliesov lift turbojets (located vertically in the forward fuselage) for direct lift. This means that the lift engines were so much dead weight except for take-off and landing, and until 1984 Western analysts were convinced that the Yak-38 was capable only of VTOL operations, which would limit its payload quite severely. Discovery that STOVL operations were indeed

possible led to a considerable upward revision of the Yak-38's warload capacity.

The Yak-38 had no inbuilt gun armament and carried its complete armament load on four hardpoints (two under each wing). The warload comprised air-to-air and air-to-surface weapons of various types, but the Yak-38's lack of electronic sophistication limited it to carrying comparatively simple weapons.

The two Yak-38 variants were the **'Forger-A'** single-seater and the **'Forger-B'** conversion trainer, with its fuselage lengthened to 17.68 mm (58 ft) to allow the insertion of a second cockpit.

Specification
Yakovlev Yak-38 'Forger-A'
Type: ship-borne single-seat multi-role warplane
Powerplant: one 8160-kg (17,989-lb) thrust Lyul'ka AL-21F-1 turbojet and two 3750-kg (7,870-lb) thrust Koliesov ZM turbojets
Performance: maximum speed 1110 km/h (627 mph); range 740 km

(460 miles)
Dimensions: span 7.32 m (24 ft 0.2 in); length 15.5 m (50 ft 10.3 in)
Weights: empty 7385 kg (16,281 lb); maximum take-off 13000 kg (28,660 lb)
Armament: up to 3600 kg (7,937 lb) of disposable stores

The Su-27 can accelerate to supersonic speed while pulling 5 g

Above: The Soviets were late converts to seaborne air power. The first Soviet carrier fighter was the Yak-38 'Forger'. This vertical take-off aircraft had separate lift-engines and was much less flexible than the Sea Harrier.

Below: Operating fighters at sea presents some unique problems. Though carriers are huge ships, by the time you have squeezed 80 aircraft into an area that on land would hold eight, you don't have much room to party!

Grumman's 'Ironworks'

The Grumman Engineering Company received its first contract to build aircraft for the US Navy in May 1931. Thus began an association between manufacturer and military service which has lasted to this day. From the start, the products of the Long Island-based company were characterised by their immense strength, so much so that the company became unofficially known as the 'Ironworks'. From the original FF-1 two-seat fighter, the chain of Grumman carrier-borne fighters has continued almost unbroken. The classic wartime F4F Wildcat and F6F Hellcat were followed by the F8F Bearcat, used in Vietnam by the French, and the F9F Panthers and Cougars, which saw action over Korea. The primary carrier fighter of today is the Gruman F-14 Tomcat, while the Grumman A-6 Intruder is the US Navy's main strike aircraft.

1948 Grumman F9F Panther

Grumman's F9F Panther and the swept-wing Cougar that was developed from it were the mainstay of US carrier wings in the early 1950s, although they were most successful as ground attack fighters. This example served in Korea with Marine Fighter Squadron 311, and is depicted in the midnight-blue colour scheme that was standard until 1955.

1970 Grumman F-14 Tomcat

The Tomcat entered squadron service in 1975, overseeing the American withdrawal from Vietnam that year. This F-14A is depicted in the colours of Navy Fighter Squadron 1 'The Wolfpack'.

Not for the first time, the Soviets sprang a surprise on the Western powers when they made public the V/STOL Yak-38 'Forger'. Using three engines instead of the Harrier's one vectored-thrust powerplant, the Soviet type was larger. Its two lift-engines are made to thrust directly downwards to blast the aircraft off the deck. Further developments were in the pipeline, but the collapse of communism put an end to dreams of a fleet of big carriers.

Apart from the Falklands war, there have been a number of 'hot' carrier operations, most involving the US fleet. Fighters have been at the forefront of these; the most dra-matic was the massive concentration of carriers in 1990-91, when the Iraqi invasion of Kuwait led to the Gulf War. US Navy carriers were tasked with preventing intervention by Iran, and were given the job of 'Scud-busting'.

During the Cold War carrier air wings continually intercepted inquisitive recon-naissance aircraft from the 'other side', guarding against any hostile moves. Pilots who flew such sorties took photographs and kept the encounters friendly. They knew that escorting the 'Bears' away made for good training. While any threat to peace exists, carrier forces remain ready to unsheath the sword.

1935
Gruman F3F

Developed from the F2F, the F3F first flew in 1935, and entered service aboard the USS *Ranger* in April 1936. The type also served with the US Marine Corps, the example depicted serving with Marine Fighter Squadron 1 at Quantico, Virginia, in the late 1930s.

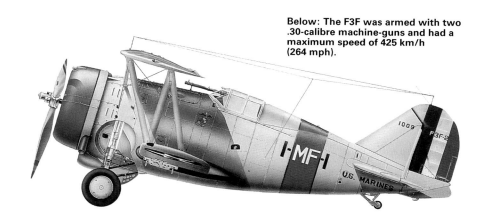

Below: The F3F was armed with two .30-calibre machine-guns and had a maximum speed of 425 km/h (264 mph).

1942
Gruman
F6F
Hellcat

Hellcats were credited with the destruction of 4,947 Japanese aircraft during the last two years of World War II. This example served with Fighter Squadron VF-27 aboard the USS *Princeton* before she was sunk in 1944.

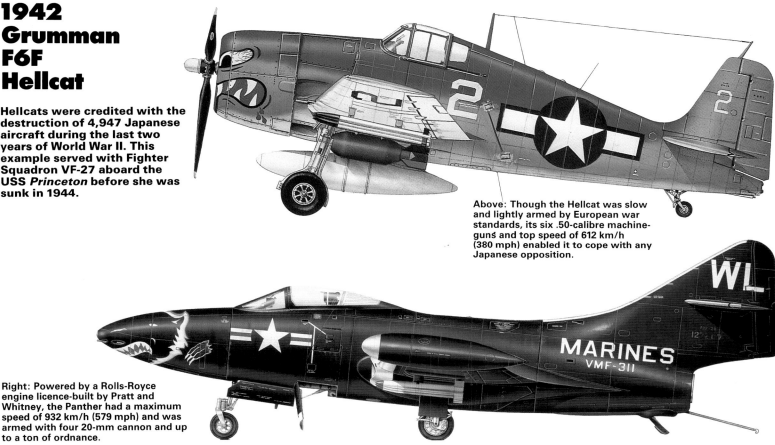

Above: Though the Hellcat was slow and lightly armed by European war standards, its six .50-calibre machine-guns and top speed of 612 km/h (380 mph) enabled it to cope with any Japanese opposition.

Right: Powered by a Rolls-Royce engine licence-built by Pratt and Whitney, the Panther had a maximum speed of 932 km/h (579 mph) and was armed with four 20-mm cannon and up to a ton of ordnance.

Below: The F-14 Tomcat can do Mach 2.34 (2517 km/h or 1,564 mph) at altitude, and is armed with a cocktail of air-to-air weapons – from a 20-mm cannon to the amazing Phoenix missile, with its 200-km (124-mile) range.

TOMCAT
The Top Gunner

Now nearly 25 years old, the Grumman F-14A remains the most capable carrier-borne interceptor in service, and Tomcat aircrew still regard themselves as the best of an elite force.

A Grumman F-14 Tomcat is ready to launch from a US Navy supercarrier. In service since 1975, the Tomcat replaced the McDonnell Douglas F-4 Phantom as the US Navy's premier fighter.

The F-14 Tomcat is no 'Turkey', although this nickname is often used. The aircraft is a lean, mean fighting machine, and at the time of its introduction was the most expensive interceptor the world had ever seen. The Tomcat's high cost is largely due to its sophisticated AIM-54 Phoenix missiles and Hughes AWG-9 fire control system.

The Phoenix missiles, priced at a cool $2 million each, have a range in excess of 100 miles and their own radar for active homing onto a target. This means that the F-14 can 'fire and forget' each missile, and does not need to keep tracking the

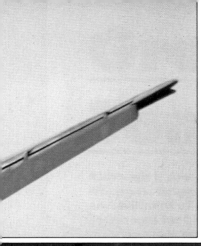

Left: Wings swept fully forward, flaps down for maximum lift, and afterburners blazing, an F-14 from Fighter Squadron 33 'Starfighters' leaves the waist catapult of USS America. The Tomcat is a big machine, with a normal carrier take-off weight of around 30 tons, and it needs all the assistance it can get to claw its way into the air.

Right: Steam from the previous launch wreathes a Tomcat as it manoeuvres onto the catapult for a launch. The size of such fighters dictates the size of the modern carrier: a 30-ton aircraft needs a 300-foot catapult, and in order to mount four such catapults, you need a 1,000-foot ship, which will weigh 75,000 tons or more.

Above: The original Tomcat was powered by a pair of Pratt and Whitney TF-30 afterburning engines, each of 9480-kg (20,900-lb) thrust. While these were enough to propel the aircraft to a maximum speed of twice the speed of sound, the low power-to-weight ratio meant that acceleration was not outstanding. The latest F-14D is powered by the General Electric F110 engine, which has engendered an electrifying improvement in performance and economy. The F-14A (Plus) is the original F-14A retro fitted with the new engine, which also powers the US Air Force's F-15s and F-16s.

Left and inset: The central aerodynamic feature of the Tomcat is its 'swing wing'. Fully extended, with a 20-degree sweep, the wings provide maximum lift for take-off, landing, and low-speed manoeuvring. For maximum high-speed efficiency and for supersonic performance, the wings can be swept back to a maximum of 68 degrees, giving the big Grumman fighter the appearance of an arrowhead.

Below: Inflight refuelling has revolutionised war in the air, at sea just as much as for land-based aircraft. Supported by Grumman KA-6 tankers, a pair of Tomcats can remain on station for hours, hundreds of kilometres out from their home carrier. The limiting factor on such long patrols becomes the endurance of the two-man crew.

Crew and cockpit

The Tomcat pilot and his back-seater, known as a RIO (Radar Intercept Officer) in US Navy parlance, sit in tandem in separate cockpits, covered by a single, upward-hingeing canopy. Once strapped in, however, the two men function as a close-knit team — so highly trained and well disciplined as almost to become a single entity. While the pilot flies the aircraft, and can control close-in engagements as though he were a single-seat fighter pilot, the RIO controls the awesomely capable weapons system, operating the radar and directing long-range engagements.

When it entered service, the F-14 was the only fighter in the world capable of engaging multiple targets simultaneously, and the only interceptor in the world with a 'fire-and-forget' BVR (beyond visual range) missile, and even today, the Tomcat has a better BVR capability than any other fighter in service.

By modern standards, the F-14's cockpit looks very old-fashioned, with its mass of analogue dials and conventional switches, dials, knobs and levers. More recent fighters tend to have three large cathode ray tubes, on which any information can be called up. The pilot's cockpit has a conventional central control column, and orthodox-looking twin throttles. Even the wing-sweep control lever would seem familiar to any F-111, Tornado or 'Flogger' pilot.

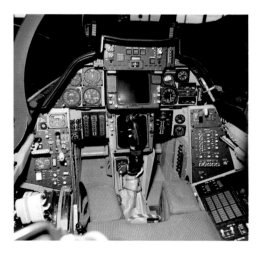

Above: As with most American fighter designs entering service from the 1970s onwards, visibility through the Tomcat's bubble canopy is excellent.

Left: Although the Tomcat's cockpit was well designed for its time, in this age of video-display units it seems positively archaic. The pilot's position (far left) is dominated by the square vertical-display indicator, with the head-up display above. The RIO's cockpit (near left) has a large circular tactical-information display, with a large armaments panel to the left.

Below: The crew of the Tomcat comprises the pilot, who is concerned with flying and fighting the aircraft, and the RIO or Radar Intercept Officer, who deals with detection, communications, electronic warfare and the like.

Weapons of the Tomcat

The Grumman F-14A Tomcat can carry a range of weapons suitable to meet and defeat any likely threat. Its armament consists of a deadly mix of close-range AIM-9 Sidewinder 'dogfight' missiles and longer-range AIM-7 Sparrow and AIM-54 Phoenix missiles, capable of downing targets at 'beyond visual range'. These are backed up by a powerful M61A1 20-mm cannon, with 675 rounds of ammunition.

Sidewinder

The AIM-9 Sidewinder is the best-known, and perhaps the most widely respected, missile in the world. Combat-proven time and again — most spectacularly in the Falklands and over the Beka'a Valley — the latest versions of the Sidewinder family have genuine 'all-aspect' capability, meaning that their seeker heads are sensitive enough to lock onto a head-on target, and not just onto the hot jet-pipe of a target flying away from you. The Sidewinder's only disadvantage is its relatively short range.

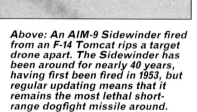

Phoenix

Although the Tomcat can carry up to six AIM-54s, such a load is extremely unusual. The big missile is very heavy, and an F-14 with six AIM-54s will always exceed the maximum carrier-landing weight, so if some were not fired, at least two of the $2 million missiles would need to be jettisoned prior to landing. For this reason, operational F-14s seldom carry more than two AIM-54s when operating from a carrier. In wartime, however, Phoenix would be the weapon to use at long ranges, against mass raids, or against cruise missiles.

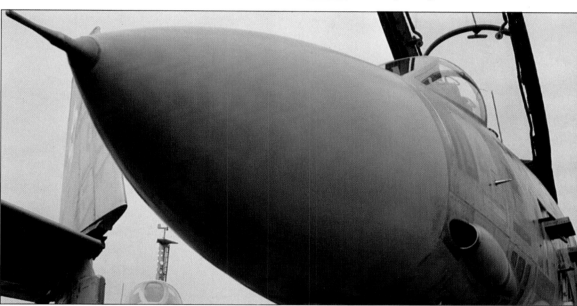

Above: An AIM-9 Sidewinder fired from an F-14 Tomcat rips a target drone apart. The Sidewinder has been around for nearly 40 years, having first been fired in 1953, but regular updating means that it remains the most lethal short-range dogfight missile around.

Left: The range of Tomcat weaponry is unparalleled. For dogfights, there is an M61 rotary 20-mm cannon in the fuselage, with Sidewinder dogfight missiles on the outside of the wing pylons. AIM-7 Sparrow medium-range radar-homing missiles are on the same pylons, while four AIM-54 Phoenix long-range missiles are carried beneath the fuselage.

Above: The Tomcat is armed with an M61A1 Vulcan cannon, firing out of the port side of the fuselage beneath the cockpit. The Vulcan is a six-barrel 20-mm Gatling gun, with an amazing rate of fire of 6,000 rounds per minute, which translates to 100 high-explosive or armour-piercing rounds every second.

Below: A Soviet 'Kashin' class destroyer which has been following a US Navy carrier battle group is framed by a Tomcat's medium- and short-range missiles. Sidewinder is a heat-seeker, with a range of eight kilometres, while the larger radar-guided Sparrow is effective out to 45 kilometres.

Guns

The M61A1 20-mm cannon works on the Gatling principle, with six revolving barrels. This gives an impressive maximum rate of fire of 6,000 rpm, although 4,000 rpm can be selected. The Tomcat carries 675 rounds of ammunition. The cannon is particularly useful for very-close-in dogfight-type engagements, or for administering a *coup de grâce* against a damaged target. The gun is also a useful option against low-value targets.

Sparrow

The AIM-7 Sparrow employs semi-active radar homing, meaning that it homes onto radar reflections transmitted at the target by the launch aircraft. The pilot has to continue flying towards the target, 'illuminating' it with his radar, while the missile is in flight. The Sparrow has proved only moderately successful, and is to be replaced by the active radar-homing AIM-120 AMRAAM.

SEA HARRIER

...and die

The Harrier had been in service for many years before it saw combat in the Falklands. Few people could have predicted how amazingly successful it would be.

A Royal Navy Sea Harrier takes off from HMS Hermes, throwing clouds of spray from the rain-soaked deck. Hermes' modest 6½-degree 'ski-jump' allowed the Harriers to take off with virtually full warloads.

Eight days had passed since the bombing raid against Port Stanley airfield. Here Flight Lieutenant Dave Morgan tells the story of air combat in the Falklands war.

"Our daily pattern then was flying combat air patrols and trying to keep the heat off the fleet while they were deploying. The GR Mk 3s did a lot of good work supporting 2 Para at Goose Green. Then on 8 June came the disaster at Bluff Cove.

"We scrambled but got there too late to catch the first wave. As I came in I saw the two great columns of smoke coming from the *Galahad* and *Lancelot*.

"We began our patrol, and below us I saw a landing craft gently trogging along the coast. I asked the control ship whether it was friendly, and it said it was. By

Below: The need to get as many fighters to the South Atlantic as possible saw both Hermes and Invincible carrying twice as many Sea Harriers as their usual complements. With limited space in the hangars, some were kept permanently on deck.

that time we had about two minutes' fuel left before we had to go back to the carrier, and we were doing a final turn from east back to the west.

"I stood the Harrier on its nose . . ."

"As I turned round I saw an enemy aircraft running in to attack the landing craft. I'd briefed my wingman, Dave Smith, that if we saw anything at low level the guy who saw it would attack and the other chap would just try to hang on and clear his tail. I was at 10,000 feet and flying fairly slowly.

Below: Sea Harriers in the Falklands were variously armed according to their tasks, but for the defence of the fleet and against Argentine fighters they carried AIM-9L Sidewinder missiles and belly-mounted cannon pods.

Right: Flight Lieutenant Dave Morgan's Sea Harrier was the only one hit in the first Port Stanley attack, taking a single 20-mm cannon shell through the tailfin. Damage was minimal, and the aircraft took a matter of minutes to repair.

I stood the Harrier on its nose and accelerated towards this aircraft, which was about eight miles away. Unfortunately, I didn't get there in time to stop him, but I locked on to the guy with my eyes and saw him miss with his bomb and then disappear.

"Okay, you'll do . . ."

"Then I saw a second guy running in from a different direction and he hit the back of the ship, which made me very angry. The angriest I've ever been in my life, because I knew from this bloody great explosion that he'd killed people, and because I hadn't been able to intercept, and because he'd had the audacity to actually kill somebody while I was there. So I decided that he was the guy who was going to get killed. As I was going for him, a third one appeared from underneath me and attacked the ship again, but missed. So I thought, 'Okay, you'll do.'

"I wound across and got in behind with a massive overtaking speed. He was rapidly getting larger in my windscreen. I locked up my missile at about 1,500 yards and fired at 1,000 yards. My missile did a quick initial jink, then went off after him and exploded near his tail; there was a huge fireball and wreckage began to fall into the water. There was no reaction at all from the others; they were in a gaggle coming off the target, with no attempt at mutual cover.

"I was going very, very fast – probably at around the speed of sound. Because I was flying so

much faster than the speed at which the machine was supposed to be flown and at which the missile was supposed to be fired, the aircraft rolled dramatically to the right – which really took me by surprise as I was only 100 feet away from the water then. That was fairly startling. I recovered and found that the roll had pointed me directly at their third guy. He began a fairly gentle turn to port across my nose, almost as if he was looking to see what had happened to the man behind. My missile locked up, broke lock, then I locked it on again and this time the lock held. I fired at the second aircraft at about 1,200

Below: During the struggle for the Falklands, the British carriers buzzed with activity. This is the hangar deck of HMS Hermes, where most of the routine service tasks and maintenance of aircraft was carried out. Rearming and refuelling of operational aircraft was performed 'topside', in the face of the worst weather the South Atlantic winter could offer.

'Black Death' and 'Nine Lima'
the deadly combination.

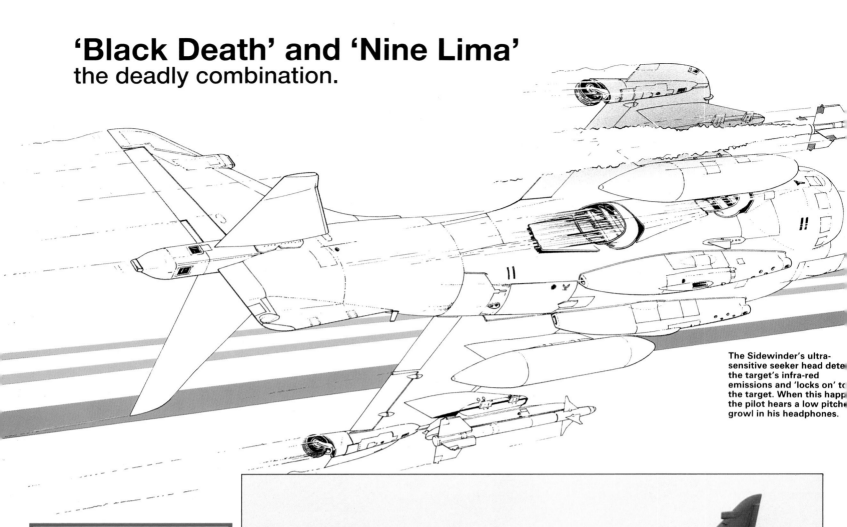

The Sidewinder's ultra-sensitive seeker head dete[cts] the target's infra-red emissions and 'locks on' to the target. When this happ[ens] the pilot hears a low pitche[d] growl in his headphones.

'Black Death' and 'Nine Lima'

There were those who did not take the Sea Harrier seriously in the early 1980s. But events in the South Atlantic soon proved them dramatically wrong; seldom has any warplane established a reputation as quickly as the Sea Harrier did in May and June 1982. It might not have had great speed, but it proved to be a ferocious fighter. The aircraft's success was helped by the superbly trained pilots who flew it, and by the highly effective AIM-9L variant of the Sidewinder heat-seeking missile with which it was armed.

A pair of Sea Harriers 'clean up' after take-off. The Harrier's light weight and powerful engine, dictated by the type's V/STOL capability, also give it stunning acceleration. Allied to good manoeuvrability, that makes the aircraft a ferocious dogfighter, as the Argentines were to discover.

yards. I think he saw it coming, because he reversed his turn and broke away to starboard. The missile reversed its turn too, cut across my nose and went straight in and hit after he had turned through about 40 degrees. It took his tail off completely and he went into the water. I thought, 'That's the end of him,' but about three seconds later a parachute opened

right in front of me and just whistled over my port wing.

"That was the two rear aircraft out. Now I was rapidly overtaking the front two. Still there was no sign that they knew we were after them. They were flying fairly close together, about 100 yards apart. Unfortunately, when I fired the second missile my head-up display went out, and I lost my magic green writing. We were down at about 50 feet at this stage, still going very fast. But

this time the other Sea Harrier was still behind me; he had lost sight of me. Dave Smith had seen my missile in flight and just aimed himself in their general direction.

Trying with cannon

"I gave them a couple of seconds' squirt with my cannon from about 1,400 yards. I didn't see any hits at all, but the No. 2 went into a steep break to port across me. And that, as it transpired, put him right in front of Dave. I followed him round, still with no gunsight, put him in the middle of my windscreen and closed from 400 to 330 yards, firing bursts at him. I had no real idea where my rounds were going; I didn't see any of them impact on the water. But Dave did – he saw

the rounds exploding and saw the Mirage flying through the explosions down at about 30 feet. He locked on one of his missiles, but he didn't want to fire because he didn't know where I was.

"I called, 'I'm out of rounds, pulling up!' I just rolled the wings to horizontal and then pulled up vertically. Dave saw me go through the horizon; meanwhile the No. 2 rolled his wings level as he saw my pull-up and sat at about 15 feet above the sea, going out to the south-west very fast. I looked

Right: Harriers were not the only things protecting the fleet. HMS Broadsword, *seen here alongside the* Hermes, *was armed with the highly effective Sea Wolf missile and served as the carrier's 'goalkeeper', or close escort.*

The main air-to-air weapon of the Sea Harrier was the AIM-9L Sidewinder, a short-range infra-red homing air-to-air missile. Known as the 'Nine Lima' to RN and RAF pilots, this advanced Sidewinder variant proved to have a genuine all-aspect capability.

When the Sidewinder is fired it drops away from the aircraft, and switches to its own internal power supply. The seeker head sends steering commands to the sensitive canard foreplanes, which guide the missile to its target. Spinning rollerons at the missile tail stabilise the missile in flight.

The missile is fitted with a sensitive optical laser fuse, which triggers the powerful annular blast fragmentation warhead. This is usually sufficient to saw the average aircraft in half!

over my shoulder and saw the steaming trail as Dave fired his missile; it went so low I could see the reflection of the trail on the water. Then, a few seconds later, there was a bloody great explosion over the coast at Hammond Point as the aircraft smashed into the ground.

"Dave then pulled up – by this stage, we were desperately short of fuel. We joined up and returned to the *Hermes*. It was 50 minutes past sunset when we got back. I made my first night landing with two minutes' worth of fuel and Dave had less than that.

"When I think about the whole campaign, the most frightening moment was on the very first raid when I saw people actually firing at me and obviously trying to kill me. I think that's what really brought it home, made me absolutely scared stiff for that fraction of a second. Then the old brain said, 'Sod it. We've got to get in there, so go do it.' I think everyone felt that on their first mission."

Right: The Harrier's cockpit reflects the 1960s technology from which it derived. Later cockpits are much less cluttered, with three or four visual displays taking the place of many of the knobs and dials seen here.

TOMCAT OPERATIONS

On the deck sits the sleek form of the Tomcat, in a moment of relative peace. A gesture from the catapult officer and the silence is shattered as the Tomcat is hurled along the deck, faster than a racing car, and hurtles into the air.

The giant aircraft carriers of the US Navy are arguably the most versatile military asset in the world: able to project US naval and air power around the globe, quickly and with lethal force. Each carrier has three squadrons of attack aircraft, a further 16 anti-submarine and anti-surface vessel planes, and a dozen or so support and control aircraft. The tasks of air defence, air superiority and fighter escort fall to the two squadrons of 12 Grumman F-14A Tomcats.

The Tomcat was designed as a weapon system – using radar to detect targets, computers to analyse the information, and weapons to kill – in an airframe designed to fly at high speed, at low or high altitude, and out to long ranges, all from the security of the carrier.

The air defence task breaks down into two roles: the combat air patrol and the deck-launched intercept. Combat air patrols are usually flown some 280 km out from the carrier. Fully bombed-up and with tanks filled, the Tomcat can maintain this patrol for some two hours or so.

In contrast, the deck-launched intercept consists of a pair of Tomcats fuelled, armed, and sitting on the catapults ready for immediate launch. Although the Tomcat can carry six Phoenix plus two Sidewinder AAMs, a more usual load is four Phoenix long-range, two Sparrow medium-range and two Sidewinder close-range AAMs (eight potential kills in all).

To launch the aircraft, the steam catapult is crucial. With the Tomcat in position, its launch bar fitted into the catapult shuttle and the blast baffle raised, the aircraft is ready for launch. The engines are run up, the pilot and deck catapult officer exchange signals, and the catapult is fired. The big fighter hits 278 km/h in just 2.5 seconds.

Landing is considered easier than the launch. On his approach, the pilot will throttle down to around 200 km/h. At about half a mile from the carrier he will be looking for the 'meatball': a series of lights and lenses which will guide him onto the correct angle of descent to the deck. The pilot will aim to hit the deck with his arrester hook catching the second or third of the four arrester wires lying across the deck. If he is successful, the aircraft will come to an abrupt, and violent, halt in just a few seconds.

F-14 Tomcat fleet defence

The catapult officer gives the catapult crew the signal to launch the Tomcat. In order to get into the air, the 30-ton fighter must be hurled to 150 knots in two or three seconds, which is three times the acceleration of the fastest supercar.

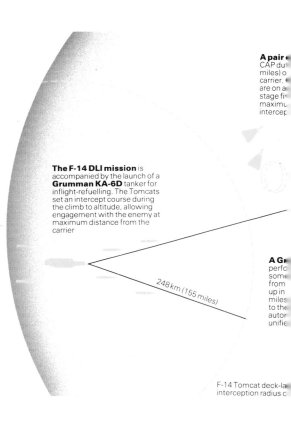

A pair CAP du miles) o carrier. are on a stage fi maximu intercep

The F-14 DLI mission is accompanied by the launch of a **Grumman KA-6D** tanker for inflight-refuelling. The Tomcats set an intercept course during the climb to altitude, allowing engagement with the enemy at maximum distance from the carrier

248km (155 miles)

A G perfo some from up in miles to the autor unifie

F-14 Tomcat deck-la interception radius c

Launch sequence

1 The Tomcat taxis forward with its nosewheels in the 'box' — a shallow groove in the deck, leading to the catapult slot. The green-shirted 'hook-up man' runs forward and kneels beside the nose gear. The nose bar is lowered to engage the catapult shuttle. The hook-up man signals for the catapult to be tensioned. The nosewheel is pulled forward, but is simultaneously restrained by the hold-back. The catapult operator signals his readiness by holding up a single finger. When he sees this, the hook-up man whirls his right hand and points forward, directing the yellow-shirted aircraft director to play his part.

2 The aircraft director has been standing in front of the aircraft with his hands above his head, fists clenched, to tell the pilot to keep his brakes on. When he sees the hook-up man whirl his hand, he unclenches his fists to signal to the pilot: "Brakes off, full power!" The hook-up man hands over to the next man, the catapult officer.

3 The catapult officer thrusts two hands into the air, two fingers extended, and waves them in a rapid, rotating motion. The hook-up officer gives the 'all-clear'. The catapult officer points at the shooter, who has both hands in the air, waiting. The pilot salutes to show his readiness, the catapult officer turns to look forward, and then turns back to face the aircraft and points forward, hitting the deck with his hand — his signal to the shooter to fire the catapult, hurtling the aircraft into the sky.

Mission profiles

The essence of the Tomcat is its phenomenal range. It can operate hundreds of miles away from its carrier — and it needs to. Modern missiles can be launched hundreds of miles from their targets. The key to defence is to destroy the attacker before he gets in range to fire, and it is easier to hit one aircraft than six missiles.

To that end, the Tomcat will fly combat air patrols. With long-range detection and control provided by Hawkeye airborne early warning aircraft, pairs of Tomcats will be held in reserve, ready to intercept any threat at a moment's notice.

The Tomcat's other main mission is the deck-launched intercept. This is a last-minute tactic, with a pair of aircraft kept at 'Alert 5'. If attackers have penetrated the barrier patrols, then these are the last airborne defence before using the missile defences of the carrier battle group itself.

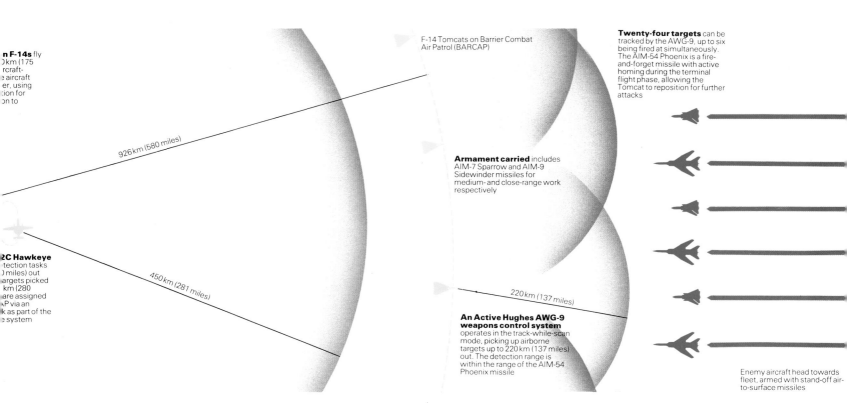

n F-14s fly)km (175 rcraft-e aircraft er, using tion for n to

2C Hawkeye tection tasks) miles) out argets picked km (280 are assigned AP via an k as part of the e system

926 km (580 miles)

450 km (281 miles)

F-14 Tomcats on Barrier Combat Air Patrol (BARCAP)

Armament carried includes AIM-7 Sparrow and AIM-9 Sidewinder missiles for medium- and close-range work respectively

220 km (137 miles)

An Active Hughes AWG-9 weapons control system operates in the track-while-scan mode, picking up airborne targets up to 220 km (137 miles) out. The detection range is within the range of the AIM-54 Phoenix missile

Twenty-four targets can be tracked by the AWG-9, up to six being fired at simultaneously. The AIM-54 Phoenix is a fire-and-forget missile with active homing during the terminal flight phase, allowing the Tomcat to reposition for further attacks

Enemy aircraft head towards fleet, armed with stand-off air-to-surface missiles

Landing the aircraft

Getting the aircraft back safely after mission completion is, obviously, terribly important. Landing on a moving runway that is pitching and rolling, and, because of the angled deck, moving sideways, is not particularly easy — in Vietnam, pilots had higher heart rates during landings than they did when fighting MiGs! If the approach is too high, then the arrester hook will not connect and the aircraft will overshoot. If the approach is too low, the aircraft will slam into the deck. The 'meatball', a device to tell the pilot when he is on the correct approach, will guide him in.

Too high: top lens illuminated

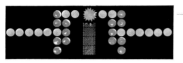

On glideslope: middle lens illuminated

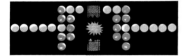

Too low: bottom lens illuminated

Co-ordinating the approach

As the carrier steams forward through the water, the angled flight deck, and thus the approach path, seem to move sideways. This is because the centreline of the deck is offset, at an angle from the centreline of the ship. This sideways movement is about 10 feet per second, which the Tomcat pilot responds to by making a succession of small sidesteps to keep himself lined up.

Sideslip 10ft/sec

Ship speed 30 knots

Using the 'meatball'

The pilot aims to place his arrester hook in the middle of the cluster of four arrester wires, which are located about a third of the way down the angled deck. To aid the pilot, the landing safety officers tell him his height, and he can also see the light landing device, or 'meatball'. The 'meatball' is a gyro-stabilised set of five Fresnel lenses surrounded by an array of green and red reference lights. The 'meatball' is set up for a glideslope angle of three degrees, and is adjusted to take account of the pitching of the deck, and the characteristics of the individual aircraft type on the approach. For lateral alignment with the deck, the pilot uses the runway centreline and a drop-line of orange lights which hang off the stern.

Left: The system of gyro-stabilised lights and lenses that gives a pilot his landing references is the ultimate development of the original mirror landing system developed in Britain in the 1950s.

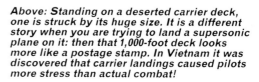

Left: A Tomcat lands, arrester hook extended. In a perfect 'trap', the hook should engage the third arrester wire; taking the first or second wire indicates a low approach. Taking the fourth wire, or missing altogether, means the aircraft is too high. In that case the pilot slams open his throttles to get back to try again.

Above: Standing on a deserted carrier deck, one is struck by its huge size. It is a different story when you are trying to land a supersonic plane on it: then that 1,000-foot deck looks more like a postage stamp. In Vietnam it was discovered that carrier landings caused pilots more stress than actual combat!

BALLISTIC MISSILE SUBMARINES

Lurking stealthily beneath the surface of the world's oceans, nuclear-powered ballistic missile submarines carry the ultimate threat of destruction.

They call it Sherwood Forest. As many as 24 closely-packed tubes like dense tree-trunks spring, four decks high, through the polished-steel grating of the floor. There may be fruit, vegetables, or loaves of bread hung in net bags between the tubes, or a crew member in jogging kit lapping 19 times round the deck to make a mile's run. Perhaps another, between watches, catches a few hours' sleep in a temporary cot slung between the tubes.

It may seem almost rural, but this is the missile compartment of a modern submarine, and all the time a game of cat-and-mouse is being played in the cold blackness, hundreds of feet below the surface of the sea.

The history of the development of the modern nuclear-powered missile submarine is closely interwoven with the political attitudes of the USSR. At the end of World War II, under Stalin's rule, the Soviet Union withdrew within a series of concentric defence perimeters. On land, there were relatively short-range missile establishments to protect her in case of attack. At sea, medium-range submarines patrolled the outer perimeter to intercept any approaching task forces.

When, however, the Korean War re-established the aircraft carrier as an essential element of US naval strategy (the supercarrier programme made it possible for nuclear bombers to strike from a distance of over 1,000 miles), a complete rethink of Soviet naval policy was necessary.

The lower missile compartment of the nuclear-powered ballistic missile submarine USS Ohio stretches away into the distance. There is more explosive power here than in all of the bombs dropped in World War II.

57

German rocket expertise shocked the Allies in World War II, and many post-war tests used captured German weapons, such as this V-2 on the deck of the USS Midway.

Rockets at sea

The US Navy started studies for taking missiles to sea as early as 1946, even going as far as firing captured German V-2 missiles off the deck of the carrier USS *Midway* in October 1947. However, such weapons were dreadfully inaccurate, and when you added the problem of firing from a moving platform such as a ship, you could not be sure that your missile would hit even a large city, let alone a smaller target.

For several years, the Navy concentrated on pilotless aircraft-type missiles, now known as cruise missiles. These were more accurate, but could be intercepted more easily by enemy air defences. By the time missile technology matured in the late 1950s, it was clear that ballistic weapons were best, and Polaris was developed wih amazing speed.

The USS Robert E. Lee was the third Polaris boat to commission into the US Navy. The Polaris system was developed astonishingly quickly, from the Navy getting the go-ahead to develop the missile and submarine in 1956 to the first submerged launch in July 1960.

After a brief period of political instability following Stalin's death in 1953, Nikita Khrushchev took power in February 1955. He quickly appointed Sergei Gorshkov as naval Commander-in-Chief and initiated a crash programme of submarine development. By August 1958, the first of the 'November' class of long-range nuclear-powered submarines had been commissioned.

Khrushchev initiated an intensive research programme into the development of subma-

BALLISTIC MISSILE SUBMARINES Reference File

275

'Lafayette' class

The boats generally known as the **'Lafayette' class** submarines in fact comprise two distinct but similar classes, namely the original 19-strong 'Lafayette' class proper and the improved 12-strong **'Benjamin Franklin' class** with quieter machinery and an increased crew.

Built from 1961, the first eight boats were produced to carry the UGM-27B Polaris A-2 submarine-launched ballistic missile with a single 800-kiloton warhead, while the remainder were completed to carry the UGM-27C Polaris A-3 with three 200-kiloton multiple re-entry vehicles. From 1970, the boats were converted to carry the Poseidon C-3 missile with between 10 and 14 40-kiloton MIRVs (Multiple

Independently-targeted Re-entry Vehicles), and from September 1978 to December 1982, 12 of the boats were extensively revised for the far more capable Trident I C-4 missile with its eight 100-kiloton MIRVs. The boats served with the US Navy's Atlantic Fleet, several of them being forward-based at Holy Loch in Scotland, with two alternating crews for 70-day patrols separated by 32-day minor overhauls.

Specification
'Lafayette' class
Type: nuclear-powered ballistic missile submarine
Displacement: 7,250 tons surfaced and 8,250 tons full load
Armament: 16 UGM-73A Poseidon

C-3 or UGM-96A Trident I C-4 underwater-launched ballistic missiles, and four 533-mm (21-in) tubes for 12 Mk 48 wire-guided torpedoes
Propulsion: one Westinghouse S5W reactor driving two steam turbines delivering 11185 kW (15,000 shp) to two shafts

Performance: maximum speed 20 kt (37 km/h; 23 mph) surfaced and 25 kt (46 km/h; 29 mph) dived
Dimensions: length overall 129.5 m (425 ft); beam 10.1 m (33 ft)
Crew: 140 or ('Benjamin Franklin' class) 168
User: USA

rine-borne ballistic missiles, with the intention not only of extending the USSR's defensive perimeter, but also of carrying the threat of attack into any potential enemy's home waters.

Early Soviet experiments

After some unsuccessful attempts with V-2 missiles towed in watertight containers, the Soviets decided to install vertical launch tubes in the conning tower of the submarine itself. Between 1956 and 1958, a number of 'Zulu' class boats were modified to take two tubes, each about 2.25 metres in diameter, in the aft part of the fin. These held SS-N-4 'Sark' missiles, giant three-stage liquid-fuel rockets measuring 15 metres long and with a diameter of about 1.8 metres.

The two main disadvantages of the SS-N-4 were the need to fire it from the surface and its short range of only 350 miles. Furthermore, the liquid fuel was extremely hazardous, and its use led to the loss of at least one Soviet boat.

Meanwhile, the USA had been engaged in more cautious submarine development. Two nuclear-powered prototypes, the *Nautilus* and *Seawolf*, were completed in 1954 and 1957 respectively. At first, the US Navy opted for solid-fuel, low-trajectory cruise missiles, the first of which, the Regulus 1, was available as early as 1954. By 1960, however, the first of the 'George Washington' class was installed with the Polaris A-1 ballistic missile: solid-fuel powered and capable of underwater launch with a range of some 1,400 miles.

The Soviet 'November' class, with a length of 358 ft and a displacement of 5,100 tons submerged, had been the largest submarines of their time; the American 'Polaris' boats were even bigger. By 1967, a fleet of 41 had been commissioned: five of the 'Washington' class

A Polaris A-3 missile is launched from a submarine, the periscope of which can be seen ahead of the missile. The A-3 entered service in 1964, and had three warheads and twice the range of the earlier models of Polaris.

276
'Ohio' class

 USA

Planned to run 18 boats, the **'Ohio' class** submarines are the world's second largest underwater craft, and of the 40 boats currently in service most are allocated to the US Navy's Pacific Fleet. The class was designed from the early 1970s as the primary launch platform for the Trident submarine-launched ballistic missile, of which no fewer than 24 are accommodated in the two rows of missile tubes abaft the sail. The first eight boats carry the Trident I C-4 with its eight 100-kiloton MIRVs, while the later units have the larger, heavier and considerably more accurate Trident II D-5 with its potent load of between eight and 14 375-kiloton MIRVs.

The programme was considerably delayed by a number of technical and production factors. The first boat was commissioned in November 1981, three years after the planned date, and the programme was finally completed in 1997. The boats are based at Bangor, Washington (Pacific Fleet) and Kings Bay, Georgia (Atlantic Fleet) and each has two crews, these alternating for 70-day patrols separated by 25-day short overhauls.

Specification
'Ohio' class
Type: nuclear-powered ballistic missile submarine
Displacement: 16,600 tons surfaced and 18,700 tons dived
Armament: 24 UGM-96A Trident I

C-4 or UGM-133A Trident II D-5 underwater-launched ballistic missiles, and four 533-mm (21-in) tubes for Mk 48 wire-guided torpedoes
Propulsion: one Westinghouse S8G reactor driving two steam turbines delivering 44740 kW (60,000 shp) to two shafts

Performance: maximum speed 28 kt (52 km/h; 32 mph) surfaced and 30 kt (55.5 km/h; 34.5 mph) dived
Dimensions: length overall 170.7 m (560 ft); beam 12.8 m (42 ft)
Crew: 155
User: USA

(382 ft; 6,900 tons), five of the 'Ethan Allen' class (410 ft; 7,900 tons) and 31 of the 'Benjamin Franklin' and 'Lafayette' classes (425 ft; 8,250 tons). These were all fitted with 16 launch tubes set in the hull aft of the conning tower.

The Soviets were unable to deploy a similar submarine until 1967. In the meantime, they went ahead with a number of interim designs. The diesel/electric 'Golf' class, the first specifically designed to carry three SS-N-4s, was clearly no match for the American 'Washington' class. It was superseded by the nuclear-powered 'Hotel' class in 1959-62 – but still only three SS-N-4s were carried. Rather late in the day, interest was aroused in cruise missiles, and SS-N-3C 'Shaddocks' were mounted, first on 'Whiskey' class boats and then on the nuclear-powered 'Echo I' class.

Britain's deterrent was initially carried by the four 'Resolution' class nuclear-powered submarines of the Royal Navy. Developed in the 1960s with some American assistance, the boats are similar to the contemporary 'Lafayette' class, although following British practice the diving planes have been moved from the fin to the bow. They were armed with Polaris A-3 missiles but are being replaced by the 'Vanguard' class armed with Trident II D-5 missiles.

277
'Resolution' class

UNITED KINGDOM

Replaced from the mid-1990s by the four 'Vanguard' class boats armed with Trident II D-5 missiles, the four submarines of the **'Resolution' class** formed the mainstay of the UK's nuclear deterrent force, and were not dissimilar to the American 'Lafayette' class. The boats were built from 1964 for commissioning dates between October 1967 and December 1969. Each had two crews for alternating 90-day patrols split by short overhaul periods.

The original UGM-27C Polaris A-3 weapons (each with three 200-kiloton re-entry vehicles designed and produced in the UK) were upgraded from the mid-1970s in the British 'Chevaline' project to A-3TK standard

with an updated bus (modified to produce a confusingly large number of credible threats on the enemy's radar screens) carrying up to three 60-kiloton re-entry vehicles hardened against the EMP (Electro-Magnetic Pulse) and fast radiation effects of nuclear explosions. It is likely that at least one re-entry vehicle in three is a dummy carrying penetration aids and decoys.

Specification
'Resolution' class
Type: nuclear-powered ballistic missile submarine
Displacement: 7,600 tons surfaced and 8,500 tons dived
Armament: 16 Polaris A-3TK underwater-launched ballistic missiles, and six 533-mm (21-in) tubes for Mk 24 Tigerfish wire-guided torpedoes
Propulsion: one Rolls-Royce PWR-1 reactor driving two steam turbines delivering 11185 kW (15,000 shp) to two

shafts
Performance: maximum speed 20 kt (37 km/h; 23 mph) surfaced and 25 kt (46 km/h; 29 mph) dived
Dimensions: length overall 129.5 m (425 ft); beam 10.1 m (33 ft)
Crew: 143
User: UK

278
'Typhoon' class

FORMER USSR

The **'Typhoon' class** submarines are the world's largest underwater vessels, and in design are truly prodigious boats whose 20 SS-N-20 'Sturgeon' missiles give the USSR a submarine-launched ballistic missile capability equal to that of the American 'Ohio' class boats.

The class was produced at Severodvinsk in 1977-89, and is based on an unusual arrangement of side-by-side main pressure hulls (probably two 'Delta III' class hulls, each complete with a propulsion system with reactor, turbine set and propeller) sandwiching a short upper pressure hull containing the command and control spaces. These three components are located inside a hydrodynamically 'clean' outer hull with features such as control of the

boundary layer for impressive performance and low operating noise. The missile compartment is unusual in its location forward of the sail. The design is optimised for operations under and through the Arctic ice, the stubby sail and retractable bow hydroplanes allowing the boat to break through thin ice; remaining inside the Arctic Circle, the boats can hit targets anywhere in the continental USA.

Specification
'Typhoon' class
Type: nuclear-powered ballistic missile submarine
Displacement: 18,500 tons surfaced and 26,500 tons dived
Armament: 20 SS-N-20 'Sturgeon'

underwater-launched ballistic missiles, plus four 650-mm (25.6-in) and two 533-mm (21-in) tubes for 36 torpedoes (Type 65 and Type 53) and anti-submarine missiles (SS-N-15 'Starfish' and SS-N-16 'Stallion')
Propulsion: two reactors driving two steam turbines delivering 60000 kW

(80,460 shp) to two shafts
Performance: maximum speed 20 kt (37 km/h; 23 mph) surfaced and 30 kt (55.5 km/h; 34.5 mph) dived
Dimensions: length overall 171.5 m (562 ft 8 in); beam 24.6 m (80 ft 8 in)
Crew: about 150
User: USSR

For a few years the strategic role was switched to land-based missiles, but then in 1967 the first of 34 Soviet 'Yankee' boats was commissioned. This type was very similar to the 'Ethan Allen' class – being fitted with 16 SS-N-6 'Sawfly' single-stage liquid-fuel missiles in hull-mounted tubes placed aft of the conning tower – and it has been suggested that the Soviets had succeeded in obtaining plans of the US submarine.

From the beginning of the 1970s, both the Soviet and US navies concentrated on the development of even larger submarines to carry even longer-range missiles. In the USSR the 'Delta I' and 'Delta II' classes were laid down, the former (443 ft; 10,000 tons) capable of carrying 12 SS-N-8 missiles, the latter (498 ft; 11,500 tons) carrying 16. The SS-N-8 missile, with a range in excess of 4,000 miles, using only a two-stage liquid-fuel rocket, was

superior to the Trident 1, for which the Americans in 1976 had begun to build the 24 missile 'Ohio' class (560 ft; 18,700 tons).

Recent developments

The 'Delta Is' and 'IIs', of which 22 are still in service, were followed by the 'Delta III', carrying 16 SS-N-18 'Stingrays', and then the 'Delta IV' (525 ft; 13,600 tons), carrying 16 SS-N-23 missiles. In 1980, the Soviets launched the first of their 'Typhoon' class – at 561 ft and 25,000 tons, the largest submarines in the world. Only four remain in service. They carry 20 of the three-stage, solid-fuel SS-N-20 'Sturgeon' missiles, with a range of 4,500 miles – capable of reaching strategic targets anywhere in the world.

Currently the US Navy has 18 'Ohio' boats

The Soviets were left at the post by Polaris, but with a great deal of effort, and with considerable help from the espionage specialists of the KGB, they had a fleet of modern ballistic missile submarines at sea by the end of the 1960s. In the early 1970s, they introduced the massive 'Delta' class boats, then the largest submarines in the world.

279
USSR

'Delta' class

This was the Russian Navy's most numerous ballistic missile class, produced at Severodvinsk since 1972 and based on the earlier 'Yankee' class.

The first variant was the **'Delta I' class** of 18 boats with a dived displacement of 10,200 tons and, because its SS-N-8 missiles offered greater capability than the SS-N-6s of the 'Yankee' class, 12 rather than 16 launch tubes in a hull 137 m (449 ft 6 in) long. From 1974, there appeared the four boats of the **'Delta II' class** with a dived displacement of 11,300 tons and a hull lengthened to 155 m (508 ft 6 in) to accommodate 16 missiles, as well as the first of 14 **'Delta III' class** boats with still greater dived displacement and length, and a revised

missile compartment for 16 of the shorter-ranged but more accurate SS-N-18 missiles. Finally, in 1984, there appeared the first of seven **'Delta IV' class** boats with dived displacement of 12,150 tons, a length of 166 m (544 ft 7 in), X-shaped rather than cruciform tail surfaces, 7750 kW (10,400 shp) more power to restore the performance lost in the two preceding classes, and 16 SS-N-23 missiles combining the range of the SS-N-8 with the MIRVed warhead of the SS-N-18.

Specification
'Delta III' class
Type: nuclear-powered ballistic missile submarine
Displacement: 9,750 tons surfaced

and 11,700 tons dived
Armament: 16 SS-N-18 'Stingray' underwater-launched ballistic missiles, and six 533-mm (21-in) tubes for 18 Type 53 and Type 40 torpedoes
Propulsion: two reactors driving two steam turbines delivering 37300 kW (50,025 shp) to two shafts

Performance: maximum speed 20 kt (37 km/h; 23 mph) surfaced and 24 kt (44 km/h; 27.5 mph) dived
Dimensions: length overall 160 m (524 ft 11 in); beam 12 m (39 ft 4 in)
Crew: 130
User: USSR

280
FRANCE

'Le Redoutable' class

The five **'Le Redoutable' class** submarines were the mainstay of the French nuclear deterrent force, and after design from 1963 were commissioned between June 1974 and May 1980.

The first two boats were each completed with a complement of 16 M1 missiles each possessing a 500-kiloton warhead, while the third boat was completed with 16 examples of the longer-ranged M2 carrying the same warhead; the first two boats were then retro-fitted with the M2. These three boats were later upgraded to the standard of the fourth and fifth boats, which were each completed with 16 examples of the M20, which had the same range and accuracy as the M2

but carried a 1.2-megaton warhead; the first three boats were retro-fitted with the M20, introduced on France's sixth strategic missile-carrying submarine, L'Inflexible. The three surviving 'Le Redoutable' class boats have been retro-fitted with the M4 missile, which is larger, heavier and longer-ranged than the M20 but also more accurate, and armed with six 150-kiloton MIRVs; the boats also carry the SM.39 underwater-launched version of the Exocet anti-ship missile.

Specification
'Le Redoutable' class
Type: nuclear-powered ballistic missile submarine
Displacement: 8,045 tons surfaced

and 8,940 tons dived
Armament: 16 M20 underwater-launched ballistic missiles, and four 533-mm (21-in) tubes for 14 L5 wire-guided torpedoes and four SM.39 Exocet anti-ship missiles
Propulsion: one reactor driving two steam turbines delivering 11925 kW

(15,990 shp) to two shafts
Performance: maximum speed 20+ kt (37+ km/h; 23+ mph) surfaced and 25 kt (46 km/h; 29 mph) dived
Dimensions: length overall 128.7 m (422 ft 3 in); beam 10.6 m (34 ft 9 in)
Crew: 135
User: France

An 'Ohio' leaves port. Like an iceberg, a missile boat gives a false impression of its true size, most of the hull being under water. These huge submarines are in fact larger than World War II heavy cruisers.

Front-Line Missile Boats

The shield that has protected East and West from the horrors of nuclear war has to a large extent been provided by the submarine forces of the respective navies. For months at a time, ballistic missile-firing boats patrol the seas, their awesome destructive power concealed and protected by the vastness of the oceans. Given the similarity of their tasks, it is not surprising that these boats share the same general outline. But there are differences, reflecting the varying philosophies of their operators.

in commission. The improved Trident II D-5 is installed in the later boats, and the four oldest will be converted to non-strategic roles to comply with the START nuclear treaty. The Royal Navy has three *Vanguard* class submarines in service, armed with 16 Trident II D-5 missiles, and a fourth under construction.

Missile boats of other nations

The French, who withdrew from NATO in 1966, then went ahead with the development of their own nuclear submarines and ballistic missiles. *Le Redoutable* (420 ft; 9,000 tons), commissioned in 1971, deployed 16 M1 missiles of a size and range similar to the Polaris A-2. These missiles were progressively improved. *L'Inflexible*, the sixth of this type, deploys the M4, which has been retro-fitted to the surviving three. A new class, of which *Le Triomphant* (453 ft; 14,200 tons) is the first launched will eventually receive the M51.

The People's Republic of China has a single Project 092 'Xia' capable of launching 12 'Ju Lang 1' (CSS-N3) missiles. She will be followed by three Project 094 boats armed with 16 'Ju Lang 2' missiles. India attempted to acquire nuclear capability by leasing a Soviet submarine in the 1980s, but she was returned. Work continues on an indigenous reactor plant in both Brazil and India, but the cost has slowed progress.

With the ratification of the SALT agreements, the number of US and Soviet missile submarines has been gradually decreased. It is noteworthy, however, that even in the new climate of *perestroika* the announced cuts in defence spending have not included submarines. So these silent, deadly weapons continue to prowl the black depths of the world's seas.

HMS *Resolution* 1967

Although completely constructed in the United Kingdom, the design of the four 'Resolution' class submarines of the Royal Navy was based to a considerable extent upon American practice. As a result, the boats are very similar to the contemporary 'Lafayette' class serving in the US Navy. They differ in that they are armed with Polaris rather than the later and heavier Poseidon missile.

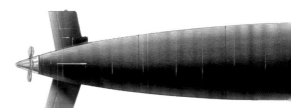

Above: *Resolution* has a maximum speed of 25 knots, and a maximum diving depth of 465 metres (1,525 feet).

'Delta III' 1976

The Soviet 'Delta' class submarines were the result of an evolutionary enlargement of the 'Yankee' design, which was itself copied from the American Polaris boats. Designed to take longer-ranged SS-N-8 missiles, the 'Deltas' represented a significant enhancement of Soviet nuclear capability. At least 17 of the large 'Delta III' variant have been built.

USS *Ohio* 1981

Although the lead ship has now been in commission for almost a decade, the 'Ohio' class still represents the cutting edge of American submarine technology. These huge boats are designed to elude any anti-submarine threat that the Soviets are known to possess or are believed to be developing. Twenty-four examples were to be built at a cost of between one and two billion dollars apiece, but with the subsequent relaxation in international relations and budget cuts by Congress, the final force is likely to be approximately 18-strong. However, even that smaller force is capable of carrying more than 6,000 nuclear warheads!

Above: The bow of the 'Delta III' is occupied by a low-frequency sonar system, and by six 21-inch torpedo tubes. The big boat carries up to 12 torpedoes.

Below: The USS *Ohio* is powered by a single reactor driving a single propeller. While it is no faster than any other missile boat, it is one of the quietest vessels ever to put to sea.

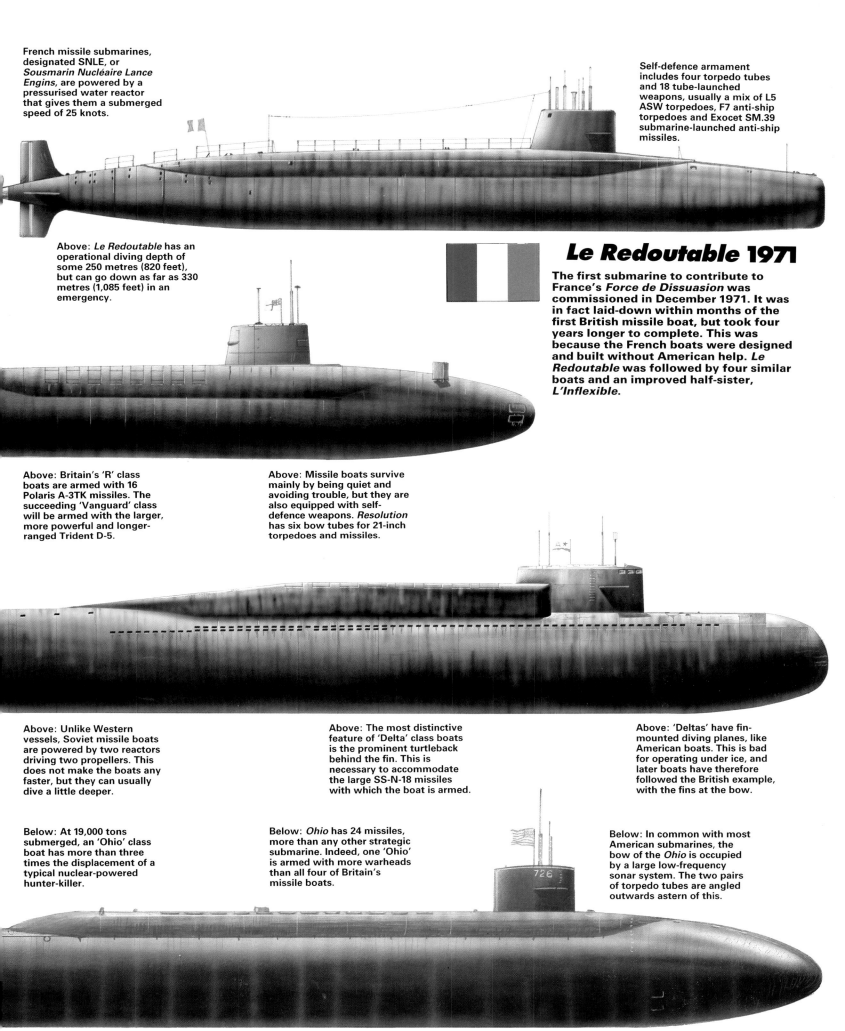

French missile submarines, designated SNLE, or *Sousmarin Nucléaire Lance Engins*, are powered by a pressurised water reactor that gives them a submerged speed of 25 knots.

Self-defence armament includes four torpedo tubes and 18 tube-launched weapons, usually a mix of L5 ASW torpedoes, F7 anti-ship torpedoes and Exocet SM.39 submarine-launched anti-ship missiles.

Above: *Le Redoutable* has an operational diving depth of some 250 metres (820 feet), but can go down as far as 330 metres (1,085 feet) in an emergency.

Le Redoutable 1971

The first submarine to contribute to France's *Force de Dissuasion* was commissioned in December 1971. It was in fact laid-down within months of the first British missile boat, but took four years longer to complete. This was because the French boats were designed and built without American help. *Le Redoutable* was followed by four similar boats and an improved half-sister, *L'Inflexible*.

Above: Britain's 'R' class boats are armed with 16 Polaris A-3TK missiles. The succeeding 'Vanguard' class will be armed with the larger, more powerful and longer-ranged Trident D-5.

Above: Missile boats survive mainly by being quiet and avoiding trouble, but they are also equipped with self-defence weapons. *Resolution* has six bow tubes for 21-inch torpedoes and missiles.

Above: Unlike Western vessels, Soviet missile boats are powered by two reactors driving two propellers. This does not make the boats any faster, but they can usually dive a little deeper.

Above: The most distinctive feature of 'Delta' class boats is the prominent turtleback behind the fin. This is necessary to accommodate the large SS-N-18 missiles with which the boat is armed.

Above: 'Deltas' have fin-mounted diving planes, like American boats. This is bad for operating under ice, and later boats have therefore followed the British example, with the fins at the bow.

Below: At 19,000 tons submerged, an 'Ohio' class boat has more than three times the displacement of a typical nuclear-powered hunter-killer.

Below: *Ohio* has 24 missiles, more than any other strategic submarine. Indeed, one 'Ohio' is armed with more warheads than all four of Britain's missile boats.

Below: In common with most American submarines, the bow of the *Ohio* is occupied by a large low-frequency sonar system. The two pairs of torpedo tubes are angled outwards astern of this.

THE BIG STICK

Below: An American 'Poseidon' boat undergoes a maintenance inspection. Some of her deadly cargo has been removed, but the white foam plastic covers indicate that six missiles are still aboard. A similar inspection on an 'Ohio' class submarine would reveal 24

The submarine-launched missile has evolved from the crude pilotless planes of the 1940s to today's weapons, able to hit targets accurately from around the world.

The lines to the shore are slipped, and the sinister bulk of the huge submarine is pushed into the centre of the channel by a tug. With unlimited range and continual regeneration and filtering of the atmosphere, the endurance of a nuclear-powered boat is limited by its food storage capacity and the stamina of its crew. Ahead lie two months of almost unbearable boredom, which are nonetheless the foundation upon which the security of the whole world rests.

They call them 'boomers' in the US Navy, and 'bombers' in the Royal Navy. But whatever their nickname, the crews of the submarines have a single mission: to ensure that their deadly cargos of nuclear-tipped ballistic missiles are ready to fire. Paradoxically, if they ever had to fire in earnest, they would have failed in their task of

Early missiles

The idea of taking strategic weapons to sea is not new: the Germans had plans to fire V-2 missiles in that fashion against New York. The US Navy built submarines to fire Loon and Regulus cruise-type missiles in the 1950s. However, these were soon surpassed by the rapid evolution of the Polaris system, and by the early 1960s the ballistic missile submarine was taking up the burden of national deterrence. The speed with which the missiles and submarines were developed left the Soviets behind, but by a determined effort they had similar 16-tube missile boats at sea by the end of the 1960s.

Above: A Poseidon missile is carefully lowered into an American missile boat. This is a tricky operation, since the missile is easily damaged, and must be aligned exactly in the tube.

Above: The first operational ballistic missile submarines in the US Navy were those of the 'George Washington' class, which were designed as hunter-killers but had a missile section added during construction.

Right: Early Soviet missiles were too large to be fitted in the hull, so 'Hotel' class nuclear submarines carried three short-range weapons in an extended conning tower.

deterrence.

The commander of the submarine takes his charge to sea. Once in open water, he dives the boat and begins a complex series of evasive manoeuvres to elude any inquisitive strangers. Secrecy is everything to missile submarines, and some navies will use surface forces and hunter-killer submarines to ensure that the missile boat is not tailed.

Secret patrol

Where it actually goes, the route taken, and the final return date are known only to the skipper and one or two people on shore. No messages are transmitted during the duration of the patrol, but messages can be received via ELF (extremely low frequency) radio.

Within its patrol zone, a submarine will travel very slowly and quietly to reduce the chances of detection. The main emphasis of daily schedules is on keeping the missiles ready to fire, and in Western boats all of them are ready at least 95 per cent of the time.

Missile boats have to be ready to take evasive action if any strange surface or submarine craft are detected. To that end, they are equipped with the most advanced passive sonar systems available. If the worst comes to the worst, the big boats are also equipped with decoys and acoustic homing torpedoes for self-defence.

Despite the easing of international tensions, larger and larger missile boats are still putting to sea with ever more deadly warloads. Although the invulnerability of the SSBN on patrol is often quoted by Western naval authorities as one of its major advantages, the Soviet Union for years made great efforts to collate intelligence information, hydrographic data, missile performance and possible targeting of British, French and American missiles, all of which suggest likely patrol areas. When this effort is considered together with the Russians' improved submarine designs and experiments in advanced detection techniques, it is possible that the claim by the Royal and US Navies that the Russians have never tailed a missile boat might yet be challenged.

Powerful deterrent

In spite of that, the nuclear-powered ballistic missile submarine remains the ultimate piece of insurance for a nation. It is likely to be many years before governments of any persuasion are ready to scrap such an effective deterrent.

Above: Le Redoutable was the first French ballistic missile submarine, commissioned in December 1971. Designed and built without American assistance, the French boats took much longer to come into service than their British contemporaries.

Western missiles

Only a small number of types of submarine launched Ballistic Missiles (SLBMs) are in service today. The Chinese Ju Lang 1 has a maximum range of only 3,600 km. The US Navy's Trident II D-5 has a range of 12,000 km. The Russian SS-N-23 'Skiff' (RSM-54) is credited with a range of 10,000 km, and its successor, the SS-NX-228, has not yet been launched successfully.

Main picture and inset: A Trident C-4 missile blasts into the sky after launch from an 'Ohio' class submarine of the US Navy. The missile is popped from its launch tube by compressed air, its motor igniting just as the nose of the missile breaks the surface. The British Polaris missile (inset) is launched in the same way from an 'R' class submarine of the Royal Navy, but can deliver fewer warheads half the distance and less accurately than the later weapon.

Warload

First-generation missiles were armed with single large warheads, designed to airburst over large cities to cause devastation over a wide area. Later, increased accuracy meant that warheads could be targeted more precisely onto high-value targets such as command centres or even missile silos. With the introduction of multiple re-entry vehicles (MRVs), a missile could deliver a number of warheads (usually three) of smaller yield against a target, thereby increasing the area of devastation.

Multiple independently-targeted re-entry vehicles (MIRVs) were the next stage, whereby each warhead carried by a missile could be directed at different targets. With the increase in accuracy, a single missile could now deal with a number of hard targets like missile silos.

The latest development is the MARV (manoeuvring re-entry vehicle). This is capable both of inflight manoeuvres to avoid enemy anti-ballistic missile defences, and of terminal in-atmosphere guidance to give much-improved accuracy. Missiles like the Trident D-5 can carry as many as a dozen 300-kiloton warheads, each capable of hitting to within 100 metres of separate targets after a flight of more than 12000 kilometres.

Below: The tracks of multiple re-entry vehicles pierce the sky over a Pacific test range after a flight of several thousand miles from the west coast of the United States. Each streak represents a single warhead, capable of exploding with the force of 400,000 tons of TNT.

Above: Beautiful and terrible, the power of the atom is unleashed. Mankind has never created anything more destructive than the hydrogen bomb, yet as long as such a horrifying weapon is available then nobody is likely to start the war that would end the world.

Right: The first atomic weapons were large, heavy devices weighing two tons or more. Modern missiles can carry a number of re-entry vehicles, each carrying nuclear devices many times more powerful than the bombs that devastated Hiroshima and Nagasaki, but at a fraction of the weight. The re-entry vehicles, or RVs, from a single missile can be programmed to attack widely-separated targets, thus spreading the destructive power of the missile over wider and wider areas.

THE LONG PATROL

A nuclear missile patrol is the most important and at the same time one of the most boring jobs a sailor can do in any modern navy.

Day 1
USS *Ohio* (SSBN 726) sets off on patrol from Kings Bay, Georgia. Clearing the end of Cape Hatteras, the huge boat passes a US Navy carrier heading north for Norfolk. Diving to 600 feet, the submarine moves off into the Atlantic at a cruising speed of 15 knots.

Day 3
Crew routine is settling down, as *Ohio* heads past the Grand Banks off Newfoundland. The submarine gives these intensively-worked fishing grounds a wide berth.

Above, inset: With nearly 300 warheads at the other end of a button, the missile control panel of the USS Ohio is possibly the most powerful single military seat in the world.

There are a number of Soviet vessels in the region, and some of their trawlers are equipped more for intelligence-gathering than fishing. In any case, getting tangled in a trawl net could be embarrassing!

Day 4
An ELF message is received. These extremely low frequency radio waves are not stopped by water, but they don't carry much information. In this case, *Ohio* receives a three-letter pre-arranged code group instructing her to come to periscope depth to receive a satellite message. Once at 60 feet, the captain orders the needle-thin ESM mast, with its sensitive radar detectors, to be raised. With no radar transmissions in evidence, the captain uses the periscope to check that the surface is clear, then raises the radio antenna. Communications are established via satellite with CINCLANT at

Norfolk, Virginia. *Ohio* is given orders to proceed with the missile patrol, heading out into the Atlantic and keeping well away from the shipping lanes. Diving to 800 feet, *Ohio* crawls south-east at less than six knots.

Day 7
After three days, *Ohio* has reached her patrol station. Now it is a task of waiting and listening. Off to the east are the north-south Atlantic shipping lanes, while to the north is the main transatlantic route. *Ohio* has her reactors powered right down and is only

Above: Submarines have changed a lot since *World War II*. Control rooms still have plenty of levers and handwheels and dials, but more and more space is taken up by warning lights, computer keyboards and visual display units. On a ballistic missile boat patrol, such screens are often the only way of knowing that you are going anywhere. In the interests of secrecy, these big boats generate very little noise, creeping about the ocean depths like titanic ghosts.

Main picture, left: The 'Ohio' class boat **USS** Alabama leaves Bangor, Washington State, on the 100th Trident patrol carried out by the US Navy. It doesn't matter whether the patrol is in the Pacific or the Atlantic: from the moment the big boat submerges, nobody will know where it is until it returns to port in two months' time.

Left: Food aboard US Navy submarines is pretty good. Indeed, one of the perils of a long patrol in confined spaces is an expanding waistline! Big though the vessel is, there's nowhere to exercise.

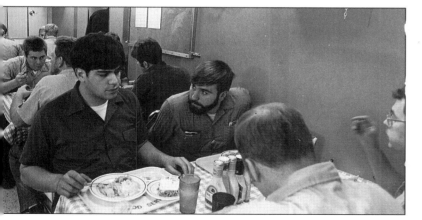

of whales. Some US Navy sonarmen have become real experts on marine mammals, which is not surprising since they hear more underwater activity in a single patrol than most marine biologists can in a lifetime.

Day 15
Sonar reports an approaching submarine. The sound patterns indicate a single-screw boat travelling at about 25 knots. It is quickly identified as a 'Los Angeles' class hunter-killer of the US Navy. At that speed, its sonar will have heard nothing but the sound of its own passage through the water. Suddenly, the engine noises are cut right back and the 'Los Angeles' slows down. This is standard practice with attack boats, involving moving in short, high-speed bursts with frequent pauses for listening, and is known as 'sprint and drift'. *Ohio*'s captain slows his own boat even further, to little more than a snail's pace. No matter that the hunter-killer is from the same navy; a 'boomer' survives by not being found, and evading the highly sophisticated systems of a state-of-the-art American boat is a pretty reliable test of how good at its job the missile submarine is.

making steerage way. The US Navy calls its missile boats 'boomers', but this is something of a misnomer, as ballistic missile submarines are among the quietest vessels ever to go to sea. All extraneous noises have been muffled, and all sonar systems are manned. So quiet is the big boat, and so sensitive are its 'ears', that if there is an unidentified

submarine in these wide-open waters it will be heard and evaded long before it gets close.

Day 11
Ohio's crewmen have settled down to a normal cruise routine. The only problems they face are those generated by boredom. Ballistic missile boats are designed to survive by being

unobtrusive, so they do nothing that is going to attract attention, and serving aboard one is not at all like being part of the crew of a hunter-killer. There are no high-speed chases, no trailing of enemy submarines, no simulated attacks on the huge supertankers passing within a few miles of this point. *Ohio* simply pretends to be a hole in the water, listening for intruders and making virtually no sound at all.

Day 12
Fresh salads run out. From now on, the crew will be eating canned and frozen vegetables.

Day 13
The submarine's sonar operators are entertained by a passing pod

Day 16

Ohio carries out a missile launch exercise. This simulates all of the procedures to be followed during a nuclear exchange. First the ELF (extremely low frequency) radio receives the standby message from the US Navy's transmitter station, which is right in the middle of the continental USA. Although ELF messages do not carry much information, they are not stopped by water, so they can get through to a deeply submerged submarine. Then the submarine rises to periscope depth, all the time listening for any hostile vessels. Now it can receive satellite messages, which go through a rigorous process of authentication. Once the captain and his senior officers are satisfied that they have been given a Presidential order, they will prepare to launch their missiles.

It takes a number of keys turned simultaneously to unlock the missile launch controls and to arm the missiles. This is a precaution to stop a single madman from starting World War III. Finally, the missiles are launched, at a rate of one per minute, until all 24 are gone. This is one area where the simulation is unlike the real thing, as one cannot truly mimic the shudder through the boat's hull as compressed air blasts the missile free from its tube. Most of the crew are happy that this is so, and most pray that they never have to do it for real.

Day 27

The monotony of the patrol is broken by the passage of an old tramp freighter overhead. It is the first man-made contact in over a week.

Day 29

Ohio cuts short her patrol, by order. The submarine has been instructed to move north, under the Arctic ice, to check the feasibility of SSBN operations in that region. It is a risk sending a missile boat into waters that are patrolled by the latest Soviet submarines, but it is a risk that must be taken.

Day 35

Ohio enters the Arctic Ocean and heads due North. She is following the same route that Commander Peary took in 1909, but the submarine's crew is a lot more comfortable several hundred feet beneath the ice than the earlier US Navy officer had been with his dog sled.

Day 38

Ohio makes a rendezvous with

USS *Sea Devil* and the British submarine HMS *Splendid* under the Pole. The two attack boats surface, carefully breaking through one of the patches of thin ice known as *polynyas*. The three submarines are testing the concept of joint UK/US operations in the Arctic environment without logistic support.

Day 40

Ohio heads south. From the North Pole, any direction is south! The course is set to return to the Atlantic.

Day 42

A faint contact is heard, moving very slowly. The sound is identified as a twin-screw nuclear-powered submarine, and the Soviets are the only people who make twin-screw nuke boats. The low noise levels and slow speed mean that it is almost certainly a missile boat. Such an encounter between SSBNs is unusual, but the *Ohio* does not stick around to think about it. Soviet missile boats are usually accompanied by one or more escorting hunter-killers, and as far as the US Navy knows, none of them has ever managed to tail an 'Ohio' class boat. The captain wants to keep it that way. Changing course, *Ohio* slips silently away like a giant ghost.

Day 43

Safely away from any possible enemy contact, the *Ohio* sends a communication buoy to the surface. This delays transmission until the missile boat is well clear, then squirts a burst-transmission lasting under one-tenth of a second towards a satellite in high orbit. This then relays it to Norfolk. *Ohio* reports the contact with the 'Typhoon', giving the big Soviet boat's last known course and speed.

Day 44

Ohio almost runs into a Norwegian diesel boat one-tenth her own size. Both are so quiet that they do not hear each other until they are very close. The Norwegian boat is on barrier patrol, lying silently, waiting for potentially hostile submarines to come within range of its torpedoes. Once again the big missile submarine has to go through its disappearing act.

Above: Missile room crew check the conditions inside the huge silos that take up so much of the ship. To be an effective deterrent, the Trident missiles must be ready to fire at all times.

Left: On the surface, the submarine is an ungainly machine, leaving behind a huge wake as it ploughs through the water. Once submerged, however, a missile boat makes about as much noise as "a virgin whale who wants to stay that way!"

Left: In many ways, being a missile crewman is one of the most boring jobs a sailor can get. Yet there is usually plenty to do, especially the continuous monitoring and maintenance of equipment that ensures the boat is always ready for action.

Below: It could be a chemical works, or some kind of oil-storage facility. But it would take a very dull mind indeed to walk without some sense of foreboding through the awesome destructive potential of a missile boat's missile deck.

Day 46
Ohio returns to her patrol area and settles down for another two weeks of silent cruising.

Day 48
The boredom of a regular missile patrol sets in. The only spark of excitement comes when the video machine in the enlisted crew's mess breaks down. In the interests of crew morale, and to head off incipient mutiny, the captain has to replace it with the video from the wardroom. The only other machine is the one from the chief petty officers' mess, and it would take more than mere rank to make them give it up.

Day 55
USS *Hawaii* left port five days before, and by now will be on station. She is the *Ohio*'s relief, and once the ELF message comes from Fleet HQ the older boat can go home. Her patrol is over.

Day 60
Ohio surfaces off the coast of Georgia at the end of her 60-day patrol.

Above: Two months at sea are made more bearable by the provision of all the services expected in the modern world. Even with air conditioning and plenty of hot water, there is always demand for the use of the laundry!

Below: Even as one huge submarine slips silently back into port after a patrol, a sister vessel is heading out to take up the deterrent burden. Every hour of every day of the year, the missile boats of four or five navies prowl the oceans of the world, their readiness for action the assurance that their deadly warload is never used in anger.

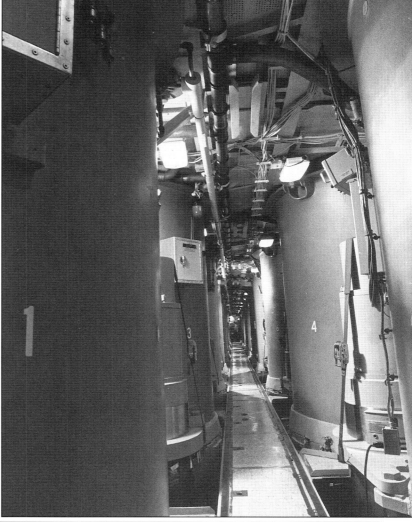

BASTIONS IN THE ICE

They are some of the bleakest military bases in the world. Cold, stormy, dark for half the year, the Kola Peninsula is nevertheless home to the powerful Russian Northern Fleet and, above all, to the majority of the USSR's missile submarines.

Russia holds what remains of the world's largest force of ballistic missile-firing submarines. Included among these are the 23 or more units of the 'Delta III/IV' classes and the 'Typhoon' class, for many years the largest submarines in the world. The 'Deltas' have since been surpassed by the American 'Ohio' class; at over 30,000 tons, a 'Typhoon' displaces more than many aircraft carriers of World War II.

Russian naval tactics have always been limited by geography. To get out into the open ocean from ice-free ports, vessels have to go through narrow choke-points at the entrances to the Black Sea or the Baltic, or operate from remote ports like Petropavlovsk on the Kamchatka Peninsula. The Northern Fleet, is limited by the stormy waters of the Arctic, the advance of the ice in winter, and the heavily-patrolled waters around Norway and in the Greenland-Iceland-UK (GIUK) gap.

The first Soviet strategic submarines operated under a number of handicaps. Early missiles had a relatively short range, so the missile boats had to run the gauntlet of NATO ASW forces in order to reach their patrol areas, less than 500 miles off the coast of the USA. They were also very noisy vessels, and were almost invariably picked up on sonar. If it had ever come to war, the 'Hotel' and early 'Yankee' class boats would have been sunk within minutes.

Modern Russian submarines

New high-technology boats and the development of long-range missiles have changed all that. No longer do Russian vessels have to brave the perils of the North Atlantic in order to threaten the US, which is still the main potential enemy, in spite of changing world conditions.

Modern Russian submarines can hit hard from within Russian dominated waters, even in the midst of the Arctic ice. Now the attack boats have to come to them, and during the Cold War British and American hunter-killers spent more and more time 'up north'. It was a challenging task for Western boats to penetrate the very lair of the bear, but even so, the threat presented to the Soviet Northern Fleet by such sophisticated antagonists was very real. As a result, Russian naval tactics still have the protection of their missile boats as their primary aim.

Above: A huge 'Typhoon' class missile boat sets off on a patrol from the Soviet Northern Fleet bases on the Kola Peninsula. With its long-range missiles, the 'Typhoon' hardly needs to leave port to be effective, but for added security the huge submarines are designed for operations under the Arctic icecap, where it is hard for Western hunter-killers to find them. There they are to break through thin areas of ice known as polynyas, from where they can fire their missiles.

Left: The diesel-powered 'Golf' class boats were the world's first ballistic missile-firing submarines. But because of their short-range missiles, the boats had to operate close to the American coast, where they were easy prey to the US Navy's anti-submarine forces.

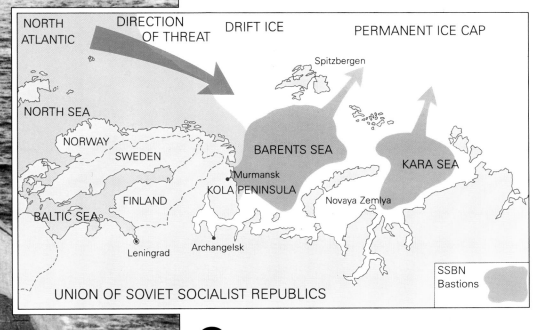

NORTH ATLANTIC | DIRECTION OF THREAT | DRIFT ICE | PERMANENT ICE CAP

Spitzbergen

NORTH SEA

NORWAY

SWEDEN

BARENTS SEA

KARA SEA

Murmansk

KOLA PENINSULA

FINLAND

Novaya Zemlya

BALTIC SEA

Leningrad   Archangelsk

SSBN Bastions

UNION OF SOVIET SOCIALIST REPUBLICS

Left: Every discussion of Russian naval strategy is dominated by geography. Most ports are either iced-in for part of the year, or, like St. Petersburg, have access to the ocean only through choke-points, which are easily blocked by an enemy. Murmansk is the only ice-free port with more open prospects. However, missile submarines no longer need to get out into the Atlantic, operating instead under air and surface protection from 'bastions' or 'sanctuaries' to the north. Any attacker must now come into Russian dominated waters to get at the missile boats.

2 Threat

Despite the marked lessening of tensions between the superpowers, as long as the United States and Russia and, to a lesser extent, Britain and France retain their submarine-launched strategic missile capability, each side will do its best to keep tabs on the other side's missile force. From the moment a Northern Fleet missile submarine leaves Russian territorial waters, it is under observation by Norwegian or American maritime reconnaissance aircraft. Once it submerges,

usually at a point about 50 miles out, which has been nicknamed 'Checkpoint Charlie' by NATO submariners, the task of tailing the boat passes to British and American attack submarines. These are advanced boats, notably quiet, and manned by highly professional crews. Their aim is to maintain contact with the Russian boats without being detected themselves, ready at all times to destroy the target if the final war were declared.

1 Situation

Russian Northern Fleet bases are located around Polyarnyy, near Murmansk on the Kola Peninsula. They have the advantage of being ice-free all the year round, offering the Russians their only unrestricted access to the North Atlantic. Over the years, the submarine force bases have been moved further west to the Rybachiy Peninsula, less than 70 kilometres from the Norwegian border. The submarines themselves are housed in hardened pens carved deep into the mountains which line the Motovskiy Inlet.

Right: The Northern Fleet's submarines are berthed in pens carved deep into the granite of the Kola Peninsula, safe from all but a direct hit from a nuclear weapon.

Above and inset: Even in this more peaceful age, the main threat to Russian missile boats comes from NATO's air and submarine forces. Maritime patrol aircraft regularly patrol the waters off North Cape, and British and American submarines operate under the ice and even penetrate deep into the Barents Sea, north of the Russian landmass.

3 Escorts

The modern Soviet navy grew from a purely coastal force after World War II to its peak in the 1980s under the guidance of Admiral Sergei Gorshkov. Gorshkov's doctrine stated that the prime purpose of the fleet was to support the submarine force, and the most important submarines in that force were the missile boats. Soviet PLRKs (*podvodnaya lodka raketna krylataya*, or ballistic missile submarines) were usually accompanied on patrol by one or more attack boats. There were intended to hunt for potentially hostile boats, and to shield the missile boat. They rarely worked alone, however, except when taking part in the potentially deadly game of hide-and-seek under the Arctic ice. Soviet doctrine, frequently exercised, stressed the importance of mounting anti-submarine operations from a variety of mutually-supporting platforms below, above, and on the surface. The complexity of such operations demands some form of centralised control, and Soviet commanders were unlikely to show the initiative displayed by Western sub-skippers in their 'lone-wolf' patrols. The end of the Cold War and the collapse of Russian military might makes such arguments academic.

Right: Soviet surface forces were also used to protect the missile boats. An anti-submarine group like this include 'Mirka' class corvettes and the helicopter-cruiser Moskva, would form a barrier between the bastion and any approaching submarine threat.

Below: This US Department of Defense illustration depicted the Soviet threat, as seen by the Pentagon. Here a 'Delta IV' class submarine is shown launching a SS-N-23 missile. Deterrence ensured that the Cold War ended, replacing the Soviet Union with a new Russian state.

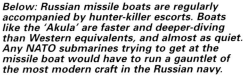

Above: The Russian navy will subordinate every other weapon system is possesses in order to protect its ballistic missile submarines. Typically, a missile boat will be assigned a regiment of maritime reconnaissance aircraft like this Il-38 'May', to clear an area of enemy submarines.

Below: Russian missile boats are regularly accompanied by hunter-killer escorts. Boats like the 'Akula' are faster and deeper-diving than Western equivalents, and almost as quiet. Any NATO submarines trying to get at the missile boat would have to run a gauntlet of the most modern craft in the Russian navy.

4 Bastions

With the longer-ranged modern missiles, Russian submarines can now take advantage of operating close to home. By setting up 'sanctuaries' or 'bastions', the Northern Fleet can cause serious problems to Western hunter-killers trying to get through to the missile boats. Minefields laid at strategic points make any penetration risky, channelling intruders into selected areas or forcing them to make wide detours under the ice. Specialist surface ASW groups operate with submarine task groups and maritime patrol aircraft groups of regimental size, all dedicated to protecting the missile submarines. Behind that covering force, the latest missile boats, such as the massive 'Typhoons', add to NATO's problems by operating under the ice pack. This is a notoriously difficult ASW environment, the constant grinding of millions of tons of ice masking the faint noises of a slow-moving submarine, and that is why British and American boats regularly patrol as far as the North Pole.

SUPERCARRIERS

The reality of modern sea power is graphically illustrated by a flight of Grumman F-14 Tomcats overflying the supercarrier USS Dwight D. Eisenhower, one of the largest and most powerful warships ever built.

Over the last 70 years, the aircraft-carrier has developed into the most powerful and flexible warship the world has seen.

Like a huge floating office block, moving faster than any city traffic, the biggest and most powerful warship the world has ever known forges steadily across the Gulf. Forced to hold a course only a few degrees off the wind, which is gusting at up to 50 knots, she is abeam to long, deceptively smooth rollers that have come from halfway across the world, and that cause her to drive forward in a strange slow corkscrew movement, interrupted every now and then by a sudden kittenish shiver that can be felt throughout the ship.

The light is failing at the end of a cold, overcast afternoon, but two of the ship's squadron of 10 S-3 Vikings are up on round-the-clock watch for submarines, two Grumman E-2C Hawkeyes and four F-14 Tomcats are on a long-range sweep for incoming enemy aircraft or missiles, and the deck crew are anxiously awaiting the last straggler of a strike force of A-6 Intruders. Close by the ship, and low over the waves, two Sea King helicopters chatter busily, ready to pick up the crew if the plane fails to make it to the flight-deck.

Hard to land

An aircraft-carrier, for all its size, is a small and continuously-moving object to an incoming pilot – "You're trying to land on something that looks like a pinball machine at the end of a football field," said one – and despite the sophistication of modern blind approach systems, all landings, whether by day or night, are visual.

The Landing Signal Officer (LSO) stands with his staff on a small platform at the stern of the ship, watching for the approaching aircraft. He is a veteran carrier pilot and, as the pilot switches on his red and green beams to illuminate the Light Landing Device – or 'meatball' – to guide the aircraft on the correct flight path, he assesses its correct height and speed and switches on a series of lights to indicate that the deck is clear.

Four arrester cables lie across the flight deck. Each has a tensile strength of 175,000 lb and, after only a few landings, is

A French navy Super Etendard prepares to launch from the catapult of the carrier Clemenceau. Since the British retired the old Ark Royal, France is the only Western nation other than the United States which has continued to develop modern conventional carriers.

thrust. Too high! He misses the fourth wire and, in a shower of sparks from the trailing arrester hook, howls off the angled flight deck, clear of the planes tightly parked around the ship's island, and 'bolters' for another attempt. If he has a previous record of poor landings, this failure may well get him busted on the recommendation of the LSO.

Meanwhile, on the forward part of the flight deck, a new patrol of two Hawkeyes, the only prop aircraft still in carrier operation, is ready to change the watch. The big four-bladed propellers churn hard against the pull of the hold-back bars on the steam catapults as the catapult officer signals 'ready' to the catapult operators in their pits.

There is a whoosh, a cloud of exhausted steam, and the first Hawkeye is hurled off the bow of the ship. The speed of take-off is quite unlike that from land, as there is no steady acceleration, and it outruns the pilot's physical response and that of his instruments. He must put his faith in the pre-setting of the flaps and the expertise of the deck crew until control is recovered several hundred feet off the bow. Thirty seconds later, the second Hawkeye follows.

thrown overboard to ensure that it cannot be used again. The pilot aims to pick up the third: if he arrests on the first or second his approach is judged too low, and the fourth indicates too high an approach.

With engines screaming the Intruder comes in at some 150 mph and, as the wheels touch the flight deck, the pilot slams on full

British ideas

It is ironic that the Royal Navy no longer possesses a single carrier that will take conventional landings, and yet the three technical developments that have kept the large carrier in modern fleets were all British: the flight deck angled off the port beam so that aircraft making an unsuccessful touchdown could take off again without danger to men and machines on the forward deck; the reflector landing sight; and the steam catapult.

After World War II the continued value of shipborne tactical aircraft was demonstrated in both the Korean and Vietnam conflicts, as well as in short-term operations such as the Suez crisis of 1956. However, the development of V/STOL aircraft, together with the RAF's insistence that land-based aircraft could carry out any necessary strike, and an

Curtiss SB2C dive-bombers pass over an 'Essex' class carrier. By the end of the war, the US Navy's carrier fleet could mount 1,000-aircraft raids on Japan.

The First Carrier War

The British were the first to use carriers in battle, but it was in the war between Japan and the USA in the Pacific that the carrier came into its own. Carriers made the strike at Pearl Harbor, carriers marked the turn of the tide at the Coral Sea and at Midway, and it was with carriers that the US Navy forced the war on to the Japanese homeland. At the start of the war the US Navy had seven carriers in service: by 1945 there were 17 fleet carriers, eight light carriers, and no less than 60 escort carriers operating in the Pacific alone. To that were added the four armoured deck fleet carriers of the Royal Navy. By that time, Japan had a grand total of three carriers afloat, all severely damaged by American air attacks.

SUPERCARRIERS Reference File

175

FRANCE

'Clemenceau' class

The two ships of the **'Clemenceau' class**, the Clemenceau and Foch, were the first French aircraft carriers to be designed and completed as such in 1961 and 1963 respectively. The hull was similar to that of the US Navy's 'Essex'. class carriers. As completed the ships had considerable gun armament, but this was steadily reduced over the years.

The flightdeck was 257 m (843 ft 2 in) long and 51.2 m (168 ft 0 in) wide, and includes an 8° angled section 165.5 m (543 ft 0in) long and 29.5 m (96 ft 9 in) wide. The angled section was served by a single steam catapult, and the bow section by another. There were two lifts, one starboard deck-edge unit abaft the

island and the other in the forward section of the flight deck. The aircraft complement was about 40, comprising about 35 fixed-wing machines and two or four utility helicopters. The fixed-wing strength comprised 10 Vought F-8E(FN) Crusader fighters, 18 Dassault Breguet Super Etendard strike/attack aircraft (with the Exocet anti-ship missile as well as nuclear weapons such as the ASMP missile and AN52 bomb) and seven Dassault-Breguet Alizé anti-submarine aircraft. The ships were taken out of service in the late 1990s and will be replaced by the new nuclear carrier 'Charles de Gaulle'.

Specification
'Clemenceau' class
Type: multi-role fleet aircraft-carrier
Displacement: 32,780 tons full load
Armament: four 100-mm (3.94-in) guns and two Naval Crotale octuple launchers for R.440 SAMs
Propulsion: two 46973-kW (63,000-

hp) steam turbines
Performance: maximum speed 32 kt (59 km/h; 37 mph); range 13900 km (8,635 miles)
Dimensions: length overall 265 m (869 ft 5 in); beam 31.7 m (104 ft 1 in)
Crew: 1,338
User: France

escalating cost, persuaded the British government in 1966 to discontinue the big carrier. However, the 1998 Strategic Defence Review provides for the construction of two 50,000-ton carriers in the next century. These will operate the new Joint Strike Fighter (JSF) in its STOVL version. This design, called CV(F) may also be built for the French Navy.

The first carriers built specifically for jet aircraft were the 'Forrestal' class of the US Navy, commissioned in 1955-9 to carry Navy nuclear bombers such as the Savage and Skywarrior. These, with standard displacements of some 60,000 tons and flight deck length of over 1,000 feet, were far larger than anything else then afloat, but they were soon sur-

The Clemenceau enters Cannes Roads. Small by American standards, the two 'Clemenceaus' nevertheless gave France considerable ability to project power around the world. They are to be replaced in 1999 by nuclear-powered vessels.

176
'Admiral Kuznetsov' class

FORMER USSR

After gaining design and operational experience with the two 'Moskva' class helicopter-carriers and four 'Kiev' class hybrid missile-cruisers and STOVL carriers, the USSR began construction of its first true aircraft-carrier in 1983. These two carriers, which were due to enter service in the first half of the 1990s, are the 'Admiral Kuznetsov' and 'Varyag'. The ships had the standard flight deck combination of a bow section (though in this instance with a 12° 'ski-jump') and an angled section, served by three lifts.

The ships were designed for accommodation of conventional aircraft, the Yakovlev Yak-38 and much improved Yak-41 STOVL types,

partnered by naval versions of the Mikoyan-Gurevich MiG-29 and/or Sukhoi Su-27 land-based fighters, giving a strength of about 50 fixed-wing aircraft within a total complement of about 70 aircraft. The Project 1143.4 design has not proved an unqualified success. After the fall of the Soviet Union, work stopped on the 'Varyag' and the Kuznetsov' has been running trials since 1987.

Specification
'Adm Kuznetsov' class
Type: multi-role fleet aircraft-carrier

Displacement: about 65,000 tons full load
Armament: several 100-mm (3.94-in) or 76-mm (3-in) guns, several hybrid 30-mm cannon/SA-19 SAM mountings, 24 octuple launchers for SA-N-9 SAMs, and several SS-N-19 anti-ship missiles
Propulsion: probably four 28000-kW

(37,555-hp) steam turbines.
Performance: maximum speed 32 kt (59 km/h; 37 mph)
Dimensions: length overall 300 m (984 ft 3 in); beam 38.0 m (124 ft 8 in)
Crew: not revealed
User: USSR

An F/A-18 Hornet manoeuvres on to the catapult for launching. Modern carrier aircraft such as the Hornet are at least as good as, if not better than, their land-based contemporaries.

With a navy crew of around 3,000 men, together with an equal number for their 90 aircraft, a hospital for 80 or more patients, a library, shops and their own TV and radio stations, these giant ships are like floating city blocks. Yet they are fast, with speeds up to 35 knots, and they are as manoeuvrable as any ship such a size can be.

French carriers

Far smaller, with a displacement something over 27,000 tons and a length of 870 feet, are the two French ships *Clemenceau and Foch*, which went into service in 1961. These carried 40 aircraft, mainly Super Etendards. The nuclear-powered carrier, 'Charles de Gaulle' class is expected to come into commission at the end of 1999.

For a long time it was assumed that carriers would be protected against attack by their own aircraft or by the guns of their escorts, and the post-war US carriers of the 'Midway' class were even stripped of their guns to allow more hangar and fuel space. The first Russian

passed by the USS *Enterprise* (nearly 76,000 tons standard, 1088 feet long), the world's first nuclear-powered carrier, which was commissioned in 1961.

Four conventionally steam-powered carriers of the 'Kitty Hawk' class were commissioned between 1961 and 1968, but thereafter the US Congress came down heavily in favour of nuclear power, resulting in the laying down of three 'Nimitz' class (91,000 tons full load), the name vessel of which was commissioned in 1975. The nuclear powerplants of these vessels are capable of keeping them at sea for 13 years.

---

177 'Nimitz' class

The **'Nimitz' class** is the world's largest aircraft-carrier class, and its individual ships are both the largest and most powerful surface combatants in service with any navy. By comparison with the *Enterprise*, which pioneered the concept of a nuclear-powered aircraft-carrier, the 'Nimitz' class has two rather than eight reactors without any loss of power, and the additional volume available for aviation ordnance and fuel gives each ship the capability for 16 rather than 12 days of sustained operations.

The first ship was commissioned in 1975 and the programme will finally be completed early in the next century. The ships are all

characterised by very advanced onboard systems in addition to their aircraft, and are the *'Nimitz'*, *'Dwight D. Eisenhower'* and *'Carl Vinson'*. The *'Theodore Roosevelt'*, *'Abraham Lincoln'*, *'George Washington'*, *'John C. Steunis'* and *'Harry S. Truman'* form a sub-class, with the *'Ronald Reagan'* and a tenth sister to be delivered in 2002-2008. Thereafter a new CVX design will be built.

Specification
'Nimitz' class
Type: multi-role fleet aircraft-carrier
Displacement: 91,485 tons full load for first three ships and 96,350 tons full load for later ships

Armament: three or (last five ships) four 20-mm Phalanx CIWS mountings and three octuple launchers for Sea Sparrow SAMs
Propulsion: four 52200-kW (70,000-hp) steam turbines powered by two nuclear reactors
Performance: maximum speed 30+kt (55.5+km/h; 34.5+mph); range essentially unlimited
Dimensions: length overall 332.9m (1,092ft 0in); beam 40.8m (134ft 0in)
Crew: 3,300 plus an air group of about 3,000
User: USA

---

178 'Kitty Hawk' class

The three ships of the **'Kitty Hawk'** class are the *Kitty Hawk, Constellation* and *America*, which were built to an improved 'Forrestal' class design and commissioned in the first half of the 1960s. A fourth unit, the *John F. Kennedy* of the **'John F. Kennedy' class** and commissioned in 1968, is basically similar apart from having the underwater protection designed for the US Navy's nuclear-powered carriers.

The ships each carry an air group of about 90 aircraft including advanced types such as the Grumman F-14 Tomcat and Lockheed S-3 Viking. This gives the ships potentially the same capabilities as the 'Nimitz' class, but only over a shorter sustained period of operations because the ships'

bunkerage requirements reduce the quantity of aviation consumables (ordnance and fuel) that can be accommodated. The flight deck is the same as each ship's length, and its width is 76.2m (250ft 0in) in the first two units, 81.1m (266ft 0in) in the third unit and 81.6m (267ft 6in) in the last unit.

Specification
'Kitty Hawk' class
Type: multi-role fleet aircraft-carrier
Displacement: 80,800 tons full load for the first three ships and 82,000 tons full load for the fourth ship
Armament: three or (in last ship) one 20-mm Phalanx CIWS mounting and

three octuple launchers for Sea Sparrow SAMs
Propulsion: four 52192-kW (70,000-hp) steam turbines
Performance: maximum speed 30+kt (55.5+km/h; 34.5+mph); range 22210km (13,800 miles)
Dimensions: length overall 324m (1,062ft 6in) for first ship, 327.1m (1,072ft 6in) for second ship and 319.5m (1,047ft 6in) for last two ships; beam 39.5m (129ft 6in) for first two ships and 39.6m (130ft 0in) for last two
Crew: 2,920 plus an air group of about 2,500
User: USA

The evolution of the carrier deck

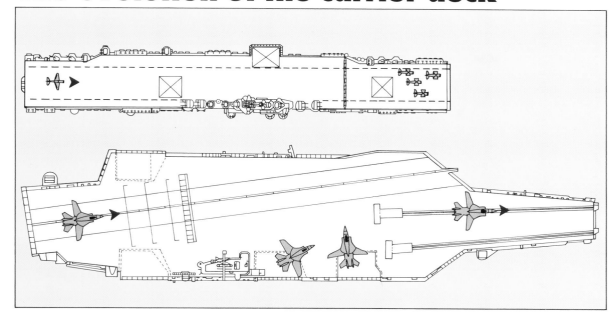

The evolution of the flight deck of the carrier was not a steady progress. The first ships to carry aircraft were built with 'flying-off' decks over the bows. These allowed planes to be launched, but getting back on to the ship was nearly impossible. The through-deck was the answer. This served well during World War II, although it was impossible to launch and land aircraft simultaneously. After the war, with bigger and faster jet-powered aircraft entering service, the straight deck became dangerous, and the accident rate rose dramatically. Many authorities felt that the carrier could go no further. The British development of the angled deck changed all that. Aircraft coming in to land now have an unobstructed deck in front of them, enabling them to go round again if the approach is wrong. It also allows the carrier to launch and recover aircraft simultaneously.

carriers, however, four ships of the 33,500-ton 'Kiev' class, which were commissioned from 1975 onwards, were provided with a formidable battery of SSM launchers. As a result, they did not have foredeck cata-pults, and were restricted to V/STOL Yak-38s and helicopters. These ships had a remarkable appearance, as they were in effect cruisers with a 620-ft, slightly angled flight deck hung off the port beam.

Only one, the 'Admiral Gossfikov', remains in service, and she may soon be sold to India.

This vessel is of 65,000 tons displace-ment; another, nuclear powered vessel,

---

179
'Forrestal' class

Conceived originally as smaller versions of the large flushdecked strike carrier *America*, which was cancelled, the four units of the **'Forrestal' class** were then redesigned along more conventional lines to appear from the mid-1950s as the USA's first aircraft-carriers built specifically to operate jet aircraft. As such the ships (the *Forrestal*, *Saratoga*, *Ranger* and *Independence*) had a conventional island superstructure to starboard and an angled flight deck arrangement that allowed the incorporation of four steam catapults as two each on the bow and angled sections.

The flight deck of the first three ships measured 316.7 m (1,039 ft 0 in) in length and 72.5 m (238 ft 0 in) in width, while the equivalent figures for the last ship were 319 m (1,046 ft 6 in) and 72.7 m (238 ft 6 in). The air group strength was about 90, roughly similar to that of the 'Nimitz' class. The ships were steadily upgraded electronically, and better protection was provided by the addition of Kevlar armour over the most vulnerable spaces. None of the class remains in service.

Specification
'Forrestal' class
Type: multi-role fleet aircraft-carrier
Displacement: 78,000 tons full load
Armament: three 20-mm Phalanx

CIWS mountings (first ship only) and three octuple launchers for Sea Sparrow SAMs
Propulsion: four 48464-kW (65,000-hp) or (last three ships) 52192-kW (70,000-hp) steam turbines
Performance: maximum speed 33 kt (61 km/h; 38 mph) or (last three ships)

34 kt (63 km/h; 39 mph); range 22210 km (13,800 miles)
Dimensions: length overall 316.7 m (1,030 ft 0 in) or (last unit) 319 m (1,046 ft 6 in); beam 39.5 m (129 ft 6 in)
Crew: 2,945 plus an air group of about 2,500
User: USA

180
'Midway' class

The two ships of the **'Midway' class** are the oldest aircraft carriers in first-line service. The ships were laid down at the end of World War II and became the world's first carriers able to operate jet-powered nuclear strike aircraft without modification. The *Midway* and *Coral Sea* outlived their sister ship *Franklin D. Roosevelt*, which was deleted in 1977.

Over the years the ships were steadily upgraded in capability despite a progressive diminution in the gun armament, the former witnessing the introduction of an angled flightdeck and modern carrier landing aids, and the latter the replacement of comparatively large numbers of small and medium-calibre guns with

missiles and close-in weapon system mountings. Served by three deck-edge lifts and two (*Midway*) or three (*Coral Sea*) steam catapults, the flightdeck measures 298.4 m (979 ft 0 in) in length and 72.5 m (238 ft 0 in) in width. This is too small for the operation of several of the US Navy's latest aircraft (notably the Grumman F-14 fighter and Lockheed S-3 anti-submarine aeroplane), so the carriers are generally deployed to areas of secondary threat with a complement of 75 aircraft. Both ships were deleted in the 1990s as more units of the 'Nimitz' class became available.

Specification
'Midway' class
Type: multi-role fleet aircraft-carrier

Displacement: 62,200 tons full load
Armament: three 20-mm Phalanx CIWS mountings and (Midway only) two octuple launchers for Sea Sparrow SAMs
Propulsion: four 39517-kW (53,000-hp) steam turbines
Performance: maximum speed 32 kt

(59 km/h; 37 mph); range 27800 km (17,275 miles)
Dimensions: length overall 298.4 m (979 ft 0 in); beam 36.9 m (121 ft 0 in)
Crew: 2,510 plus an air group of about 1,950
User: USA

Carrier Evolution

Half a century has seen the capability of the aircraft-carrier grow from HMS *Hermes*, the first carrier built as such, to the might of the nuclear-powered USS *Nimitz*.

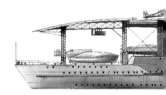

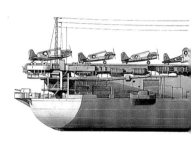

Above: The carrier's superstructure carries all of the myriad radar, electronic warfare and communications antennas necessary to fight a capital ship in modern battle.

Below: The 1980s saw the old capital ship and the new operating together for the first time since World War II. Here, Saratoga accompanies the battleship Iowa.

Ulyanovsk – laid down in 1988 – was broken up on the ·slipway during construction. This effectively put an end to Russian hopes of challenging the American lead in carriers.

For the US and Russian navies, these supercarriers have an obvious importance. They can approach close to an enemy coastline almost anywhere in the world, and launch a tactical strike without the need for any land base – as was dramatically illustrated by the veteran *Coral Sea* in th bombing of Libya in 1986. Their mobility, and the threat of their mighty armament, plays a vital peace-keeping role in the world today.

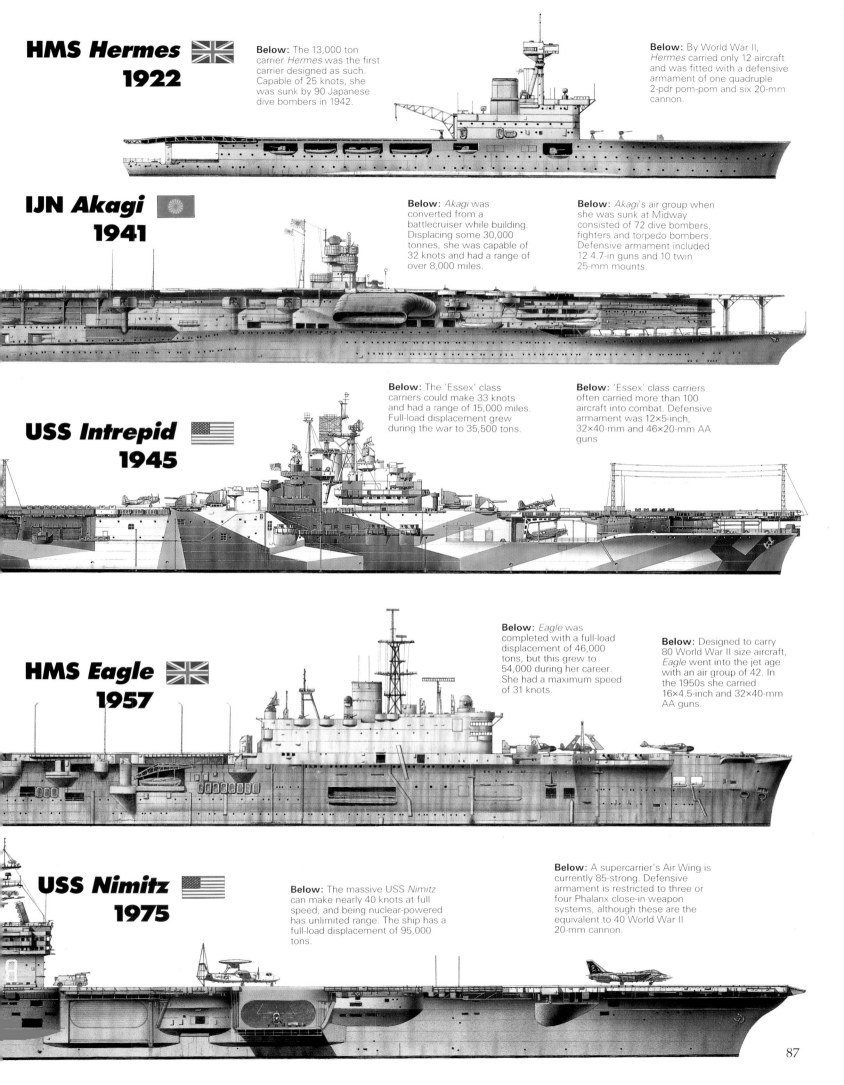

HMS *Hermes*
1922

Below: The 13,000 ton carrier *Hermes* was the first carrier designed as such. Capable of 25 knots, she was sunk by 90 Japanese dive bombers in 1942.

Below: By World War II, *Hermes* carried only 12 aircraft and was fitted with a defensive armament of one quadruple 2-pdr pom-pom and six 20-mm cannon.

IJN *Akagi*
1941

Below: *Akagi* was converted from a battlecruiser while building. Displacing some 30,000 tonnes, she was capable of 32 knots and had a range of over 8,000 miles.

Below: *Akagi*'s air group when she was sunk at Midway consisted of 72 dive bombers, fighters and torpedo bombers. Defensive armament included 12 4.7-in guns and 10 twin 25-mm mounts.

USS *Intrepid*
1945

Below: The 'Essex' class carriers could make 33 knots and had a range of 15,000 miles. Full-load displacement grew during the war to 35,500 tons.

Below: 'Essex' class carriers often carried more than 100 aircraft into combat. Defensive armament was 12×5-inch, 32×40-mm and 46×20-mm AA guns

HMS *Eagle*
1957

Below: *Eagle* was completed with a full-load displacement of 46,000 tons, but this grew to 54,000 during her career. She had a maximum speed of 31 knots.

Below: Designed to carry 80 World War II size aircraft, *Eagle* went into the jet age with an air group of 42. In the 1950s she carried 16×4.5-inch and 32×40-mm AA guns.

USS *Nimitz*
1975

Below: The massive USS *Nimitz* can make nearly 40 knots at full speed, and being nuclear-powered has unlimited range. The ship has a full-load displacement of 95,000 tons.

Below: A supercarrier's Air Wing is currently 85-strong. Defensive armament is restricted to three or four Phalanx close-in weapon systems, although these are the equivalent to 40 World War II 20-mm cannon.

The USS Kitty Hawk cruises the oceans with a fair proportion of her air wing covering the broad expanse of her flight deck. Her massive crew is dedicated to keeping those aircraft flying and fighting.

Big though a carrier is, moving 30-tonne aircraft about the deck is a highly intricate task. The deck crew are experts at weaving aircraft through the pack to get them in position for launch, and have evolved a series of 'traffic signals' to tell the pilot where to steer next.

Flight deck crew

A carrier's flight deck is big. Over 1,000 feet long and 250 feet wide, it is as large as three football pitches. But when you are operating 80 aircraft, it can get pretty crowded. And working on that deck is hot, dirty, and potentially deadly. 'Deck Apes' come in a variety of colours, wearing shirts that instantly indicate their function. Green Shirts are the maintenance crew, who do a variety of jobs including the highly dangerous ones of hooking aircraft onto the catapult at launch, and checking whether the tailhook has safely caught on recovery. Yellow Shirts direct traffic, and are responsible for the delicate task of moving 80 or more aircraft around on limited flight deck space. It is the yellow-shirted catapult officer who gives the final clearance for an aircraft to launch. Brown Shirts are the aircraft maintenance crews, looking after their charges like a mother looks after her babies. Blue Shirts are the shunters and movers, the tractor drivers and the like. No matter what the colour of the shirt, one thing is constant. A carrier's deck is dangerous, and it takes teamwork to ensure that accidents do not happen.

Left: Launching a fighter is a complex operation, which must be done in the correct fashion or disaster follows. Once on the catapult, the pilot and flight deck crew will exchange a series of signals as each stage of hooking up and preparing to launch is carried out. Once the pilot is ready to go he will salute the catapult officer, who will return it. The pilot then puts his head back into his seat restraint, and the catapult officer will instruct the operators to launch the aircraft.

THE FLOATING CITY

The 6,300-strong crew of a carrier are dedicated to a single task; getting the air wing into battle.

Supercarriers like the USS *Nimitz* are the most powerful and flexible warships ever built. They can respond to any situation, from disaster relief and civilian evacuation, right up to fleet battles and nuclear war. That power and flexibility come from the 80 aircraft of the carrier's Air Wing.

But USS *Nimitz* and her sisters are much more than floating aerodromes. Three thousand officers and men are required to keep the aircraft flying and fighting. Pilots may be the 'Top Guns' of the business, but without the maintenance men, the ordnance handlers, the flight deck crew and all the other support personnel, they would be about as much use in the air as a penguin.

While the aircraft and the personnel of the air group are vital to the vessel's fighting ability, it should be remembered that an aircraft-carrier is first and foremost a very large ship, and it requires an equally large crew to make it run. The 3,300 men of the ship's complement handle everything from manning the nuclear reactors and steam turbines that power the ship to providing all the services that a community of 6,300 requires. Just feeding such a huge crew is a major task, and the 24-hour catering arrangements are extensive. Other onboard facilities include hospitals, laundries, shops and that most important of military establishments, the barber's shop. The ship even has its own television station.

Administration of such a complex system is a major task in itself. The supercarrier community is run like a major corporation, with the Captain as chairman of the board and the Executive Officer (known as 'XO') as managing director. The ship is split into departments, like the operating divisions of a company. The departments are Air, Air Wing, Aircraft Maintenance, Operations, Navigation, Communications, Engineering, Safety, Administration, Supply, Training, Medical, and Dental.

At one and the same time, a carrier is a weapons platform, an oil tanker, a town of 6,000 souls, a factory, and an airport. These characteristics, and the skills of the men who make up the crew, go together to make it the largest, most powerful, most flexible warship ever to sail the seas.

Above: Green Shirts – the hook runners – have some of the most dangerous jobs on the flight deck. When a plane lands, the hook runner has to move in close to check that the arrester wire is safely caught. If the wire snaps, the ends could whip round with enough force to cut a man in half.

Left: At the other end of the flight deck, the hook-up man connects the aircraft's catapult bar to the steam catapult. This is also a high-risk job. If anything breaks, the plane could be free to move forward and run him over. If he moves in the wrong direction, he could be sucked up into the jet intake.

Aircraft stores

Movement and maintenance of aircraft is important, but a warplane needs more in order to fly and fight. The Red Shirts are 'ordies', or ordnance handlers. They look after the aircraft's weapons, taking them from the magazines and loading them onto the aircraft. They deal in missiles and cannon ammunition for the fighters, tons of bombs and air-to-surface missiles for the attack birds, and torpedoes, depth charges and the like for the carrier's anti-submarine aircraft and helicopters. The Purple Shirts are another team in a dangerous trade. They are responsible for fuelling the aircraft. Both Red Shirts and Purple Shirts have to be highly safety-conscious. Fire is a real danger aboard a carrier, packed as it is with highly explosive stores, so fuelling aircraft is carried with as much care as possible. On the rare occasions that there are accidents, it is usually under combat conditions. It was accidental firing of weapons that caused the disastrous fires aboard the USS *Oriskany*, *Forrestal* and the *Enterprise* at various times during the Vietnam War.

Right: A variety of flight-deck crew types work on a Grumman A-6 Intruder. Those nearest the camera in purple shirts are responsible for fuelling the aircraft.

Below: Red-shirted ordnance technicians, known as 'ordies', wheel a trolley with three Rockeye cluster bombs along the flight deck towards the aircraft that they are arming.

Above: A Purple Shirt unreels a fuel hose aboard USS Nimitz. Deck fuel points mean that planes do not have to be struck down to the hangar to refuel.

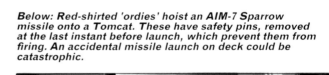
Below: Red-shirted 'ordies' hoist an AIM-7 Sparrow missile onto a Tomcat. These have safety pins, removed at the last instant before launch, which prevent them from firing. An accidental missile launch on deck could be catastrophic.

Right: Fire has always been a major hazard at sea, and nowhere is it more threatening than on the flight deck of a carrier. Any accident could cause a multi-million dollar blaze, and the deck crew is trained to take immediate action.

Ship handling

An aircraft-carrier is just that: a ship that carries, launches, and recovers aircraft. All possible space is dedicated to the operation of its air wing. But it is still a warship. The seamen who keep the ship running work shifts around the clock, as they would on any other fighting vessel. All the usual tasks have to be performed, from steering and navigation to hull-painting and anchor maintenance. The only thing to break the flight deck is the carrier's island, and it is from here that its operations are controlled. In addition to the seamen, another important element is those who make a carrier fight. Operating at the heart of a major naval formation, a carrier will usually carry a flag officer and his staff. The admiral decides on what he wants the carrier to do, and it is up to the staff to decide how the carrier force will deliver the strike.

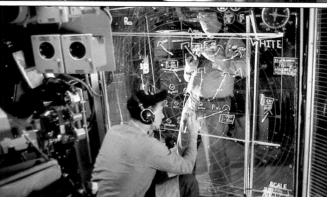

Above right: An aircraft-carrier might be a floating airfield, but it is also a warship. Handling such a huge vessel is an intricate business, especially when the bridge is some 600 feet back from the bows. This is the bridge of the USS Nimitz, seen on her first commission in 1975.

Right: The heart of a ship in battle is no longer the bridge. Now, with electronic sensors reaching out for hundreds of miles around the battle group, it is from the darkened world of the Combat Information Center that the battle is fought.

Living on a carrier

Big though it is, a carrier is not the most spacious of vessels to live on. Eighty aircraft take up a lot of room, to say nothing of the equipment to keep them running and fighting, the massive engines which power the carrier, millions of gallons of aviation fuel, and thousands of tons of stores and supplies. There is little privacy for any but the most senior officers of the 6,300 men who comprise the carrier community. Yet every effort is made to make life bearable. Food is plentiful and varied, although the fact that the ship's bakery prepares over 6,000 hamburger and hot dog rolls every day indicates that fast food is as popular aboard ship as it is back home. Some canteens are open round the clock to cater for sea-going watch

Above: Nuclear power gives a carrier almost unlimited range, but men and aircraft are not nuclear-powered. Big though it is, a carrier can carry only enough food and fuel for about two weeks of operations, and must be replenished regularly. To save wasting time, this usually takes place at sea.

Right: If you put 6,300 men into a restricted space for months at a time, you are going to get medical problems, and a carrier has a fully equipped hospital and dental surgery.

routines. There are shops, and movie shows, and a ship's television station. You might think such comforts overly luxurious in a fighting ship, but they are absolutely vital in a vessel which might be on deployment, far from home and loved ones, for up to half a year at a time.

Right: Keeping order among the aircraft in the air is just as important as handling them efficiently on the flight deck. In the carrier's control centre a close check is kept on which aircraft are flying, assisted by information from the carrier's radar and from the airborne radar carried by the Air Wing's Grumman E-2 Hawkeyes.

Above: A carrier will often carry a *Rear Admiral,* with his own bridge, staff, cabin, and dining room. He is responsible for handling the whole battle group, as a captain is responsible for handling his ship. Most modern battle group commanders are ex-fliers who have also commanded carriers.

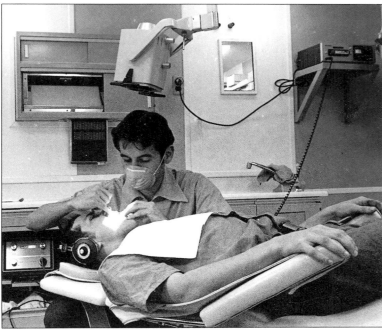

Above: The enlisted men's barber shop aboard the *USS* Nimitz might be expected to deal with over 100 heads per day, a level of custom that any hairdresser ashore would be delighted to have. But fancy hairstyles, permanent waves and dye jobs are unlikely to be on the menu!

Right: Living conditions aboard warships have improved out of all recognition. Large ships like carriers even have their own supermarkets. But one thing that you cannot get is alcohol: the *US* Navy afloat is strictly dry, and does not even allow beer.

Engineering

The sheer size of a supercarrier is awesome. At 90,000 tons, it is the largest warship ever built. It is also among the fastest ships afloat, and can force its bulk through the water at nearly 65 kilometres per hour (40 mph). Obviously, something pretty potent must be happening down in the engine rooms. All carriers are steam-powered, although that steam can be generated by a nuclear reactor or by conventional boilers. The steam drives four huge turbines, turning four propellers. The entire system generates over 280,000 shaft horsepower. Looking after these mighty machines is another highly skilled trade, one that calls for men to work under conditions of high temperature and almost deafening noise. Without those men, however, steam would not be generated and the ship would not move. Without steam, there would be no fresh drinking water, no catapult launches, no heating or air conditioning, no electricity to light the vessel, or to cook the 20,000 meals a day necessary to feed the crew. It may not be the most glamorous of jobs, but working in the engineering spaces is vital.

Right: A carrier and its air wing make up a large chunk of complex machinery. Carriers are fully equipped with engineering workshops, capable of a wide variety of repair work.

Left: Keeping a carrier running is the task of the engine-room crew. In the case of a nuclear-powered vessel they follow the US Navy's unofficial first nuclear safety commandment: "Thou shalt watch all of the dials, all of the time."

Left: When there are no flight operations, a carrier is one of the few vessels where you can jog a reasonable distance: twice around the flight deck is almost a mile.

Above: You can't run a ship on office hours. The 24-hour sea-going watch routines mean that a proportion of the crew is awake and working at all hours of the day and night. They must be catered for, and a carrier has a number of cafeterias and dining areas serving food around the clock. This is one of the messes for enlisted men: petty officers and officers have their own facilities elsewhere.

Left: Food at sea has always been of major interest to sailors. Salt pork, salt beef, and rock-hard biscuits that had been the standard fare for hundreds of years up until the beginning of this century gave way to canned food. Refrigeration and regular replenishment now mean that fresh food is the rule, rather than the exception. The United States has always tried to make its servicemen as comfortable as possible, and the food served aboard a carrier is plentiful and of good quality. Enlisted men get their food free, but officers have to pay for their meals!

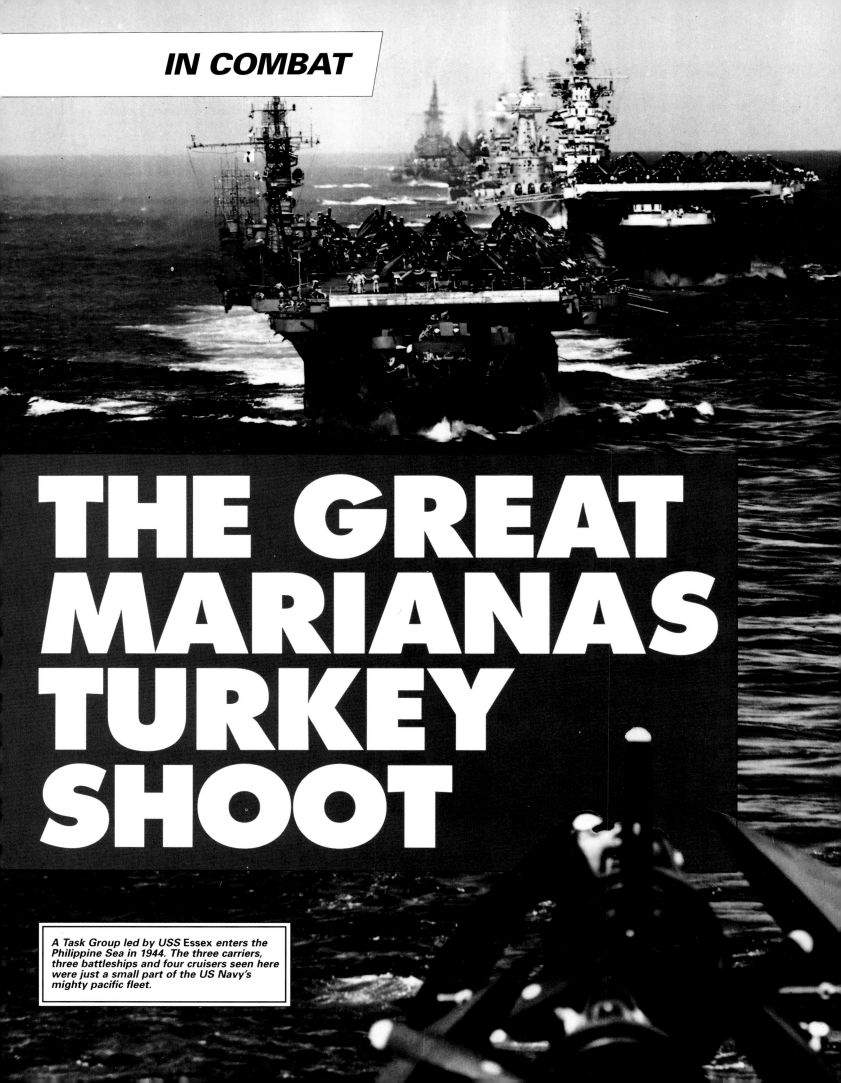

THE GREAT MARIANAS TURKEY SHOOT

A Task Group led by USS Essex enters the Philippine Sea in 1944. The three carriers, three battleships and four cruisers seen here were just a small part of the US Navy's mighty pacific fleet.

The climactic sea battle of the Pacific War did not appear important at the time, but the 'Turkey Shoot' in the Philippine Sea signalled the end of Japanese naval air power.

It took an astonishingly short time – less than a generation – for the aircraft-carrier to replace the battleship as the new capital ship. For hundreds of years, dominion over the oceans went to the navy with the biggest guns. From the defeat of the Spanish Armada to the sinking of the *Bismarck*, the battleship was queen of the seas. But war at sea had changed even as the gun-battles of World War II were being fought. The era of the battleship was over, and that of the aircraft-carrier had begun.

The Pacific War was to a large extent the war of the aircraft-carrier. From Pearl Harbor to Okinawa, it was the effective use of air power at sea that proved decisive. Battles took place across hundreds of miles of ocean without the major participants even seeing each other. And of all the many engagements, the Battle of the Philippine Sea was the most decisive. There were battles in plenty to come, but the two-day fight in June 1944 finally smashed Japanese naval aviation, and the power of the Imperial Japanese Navy.

The invasion of Saipan by American forces in mid-June 1944 forced the Japanese to react in strength. The reason was quite simple: from bases in the Marianas Islands American bombers would be able to bomb targets in Japan itself. To avoid this, the Imperial Japanese Navy decided to throw in its remaining carriers and trained aircrews.

Admiral Jisaburo Ozawa, commanding the newly established First Mobile Fleet, planned to put large numbers of land-based aircraft into the islands of Guam, Yap and Rota. These would attack the US carriers west of Saipan, greatly outnumbering the carrier aircraft. As his lightly constructed carrier aircraft had just over 320 km (200 miles) more range than the US carrier planes he would be able to launch his own carrier strike outside the range of the American aircraft, attack the fast carriers, refuel and rearm at Guam, and attack a second time on the way back. In theory the carrier strikes should have been very destructive, for the American carriers would already have suffered severe damage from the land strikes.

In practice it went very wrong. Right at the beginning the commander of the land-based air forces, Vice Admiral Kakuta, failed to inflict significant damage on the carrier aircraft. Instead the American Admiral Raymond Spruance had launched heavy attacks on the Japanese airfields, wiping out the aircraft on Guam and Rota. What remains unexplained to this day is the fact that Kakuta failed to warn Ozawa of this failure in the plan, and continued to reassure him that the Americans were suffering a heavy rate of attrition. Nor were the Americans short of intelligence about Ozawa's movements, for their submarines had spotted the carriers moving through the Philippines.

The Japanese carrier force was out in strength: the light carriers *Zuiho, Chitose, Chiyoda, Hiyo, Junyo* and *Ryuho* and the fleet

Left: The all-conquering Zero of 1941 could hold its own with the the faster, tougher American fighters in service in 1944. But good Japanese pilots were in short supply.

Above: A Japanese land-based fighter is shot down in the first stage of the battle, as it attempts in vain to attack the American invasion fleet approaching the Marianas Islands.

The Grumman F-6F Hellcat was the primary American carrier fighter in the Philippine Sea. Swarms of these big, beefy machines went up to meet the enemy attack, and they tore apart the formations of lightly-built Japanese aircraft.

IJN *Taiho*

carriers *Taiho, Shokaku* and *Zuikaku,* as well as five battleships, 12 cruisers and 27 destroyers, and 24 submarines. But this force was dwarfed by Task Force 58: the light carriers *Langley, Cowpens, San Jacinto, Princeton, Monterey, Cabot, Belleau Wood* and *Bataan,* the fleet carriers *Hornet, Yorktown, Bunker Hill, Wasp, Enterprise, Lexington* and *Essex,* as well as seven battleships, 21 cruisers, 62 destroyers and 25 submarines. Even these heavy odds were lengthened by the superior training of the American aircrews, for the Japanese pilot-training programme had totally failed to keep up with wartime attrition, and many of Ozawa's pilots were barely capable of landing on board their carriers.

Spruance divided his force into four task groups (TGs 58.1, 58.2, 58.3 and 58.4) and a Battle Line (TG 58.7) under Admiral Willis A. Lee. To attack the carriers the Japanese aircraft would first have to fly through a barrage of anti-aircraft fire from the Battle Line, and then fight off each carrier task group's combat air patrol and face the fire from their escorts. The land attacks had done nothing to weaken this defence in depth, but Ozawa had no idea of what sort of opposition his pilots would be facing.

On 18 June the main Japanese force moved into position to the west of the Marianas, and detached the Van Force of three light carriers under Vice Admiral Takeo Kurita, with the intention of launching the first strikes next morning. When the Van Force launched its strike of 16 fighters and 53 bombers it was detected by the Battle Line on radar, giving time for the US carriers to launch every available fighter. They inflicted grievous losses on the Japanese (42 aircraft) and the only damage achieved was a bomb hit on the battleship *South Dakota.*

A second strike was launched from the six carriers of the Main Body: 48 fighters and 62 bombers, but 10 minutes after the launch-sequence had begun, the US submarine *Albacore* torpedoed the carrier *Taiho.* Once again the massed anti-aircraft fire of the Battle Line slaughtered the air strike, shooting down 79 out of the 110 aircraft, and all that was achieved was a near-miss. A third strike of 47 aircraft managed to avoid the Battle Line but found very few targets, and lost only seven planes. A fourth strike launched from 11.30 also lost its way; only 33 out of 82 aircraft found TG 58.2, and suffered heavy losses.

The Japanese carriers had made the strongest possible effort and had failed to inflict more than trifling damage on TF 58. At 12.22 Ozawa suffered a further setback when the submarine USS *Cavalla* put four torpedoes into the *Shokaku.* She blew up and sank at 15.10, followed shortly afterwards by the *Taiho.* But Ozawa had no intention of giving up, for he still believed that Kakuta's land-based forces had inflicted heavy casualties, and he therefore felt that his 102 remaining aircraft could turn the tables on Spruance. In addition Kakuta had told him that many of the survivors of the carrier strikes had landed safely on Guam.

Next day the two opposing fleets were moving to the north west on roughly parallel courses. When Spruance learned of Ozawa's position it was late in the afternoon, and he was faced with a difficult choice. A strike against the Japanese carriers would be at maximum distance, and the return flight to the carriers would have to be made in darkness. Nevertheless at 16.20 he ordered an all-out strike by 85 fighters, 77 dive-bombers and 54 torpedo-bombers.

The Japanese could only launch 80 aircraft before TF 58's tempest overwhelmed them. The light carrier *Hiyo* was sunk by two torpedoes; the *Zuikaku, Junyo*

Above: The overriding American aim was to protect the Marine amphibious force. The Japanese had to stop the Americans from taking the islands; failure to do so would bring Tokyo into range of the US Air Force's B-29 bombers.

Right: A Japanese dive bomber crashes blazing into the sea off the Marianas, watched by American seamen on the deck of an aircraft carrier. Few Japanese aircraft managed to get through the massive anti-air defences of the US Navy's carrier task forces.

USS Enterprise

Above: Flak covers the skies above an American carrier task force. Anti-aircraft defences grew dramatically during the Pacific War, when the main offensive weapon was the aircraft.

Right: Major warships began the war with very light AA armament. By 1944, an 'Essex' class carrier might have 40 40-mm and 50 20-mm cannon, and be escorted by a battleship with even more guns.

Above: Japanese air power in the Pacific was destroyed over the Philippine Sea, not through sinking carriers but by wiping out the last of Japan's experienced carrier pilots.

and *Chiyoda* were badly damaged, and other ships were also hit. Ozawa managed to extricate the remnants of his forces without further loss, but he had lost what he knew to be the last chance of a decisive victory. His inexperienced pilots had been shot down in such numbers that the American pilots had called the air battle on 19 June the 'Great Marianas Turkey Shoot'. Even when stretched to the limit, the US Navy's pilots were more skilled: after the strike on 20 June the aircraft returned to their carriers at 22.45, many of them virtually out of fuel. In a classic signal Vice-Admiral Mitscher ordered the carriers to turn on their landing lights, to make sure that the pilots could find a friendly deck in the darkness. Losses were heavy, but 116 aircraft landed safely. The remaining 80 crash-landed or 'ditched' nearby, allowing destroyers to pick up the majority of the aircrew.

In retrospect it is difficult to criticise Ozawa's handling of the battle. The major tactical error, attacking the Battle Line, was the result of the naval pilots' lack of experience. The extraordinary lies told by Kakuta led Ozawa to believe that his four strikes would have much more effect than they did, and he was even misled into believing that his aircraft were safe in Guam, whereas in fact they had been destroyed. Given those circumstances, and the fact that he was vastly outnumbered, it would have been difficult to do better.

Even if Ozawa had been blessed with better luck and a more capable subordinate he would have needed a miracle to give him victory against TF 58. The best that could have happened would have been a few US carriers badly damaged or even sunk. That would have resulted in a short respite, but the Japanese were now being overwhelmed by sheer numbers. Not only were trained pilots in short supply; even the raw materials and oil for which Japan had gone to war were difficult to transport to Japan, because of the lack of shipping. It was now impossible for Japanese shipyards to maintain shipping at pre-war levels. The fleet could not get sufficient refined oil, and was forced to use volatile oil from Borneo – a major cause of the explosions which destroyed the *Taiho* and *Shokaku*.

On the American side there were bitter recriminations against Spruance, particularly by Admiral William Halsey and his supporters. They felt that the caution of Spruance had lost TF 58 the opportunity to sink all Ozawa's carriers, and thus eliminate the Imperial Japanese Navy. What the critics could not accept was that Spruance's dispositions at all times took account of the overriding need to prevent Ozawa from evading his task groups and getting at the vulnerable amphibious forces off Saipan. No mercy would have been shown to Spruance if his carriers had lost Ozawa, and massive losses had thus been inflicted on the invasion force. The critics tend to overlook the fact that only three months later at Leyte Halsey swallowed the bait offered by Ozawa. Although the Japanese carriers were severely punished the main force under Admiral Kurita got through to the invasion area, and only the desperate bravery of the defending light carriers and escorts saved the Americans from disaster. Historians have been kinder to Spruance than his fellow admirals in 1944.

BATTLEGROUP DEFENDERS

The carrier battle group is a multi-billion dollar investment in power projection, but it is also a prime target in combat. As a result, many of its resources are dedicated to defence.

A modern carrier Battle Group is just about the most potent military unit the world has ever seen. It can project power around the world, in ways that range from 'show-the-flag' visits right through to all-out nuclear strikes.

That power and versatility makes the Battle Group a primary target in time of war. Current US defensive measures were developed in the face of a potent Soviet missile threat. Although the collapse of the Soviet Union makes naval conflicts a remote possibility, the Russian fleet still has great potential in military planning; it is of what the enemy is capable for which you prepare, not for what you think he is actually going to do. And the Russians have been replaced by multiple threats.

The defence of a Battle Group is split into three zones.

1 The outer air battle area is an air combat zone, covered by naval fighters mounting Combat Air Patrols (CAPs). Targets are detected and the fighters are controlled by Airborne Early Warning (AEW) aircraft patrolling above the fleet.

2 The surface-to-air missile zone is covered by medium- and long-range SAMs. These are launched from the carrier's escorts and are intended to engage aircraft which have eluded the defending fighters as well as any missiles which might have been launched by the attackers.

3 The inner zone is the domain of the hard- and soft-kill weapons. Soft-kill weapons are the decoys and electronic counter-measures designed to fool the guidance systems of missiles which have 'leaked' through the outer defences. Hard-kill systems include rapid-firing guns and high-speed missiles.

The Midway Battle Group steams into the Pacific from its base at Yokosuka, with the venerable carrier USS Midway at the heart of the formation and surrounded by escorts.

1 Tomcat CAP

The outer ring of the Battle Group's layered defence is provided by Grumman F-14 Tomcats. In high alert states, pairs of F-14s will mount Combat Air Patrols (CAPs) some 350 kilometres out from the carrier. The Tomcat's powerful AWG-9 radar can track many targets simultaneously, even when the aircraft is at high altitude and the targets are skimming the sea, and it can control up to six missiles at once to allow the fighter to engage multiple targets. The huge AIM-54 Phoenix air-to-air missile has a Mach 5 top speed and a range of 150 kilometres, extending the carrier's defences to a radius of 500 kilometres.

2 The Threat

The post-World War II technological revolution has seen a vast change in the threat to capital ships. The anti-ship missile has taken the place of the bomb and the torpedo. It can be launched from submarines, surface ships, and aircraft. The latest Soviet air-launched anti-ship missiles are thought to have ranges in excess of 800 kilometres, which means that attacking aircraft can now strike from outside the Battle Group's defensive perimeter. The CAP fighters must now engage the missiles rather than the aircraft which launch them.

Three aircraft from the air wing aboard the nuclear-powered aircraft-carrier USS Dwight D. Eisenhower are typical of the outer ring of defences around the battle group. One Tomcat comes from each of the carrier's two fighter squadrons, VF-142 'Grim Reapers' and VF-143 'Pukin' Dogs', and they are both under the direction of a Grumman E-2C Hawkeye from VAW-121. The Hawkeye's powerful radar can detect targets at many hundreds of miles' range, while the Tomcats have a missile-and-radar combination that can knock enemies out of the skies at ranges of 100 miles or more.

3 Command and Control

The first warning of a missile attack will probably come from the Grumman E-2 Hawkeye airborne early warning and control aircraft. The carrier has four Hawkeyes. Flying at an altitude of 30,000 feet on the edge of the defensive perimeter, 350 kilometres from the carrier, the Hawkeye's AN/APS radar can detect aircraft at ranges of 450 kilometres. It is more than a flying radar station, however. The command and control system can simultaneously track up to 2,000 targets and at the same time direct more than 40 airborne intercepts.

Information from the many and varied sensors of the battle group comes by data-link to the Combat Information Center of the carrier, from where the captain fights the carrier and the two-star admiral in command of the group makes his plans.

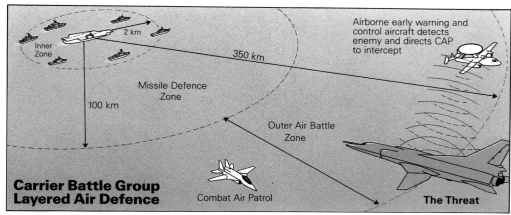

Airborne early warning and control aircraft detects enemy and directs CAP to intercept

2 km

Inner Zone

350 km

Missile Defence Zone

100 km

Outer Air Battle Zone

Carrier Battle Group Layered Air Defence

Combat Air Patrol

The Threat

For ease of control, the defence of the battle group is split into zones. The outer area is the preserve of the fighter armed with long-range missiles. This could stretch 300 kilometres out from the carrier. A Hawkeye high above this zone extends the carrier's radar horizon out to almost 1000 kilometres. Inwards from that is the inner, or missile-defence zone. This is covered by long- and medium-range surface-to-air missiles from the carrier's escort, and extends out to 150 kilometres. Anything getting through that has to engage the group's close-in defences, which are short-range, fast-reacting, radar-guided guns and missiles, effective from a couple of kilometres down to 50 metres or less.

4 The Escort Battle

The surface-to-air zone extends out to about 100 kilometres around the Battle Group. Most of the US Navy's escort vessels have some SAM capability, of which about half will be dedicated to the anti-air battle. Each Battle Group will probably contain an AEGIS cruiser. AEGIS cruisers are the most sophisticated air defence vessels ever built. Their SPY-1 radars can detect and track hundreds of targets. Computerised systems assess and engage each threat in turn, firing missiles in quick succession from vertical launch systems. AEGIS cruisers also have advanced control and communication systems, gathering information from other vessels in the Battle Group as well as from the patrolling Hawkeyes. In its ultimate form a single AEGIS cruiser will control all of the missile launchers of all the ships in the Battle Group.

The Standard surface-to-air-missile equips most of the carrier's escorts. The latest SM2-ER variant is highly accurate, with a range extended to over 120 kilometres, while the medium-range variant seen here is effective out to about 40 kilometres.

5 Last Ditch Defence

Any aircraft or missile which penetrates the Battle Group's outer and middle defence zones still has to penetrate the close-in defences. These can take a variety of forms. Counter-measures are designed to fool missile guidance systems, diverting them harmlessly away from the main targets. 'Hard-kill' systems include anti-missile missiles like the BPDMS developed from the AIM-7 Sparrow air-to-air missile. In many cases these have been replaced by Close-In Weapon Systems (CIWS), effective when a missile gets to within 2000 metres of the target. These are rapid-firing cannon spitting radar-directed streams of shells into the path of an oncoming missile. A carrier usually has four such weapons, and the other vessels in the group add another 10 or 12 weapons to the total.

Left: The Phalanx CIWS, or Close-In Weapon System, is a rapid-firing Gatling-type gun adapted from the Vulcan developed for the USAF's first supersonic fighters. Mounted on a fast-rotating and swivelling mount, it is radar-directed. The radar tracks incoming targets, directing the outgoing stream of depleted uranium projectiles to bring the two together.

The Tarawa class amphibious assault ship USS Saipan, which can carry up to 26 helicopters or Harrier AV-8B VSTOL aircraft, plus an assault force of 1,900 US Marines.

AMPHIBIOUS ASSAULT

They can range the world's oceans. They can land in any country that has a coastline. From small landing parties to multi-division assaults, amphibious forces are a vital part of 20th century warfare.

It is the darkest hour before dawn. For 40 minutes two destroyers, several miles offshore, have laid down a murderous barrage on enemy positions along the coast. But lying closer to the shore, under the huffing shells as they pass overhead, a larger vessel has been flooding its tanks, settling lower in the water.

The gate that closes the big well dock in the stern has been lowered, and the four landing craft bounce uneasily in the swell from the ship's wake. Two of them hold 250 men each, tightly packed together in their bulky equipment and queasily joking in quiet voices; two carry a Chieftain tank apiece. Slung from davits high on the ship's sides are four other, smaller craft that transport four Land Rovers and another 70 men – HQ staff, signallers, medics and mechanics.

Above the heads of the men in the well, the first helicopter starts its engines. The edges of the banked grey clouds hanging low overhead are touched with a faint pink glow, and a tiny streak of light shows along the eastern horizon. On the cramped bridges of the landing craft, naval crews are at the wheel. Unsecured, the craft wallow as the first eases its way out of the stern, the noise of its engines

US Marines storm ashore from their AAV-7P amphibious assault vehicles, supported by rocket- and cannon-firing AH-1 Sea Cobra attack helicopters. The Marines are by far the world's largest amphibious force.

Two American 'Tarawa' class assault ships could have landed the entire British Falklands invasion force

beginning to drown the roar of the helicopter lifting off. One by one the others follow, increasing speed and starting their race for the beach. The assault is on.

Putting an army ashore has always been a difficult operation, and as naval vessels and transports grew in size the difficulty increased. Men were at their greatest disadvantage as they struggled out of boats, through the breaking waves and the soft surface of the beach, and speed was the first essential. World War II saw the first development of specialised landing craft: little more than flat-bottomed steel boxes that could be driven almost onto the land, with a bow ramp that could be lowered to enable troops and tanks to storm ashore.

Landing Ship Dock

To carry these Landing Craft Vehicles and Personnel (LCVP) and Landing Craft Tanks (LCT), the Landing Ship Dock (LSD) was developed. In this, the after part of the ship was built as a single deep well that could be flooded to a depth sufficient to float the LCVPs and

Troop-carrying helicopters were soon seen as valuable additions to amphibious forces, and in the 1950s the Americans used small carriers as helicopter assault ships, developing many of the tactics in use today.

Amphibious assault in World War II

Amphibious warfare has been around for thousands of years, for as long as countries have been separated from their enemies by water. Not until World War II, however, did it begin to take the form that we know today. Specialised landing craft, and ships to support those landing craft, made their appearance on an unprecedented scale. Without such craft, the invasion and liberation of Europe would have been almost impossible.

Normandy was the biggest of them all. For the 1944 landings in North West Europe, the Allies gathered together over 4,000 landing ships and craft supported by more than 1,000 warships and some 14,000 aircraft. Preceded by massive airborne landings, the Allies pushed more than 150,000 men ashore on 6 June alone. Within two months, the Allies were to bring more than two million men, 500,000 vehicles, and over three million tons of supplies into Europe over the beaches of Normandy.

LCTs. While the ship was at sea a huge hydraulically operated gate kept the stern sealed, but once the well was flooded this gate could be lowered so that the landing craft could leave.

Few of these vessels, and not many landing craft, were kept in commission after the war, and when General MacArthur planned his seaborne assault on Inchon in September 1950 only one, the USS *Fort Marion*, was available. However, the success of the Inchon landings revived interest in this type of vessel, and between 1954 and 1957 the US Navy commissioned eight new craft, the class being named after the first, USS *Thomaston*.

The 'Thomaston' class was essentially a more modern version of the World War II LSD; they were built larger, and much more seaworthy, with a sustained speed of over 20 knots compared with the previous maximum of only 15. A platform deck covered the after part of the well, and could be used for cargo-carrying helicopters, but no hangar nor maintenance facilities were provided.

A later development of the 'Thomaston' class was the 'Anchorage' class, of which five were commissioned between 1969 and 1972.

AMPHIBIOUS ASSAULT Reference File

121
USA

'Tarawa' and 'Wasp' classes

The five ships of the **'Tarawa' class** were until recently the world's largest amphibious warfare vessels, each combining in a single hull the capabilities of the assault ship (helicopter), transport dock, amphibious command ship and amphibious cargo ship. The accommodation is one 1,903-man reinforced Marine Corps infantry battalion plus large quantities of vehicles, freight and fuel. These can be landed from the large flightdeck by an embarked strength of up to 26 Boeing Vertol CH-46 Sea Knight or 19 Sikorsky CH-53 Sea Stallion helicopters, or from the floodable docking well which measures 81.7 m (268 ft) in length and 23.8 m (78 ft) in width for use by 40 AAV-7P amphibious carriers and by

landing craft (four utility craft or larger numbers of smaller craft).

A similar configuration is used in the **'Wasp' class**, now the world's largest amphibious warfare type and planned to a strength of seven units. Displacing 40,350 tons, each 'Wasp' class ship can carry a 1,873-man reinforced marine battalion and large quantities of equipment that can be landed by up to 42 CH-46 or a smaller number of CH-53 helicopters, or by AAV-7Ps, landing craft and assault hovercraft operating from a sizeable docking well. The ships can also embark STOVL aircraft and battlefield helicopters for support of landings.

Specification
'Tarawa' class
Type: general-purpose amphibious assault ship
Displacement: 39,300 tons full load
Armament: three 127-mm (5-in) guns, six 20-mm AA guns, and two 20-mm Phalanx CIWS mountings

Propulsion: two 26096-kW (35,000-hp) steam turbines
Performance: maximum speed 24 kt (44.5 km/h; 27.5 mph); range 18500 km (11,500 miles)
Dimensions: length overall 249.9 m (820 ft 0 in); beam 32.5 m (106 ft 8 in)
Crew: 937

These are bigger and faster than their predecessors, but otherwise similar.

By 1955 the US Marine Corps was very interested in the use of helicopters for amphibious operations, and this led to the laying-down of the 'Iwo Jima' class, built to carry 25 helicopters and a full Marine battalion with all its essential supplies. Between 1961 and 1970 seven of this class were commissioned, with the designation LPH (Landing/Platform/Helicopter).

At the same time the first 'balanced force' ships were laid down, capable of transporting troops and heavy cargo as well as landing craft and tanks in the docking well. Two of these LPDs were built, the USS *Raleigh* and USS *Vancouver*.

Following suit

Other countries were quick to follow the American example, the French with the *Jeanne d'Arc* helicopter and troop carrier, commissioned in 1964, and the 'Ouragan' class LSD; and the Royal Navy with the 'Sir Lancelot' and 'Sir Bedivere' class LSLs (Landing Ship

Below: World War II also saw the development of dock landing ships, ocean-going ships enabling landing craft to cross large sea distances and to take heavy loads without the need for port facilities.

Above: The early experiments with converted World War II escort carriers led to the development of the LPH helicopter assault ship. The Americans were the only ones able to build such vessels, like the USS Guam seen here. Smaller nations like Britain had to continue to use light carriers for the task.

122

USA

'Iwo Jima' and 'Blue Ridge' classes

The seven ships of the **'Iwo Jima' class** are a very important part of US amphibious capability. Unlike most other amphibious warfare vessels, however, they were designed to use helicopters rather than landing craft to move men and equipment. The design was therefore based on that of the World War II escort carrier, and each ship can carry a 2,090-man reinforced Marine Corps infantry battalion landing team as well as large numbers of vehicles, much palletised equipment and stores, and considerable volume of fuel. The hangar can accommodate 19 Boeing Vertol CH-46 Sea Knight or Sikorsky CH-53 Sea Stallion helicopters, and the embarked helicopter strength is about 24. The landing deck can handle

seven CH-46s or four CH-53s simultaneously, and in emergencies each ship can accommodate STOVL aircraft such as the McDonnell Douglas AV-8B Harrier II. Each ship has a 300-bed hospital.

The same basic hull is used for the two **'Blue Ridge' class** amphibious command ships, the world's only vessels of their type. Extensive shipboard and communications facilities are provided for the 700-man command group, which is designed for control of high-level amphibious operations involving sea, land and air forces. So successful have they been that they now serve as fleet flagships in the Atlantic and Pacific.

Specification
'Iwo Jima' class
Type: amphibious assault ship (helicopter)
Displacement: 18,300 tons full load
Armament: two twin 76-mm (3-in) gun mountings, two 20-mm Phalanx CIWS mountings, and two octuple Sea

Sparrow SAM launchers
Propulsion: one 16403-kW (22,000-hp) steam turbine
Performance: maximum speed 23 kt (43 km/h; 26.5 mph); range 18500 km (11,500 miles)
Dimensions: length overall 180.5 m (592 ft 0 in); beam 25.6 m (84 ft 0 in)

Logistic) and the 'Fearless' class LPDs.

The six 'Sir' class ships possessed certain shortcomings as assault ships: they were designed with bow and stern doors for ro-ro (roll-on/roll-off) disembarkation of MBTs and trucks over ramps to the beach, but they had no docking facilities, and troops had to be offloaded into small landing craft or Mexeflotte pontoons. All six were employed during the Falklands landings in 1982, and *Sir Galahad* and *Sir Tristram* were badly damaged in the campaign.

All major navies now possess assault vessels of various types, and a bewildering variety of initials is used to designate them:

LST Landing Ship Tank
LCC Amphibious Command
LPD Amphibious Transport Dock
LSL Landing Ship Logistic
LKA Amphibious Cargo Ship
LHA Amphibious Assault Ship
LPH Amphibious Assault Ship/Helicopter

France has developed dock landing ships, tank landing ships, and landing craft. L9096, seen here unloading AML armoured cars, is a 650-ton EDIC (Engin de Débarquement Infanterie Chars, or tank landing craft) based at Lorient. For a period in the 1980s this vessel was transferred to the Lebanon.

123 'Raleigh' and 'Austin' classes

USA

The three **'Raleigh' class** ships are 13,600-ton amphibious transport docks, a type developed from the dock landing ship with an increase in troop and vehicle capacities secured by a decrease in the size of the docking well. In the ships of this class the floodable well is 51.2 m (168 ft) long and 15.2 m (50 ft) wide, which is sufficient to accommodate one large and three small landing craft or 20 AAA-7P amphibious personnel carriers, complemented by two more small landing craft that can be lowered by crane from the helicopter deck, which can also carry six Boeing Vertol CH-46 Sea Knight helicopters. The troop accommodation is between 930 and 1,139. The *La Salle* of this class has

been converted as a flagship for deployment in the Indian Ocean.

The **'Austin' class** design is basically an enlargement of the 'Raleigh' class design, and numbers 12 ships including the *Coronado* which has been modified as a flagship. The docking well is the same size as that on the 'Raleigh' class, but the 12-m (39.4-ft) lengthening of the hull forward of this point increases vehicle and cargo capacities as well as boosting to 28 the number of AAA-7Ps that can be embarked; landing craft numbers remain unaltered. The helicopter platform has a telescoping hangar for one of the six CH-46s.

Specification
'Austin' class
Type: amphibious transport dock
Displacement: 15,900 to 17,000 tons full load
Armament: one twin 76-mm (3-in) gun mounting, and two 20-mm Phalanx CIWS mountings

Propulsion: two 9796-kW (12,000-hp) steam turbines
Performance: maximum speed 21 kt (39 km/h; 24 mph); range 14265 km (8,865 miles)
Dimensions: length overall 173.8 m (570 ft 0 in); beam 30.5 m (100 ft 0 in)
Crew: 473

124 'Newport' class

USA

The 20 ships of the **'Newport' class** were built as the US Navy's last dedicated tank landing ships with a direct descent from World War II experience, but were built with pointed rather than rounded bows so that a higher cruising speed could be sustained. Instead of a ramp inside bow doors, the ships of this class have a 34.12-m (112-ft) bow ramp of aluminium construction, and this is handled by two supporting derrick arms. There is also a stern ramp providing access from the lower vehicle deck to the water for AAA-7P amphibious personnel carriers, and landing craft can also accept loads from this ramp. Four sections of pontoon causeway can also be carried on the hull sides, and these are handled

The unique bow ramp of the 'Newport' class is evident in this photo, as are the four pontoon sections attached to the stern.

by two cranes.

Each of the ships has a small helicopter platform, and can carry four small landing craft. Accommodation is provided for 431 troops, while the vehicle decks can carry 500 tons of freight or various assortments of vehicles such as 17 trucks in addition to 21 MBTs or 25 AAA-7Ps. There is also provision for comparatively small quantities of vehicle and helicopter fuel. Only ten remain in US service, the rest serving with friendly navies.

Specification
'Newport' class
Type: tank landing ship
Displacement: 8,450 tons full load
Armament: two twin 76-mm (3-in) gun mountings, being replaced by two 20-mm Phalanx CIWS mountings
Propulsion: six 1976-kW (2,650-hp)

Alco or General Motors diesels
Performance: maximum speed 20 kt (37 km/h; 23 mph); range 4625 km (2,875 miles)
Dimensions: length overall 159.2 m (522 ft 4 in); beam 21.2 m (69 ft 6 in)
Crew: 225

Above: The Soviets always had a small amphibious capability, but the massive growth in the Soviet navy saw that capability expand with the addition of tank landing ships like the 'Ropucha' class.

Above: At the end of World War II the Royal Navy had literally hundreds of landing ships and landing craft, but today it is considerably smaller. The Royal Fleet Auxiliary Sir Percival is a Logistic Landing Ship (LSL) able to land a squadron of tanks.

By far the largest amphibious fleet is American, comprising more than 60 vessels, and the largest vessels are also American. These are the 'Tarawa' class LHAs, and their size is dictated by the need to provide full-size helicopter facilities as well as a docking well.

As a result, these vessels have some characteristics of a conventional aircraft carrier. The most recent additions to the American fleet are the LSD 41s, the first of which, the USS *Whidbey Island*, was completed in 1984. They

---

125 'Tobruk' class

 AUSTRALIA

Australia's vast size and long coasts make it a natural environment for amphibious warfare vessels. The only major vessel in service is HMAS *Tobruk*. Developed as an improved version of the British 'Sir Galahad' logistic landing ship design, *Tobruk* features a heavy lifting system capable of dealing with large loads up to 70 tons.

Tobruk has helicopter facilities, but no hangar. Two waterjet-powered LCVPs are carried, each of which can do 20 knots. Amphibians and landing craft can also be operated, and pontoons can be carried and deployed from the ship's sides. Normal troop load is 350, but 500 can be carried for short periods. *Tobruk* can also carry a

The relationship between **Tobruk** and the British **'Sir Lancelot' class** LSL can readily be seen by comparing the Australian vessel with the Royal Fleet Auxiliary seen at the top of the page. The main difference lies in the **Tobruk's** heavy lifting gear, forward of the superstructure.

10-tank squadron of Leopard 1 tanks, together with wheeled vehicles and artillery pieces. Total cargo capacity is 1,300 tons. The ship has been laid up in reserve to provide crews for new ships.

Specification
'Tobruk' class
Type: amphibious heavy lift ship
Displacement: 5,800 tons
Armament: two 40-mm guns
Propulsion: two diesels delivering 7160 kW (9,600 hp)
Performance: maximum speed 18

knots (33 km/h; 20.7 mph); range c.12800 km (8,000 miles) at 15 knots
Dimensions: length 127 m (417 ft); beam 18.3 m (60 ft)
Crew: 130
User: Australia

---

126 'Ouragan' class

 FRANCE

Built in the 1960s, the two **'Ouragan' class** vessels were obviously inspired by the American LSD designs, but they have a number of features that make them more versatile vessels. The large 120-metre docking well permits two 650-ton EDIC tank landing craft to be carried, each of which can be loaded with 11 light tanks. A temporary deck can be added for vehicles, while flight decks over the dock and to the left of the superstructure allow the simultaneous operation of four large Super Frélon helicopters. Three hundred and forty three troops can be carried.

Both 'Ouragans' are fitted with command facilities for directing amphibious operations, but *Orage* has

The small island superstructure of the 'Ouragan' class is apparent in this picture. Offset to one side, it provides space for a helicopter landing deck, which allows the French design to operate as many helicopters as much larger Soviet, British or American dock landing ships.

spent many years as support ship to France's nuclear test facility in the Pacific.

France has built a much improved class of TCD (Transports de chalands de débarquement, or Landing Ship Dock), the *Fourdre* and 'Sciroco'.

Specification
'Ouragan' class
Type: *Transports de chalands de débarquement*, or Landing Ship Dock
Displacement: 8,500 tons full load
Armament: two 120-mm (4.7-in) mortars and four 40-mm guns
Propulsion: two diesels delivering

6410 kW (8,600 hp)
Performance: maximum speed 17 knots (31.5 km/h; 19.5 mph)
Dimensions: length 149 m (489 ft); beam 23 m (75 ft 5 in)
Crew: 238
User: France

Future operations will make use of the naturally amphibious air-cushion vehicle, although their expense and running costs mean that they will probably be limited to the major navies. This is an LCAC (landing-craft air-cushion) of the US Navy.

are designed to take the new generation of landing craft: LCUs are being replaced by air-cushion vehicles, which are capable of taking their loads across shallow water, shoals and marshes, and delivering them right up on firm ground.

The Russians, have led the way with air cushion vehicles (ACVs): the 'Aist' class, laid down in 1975, were the world's largest air-cushion assault vessels, and are designed for operation independent of any Russian docking ship. Most Russian assault vessels are LSTs of various sizes, and the only

The Soviets are the largest users of military air-cushion vehicles. The 250-ton 'Aist' class was for a long time the largest military hovercraft, and is capable of carrying two tanks, or 150 troops, or three light armoured vehicles and 50 troops.

docking ships are of the 'Ivan Rogov' class, known in Russian as *Bolshoy Desantnyy Korabl* (BDK). These have bow doors for the unloading of tanks, and a stern gate opening onto a well that will accommodate two troop-carrying ACVs.

Without doubt, ACVs will be increasingly adopted by the world's navies. Apart from their most obvious advantage of being able to operate where even the shallowest-draught LCU cannot approach, and their ability to deliver their load over dry land, they can also skim through minefields at sea with little danger.

Nevertheless, there is probably still a role to be played by the more conventional ship. Historically, assault vessels have primarily played the part of 'mothers', and until now few have been provided with any armament other than that necessary for their own defence. However, as naval vessels become ever faster there may well be a tendency for them to operate more independently.

An assault force needs gunnery support, and an ACV is unsuitable for this role. Naval gunnery, which must be accurate, requires a relatively stable platform, and it is likely that a new generation of assault vessels will not only carry the helicopters, stores and maintenance facilities, heavy vehicles, command and hospital installations – everything to provide logistic support for the forces ashore, but will also be able to provide accurate surface-to-surface bombardment of enemy positions.

Recent events in the eastern Mediterranean have shown the value of an alert amphibious assault force in containing 'brush fire' wars. We are seeing the end of the big battleships, but in future the amphibious forces of the principal navies may well become the peacekeepers of the world.

Combat Comparison

127   UNITED KINGDOM

'Fearless' class

The UK's amphibious power-projection capability has rested primarily on the two units of the **'Fearless' class**. These are amphibious docks transport, and were each designed to carry a Royal Marine amphibious group of 330, 500 or 670 men under normal, overload and austere conditions respectively. Each ship also has the command and communication facilities for control of all sea, land and air forces involved in a brigade-level landing operation. The ships are being replaced by two new LPDs, to be named 'Albion' and 'Bulwark'.

The docking well is over 60 metres in length, and can house four 176-ton LCM9 landing craft. Ramps from the vehicle decks allow trucks and AFVs to be loaded at sea.

128   FORMER USSR

'Ivan Rogov' class

The **'Ivan Rogov' class** currently comprises two ships and is expected finally to total four units, one for each of the USSR's fleets. The type is an amphibious transport dock, and accommodation in provided for either one reinforced battalion of Naval Infantry (550 men and all their armoured personnel carriers plus 10 PT-76 amphibious light tanks) or a Naval Infantry MBT tank battalion.

Each ship carries up to five Kamov Ka-25 'Hormone' or Ka-27 'Helix' assault transport helicopters in a hangar inside the main superstructure, which has landing platforms forward and aft of it, accessed forward by a ramp and aft through the hangar doors. There is also a bow ramp inside outward-opening doors for use by amphibious vehicles, while at the stern there is a floodable docking well. This is 79 m (259.2 ft) long and 13 m (42.6 ft) wide at the door, and can accommodate either two pre-loaded 'Lebed' class hovercraft and one

The docking well is 79 metres long and 13 metres wide, which is deeper but narrower than the 'Fearless' class. As in the British ship, the well connects with the vehicle decks by ramp.

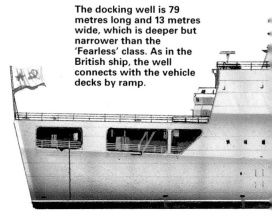

Each ship's three vehicle decks can accommodate 20 MBTs, one beach armoured recovery vehicle and 45 4-ton trucks with 50 tons of stores, or alternatively 2,100 tons of other freight. Amphibious landings are made possible by carriage of four utility and four personnel landing craft, which can use the floodable docking well in the stern. Over this dock is a helicopter platform, measuring 50.3 m (165 ft) in length and 22.9 m (75 ft) in width, for each ship's complement of four Westland Sea King HC.Mk 4 transport helicopters plus three Aérospatiale Gazelle or Westland Lynx light helicopters.

Specification
'Fearless' class
Type: amphibious transport dock
Displacement: 12,210 tons full load
Armament: two 40-mm AA guns and four quadruple Sea Cat SAM launchers
Propulsion: two 8200-kW (11,000-hp) steam turbines
Performance: maximum speed 21 kt (39 km/h; 24 mph); range 9250 km (5,750 miles)
Dimensions: length overall 158.5 m (520 ft 0 in); beam 24.4 m (80 ft 0 in)
Crew: 617

HMS Fearless is normally equipped to operate four Westland Wessex helicopters, each of which can carry 16 troops, but the flight deck is large enough to operate all NATO helicopters.

HMS 'Fearless' class is armed with two Mk 15 Phalanx 20-mm CIWS and two 40-mm anti-aircraft guns. This can be augmented by the machine-guns and hand-held SAMs of any troops being carried into action.

The two 'Fearless' class vessels are much more seaworthy than older designs of tank landing ship. Their range of 5,000 miles is achieved at close to maximum speed.

Each of the four LCM landing craft can carry two tanks or 100 tons of cargo. In addition, the 'Fearless' class has four 35-man LCVPs in davits.

145-ton 'Ondatra' class landing craft, or three 'Gus' class troop-carrier hovercraft. The armament is optimised for defence against air attack, where the SAM launcher and 30-mm cannon provide medium- and short-range capability respectively, while a 40-tube rocket launcher on the deckhouse forward of the superstructure can provide saturation fire support for a landing.

Specification
'Ivan Rogov' class
Type: amphibious transport dock
Displacement: 14,000 tons full load
Armament: one twin 76-mm (3-in) gun mounting, four 30-mm multi-barrel cannon, one twin-arm launcher for SA-N-4 'Gecko' SAMs, and one 122-mm (4.8-in) multiple rocket launcher
Propulsion: two 16775-kW (22,499-hp) gas turbines
Performance: maximum speed 26 kt (48 km/h; 30 mph); range 18500 km (11,500 miles)
Dimensions: length overall 159 m (521 ft 8 in); beam 24.5 m (80 ft 5 in)
Crew: 250

The 'Ivan Rogov' class has hangar space for up to five 14-man capacity 'Helix' helicopters, which use landing spaces in front of and behind the main superstructure.

Following standard Russian practice, the 'Ivan Rogov' is more heavily armed than its British equivalent. It has twin 76-mm guns, SAMs, close-in weapons and a multiple rocket launcher.

In spite of having a front loading ramp, which normally limits the speed of an assault ship, 'Ivan Rogov' is faster than any comparable Western vessel.

'Ivan Rogov' vessels are designed to operate with a variety of landing craft, but usually ship a combination of three or four hovercraft and 145-ton LCMs.

TARAWA
THE ONE-SHIP INVASION FLEET

Its massive slab sides tower out of the water, as if a huge building had somehow floated out to sea. But the USS *Tarawa* is one of the most capable assault ships ever built.

Amphibious warfare has been around for a long time in one form or another. Julius Caesar transported an army across what was to become the English Channel in the 1st century BC. The English transported armies the other way during the 100 Years' War with France. But the art and tactics of conducting amphibious assaults reached their peak in the Pacific campaigns of World War II and in the massive invasion of Normandy in June 1944.

New designs of ship and landing craft were evolved by the Royal and US Navies for these operations. Some were specialised cargo ships, with landing craft carried in place of lifeboats. Some had docking wells to allow large landing craft to be carried. Others were designed to carry tanks and heavy equipment.

After the war, the advent of the helicopter saw specialised helicopter-carriers appear, often converted from light aircraft-carriers. These saw action for the first time during the 1956 Anglo-French landings at Suez.

Specialised amphibious vessels are expensive, and with the decline of the European colonial empires only the United States needed that kind of long-range power projection capability. More to the point, only the US Navy could afford to maintain and improve such a massive amphibious fleet.

New designs of amphibious vessel appeared, usually upgraded variants of the types developed in the 1940s. The 'Tarawas', which were commissioned in the 1970s, are something else.

They are big. Twice the displacement of Britain's 'Invincible'-class carriers, they are known as LHAs, or general-purpose amphibious warfare ships. One 'Tarawa' combines the aviation capacity of the LPH helicopter carrier, the docking well of the LPD amphibious transport dock, the command and control facilities of the LCC amphibious flagship, and the cargo capacity of the LKA attack transport. Capable of carrying the 1,900 men of a reinforced Marine battalion, together with all their equipment, the 'Tarawas' and the succeeding 'Wasp' class LHDs are virtually complete landing forces contained within a single ship.

Amphibious assault

The main function of an assault ship is to get troops ashore in the shortest possible time. Landing craft can use the docking well at the stern of the ship to load troops and heavy equipment like tanks, while assault troops can drive their AAV-7 amphibious assault vehicles straight from their garage decks into the water and on to the beach.

An AV-8 Harrier comes in to land on the broad expanse of deck of the deck of the first of the LHA General Purpose Amphibious Ships, USS Tarawa. There are five more 'Tarawa'-class vessels in service, and another 12 of the even larger 'Wasp'-class is projected.

Command and co

An amphibious task force commander needs to maintain control of his forces at all times. The 'Tarawa' class is fitted with comprehensive command and control equipment and satellite communications gear to enable the most effective use of an amphibious group's aircraft, weapons, landing craft and sensors.

Left: A US Navy LCU utility landing craft is dwarfed by the massive bulk of the second of the 'Tarawa' class general purpose assault ships, USS Saipan (LHA-2), as it enters the assault ship's docking well.

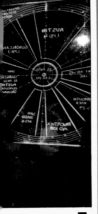

Above: The task force command centre looks more like a starship's bridge than anything else, but from here whole fleets can be controlled.

Air power

Helicopters have been an important part of the US Navy's amphibious capability since the 1950s, when the US Marines first developed the concept of 'vertical envelopment' — avoiding enemy defences by going over them — but the acquisition of the British-designed Harrier V/STOL fighter bomber has given the Marines and the US Navy's amphibious fleet real, instantly available air power.

An AV-8B Harrier II prepares to make a short-take off past the island of USS Belleau Wood (LHA-3). The Harrier II is a highly capable aircraft, giving the Marines the closest of close support and able to operate from almost any helicopter deck, or from temporary facilities ashore.

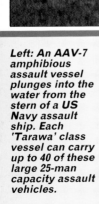

Left: An AAV-7 amphibious assault vessel plunges into the water from the stern of a US Navy assault ship. Each 'Tarawa' class vessel can carry up to 40 of these large 25-man capacity assault vehicles.

Left: The AAV-7 can swim at speeds of 12 km per hour and can handle surf up to 10 feet high. Once ashore, it can unload its cargo of Marines and support them with .50-calibre fire.

Above: A Marine Corps artillery battery goes into action after having been ferried from an assult ship into the operating area. Massive CH-53 Sea Stallion helicopters can hoist the seven-ton artillery pieces, while ammunition and other equipment can be loaded into it or hoisted by the smaller twin-rotor CH-46 Sea Knight.

114

'Tarawa' class vessel can carry large numbers of 'Hummers' (above) and 2½-ton trucks (above right).

Right: It is vital that the equipment be loaded on to the assault ship in the reverse order that it will be needed during the landing.

Artillery: The M198 howitzer has a range of over 20 km. It can be lifted by CH-53 helicopters.

Troop transport: Twelve CH-46s can move over 300 troops at a time. The Sea Knight can also be used to carry cargo.

Light Armored Vehicles: The LAV is more mobile than tracked armour, and can be used for reconnaissance.

Tanks: A company of M60A3 main battle tanks gives a Marine landing real punch.

The **AAV-7 amphibious assault vehicle** is the heart of a Marine assault. *Tarawa* can carry 40.

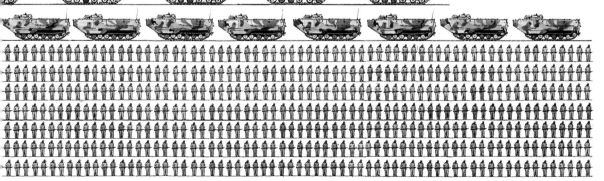

All of the equipment in the world will do you no good if you do not have the men to operate it. Tarawa can carry the **1,900 men of a Reinforced Marine Battalion**, and land them with all of their equipment.

Utility landing craft from HMS *Fearless* butt through tempestuous South Atlantic waters as the British Task Force prepares to land on the Falklands. Had the Royal Navy not had an amphibious capability, the islands would almost certainly be known as the Malvinas today

EYE WITNESS
by those who fought

D-DAY
SAN CARLOS

"The sergeant-major said, 'Party frocks and make-up on, girls, it's time to go.' And it was. Full camouflage clothing, black cream smeared over all exposed parts, 'so your little faces don't shine out like the Eddystone Light.' The heavy Bergens were pulled on. All this at one in the morning."

It was the first hour of 21 May 1982, and Jeremy Hands of ITN was about to go ashore from HMS *Fearless* in San Carlos Bay with the HQ company and the CO of 40 Commando RM.

"Whatever else the assault ships *Fearless* and *Intrepid* were designed for, it was not for assaulting. Both these ageing, rusting and overcrowded scrapyard escapees were to be the spearhead for the British landings."

After six weeks of sailing southward in the *Canberra*, the

The Falklands campaign involved the largest British landing since World War II. It showed that amphibious forces still have a vital role to play in modern warfare.

troops had been transferred by landing craft to the well decks of the assault ships. "In these caverns of steel, piping, heavy equipment and men shouting like banshees to make themselves heard . . . thick choking diesel fumes hung like a fog . . . So cramped were the ships with everything from men to equipment, floors were literally carpeted with cardboard boxes of 'ratpacks', the 24-hour ration

packs the fighting men would live on once ashore."

Captain Hugh McManners, of 148 Battery RA, whose job was to direct Naval Gunnery Support (NGS) from shore, described similar scenes aboard *Intrepid*:

"Our home base was HMS *Intrepid*, where we kept our Gemini and the outboard motors, the spare radios and batteries, the huge pile of rations and ammunition and all our spare

personal kit. . . An empty cabin, with me on my own, would suddenly be filled, stealthily, without the lights being turned on, and in the morning there would be snoring, dead-tired bodies on all the bunks and floor space, and weapons ranging from pistols to rocket launchers hanging on pegs and lying on desk tops. The corridor outside would be blocked with muddy Bergens and neatly-piled webbing with the peculiarly distinct smell of peat and rifle oil."

Aboard *Fearless* men in full kit eased their way along slippery companionways half as wide as themselves, and down narrow ladders. "Then into the dim red glow of the dock, with the landing craft waiting. Queues of men from other parts of the ship were slowly balancing their way along narrow walls to get to them too. . .

"'Good luck and God speed, 40

San Carlos landings, 21 May 1982

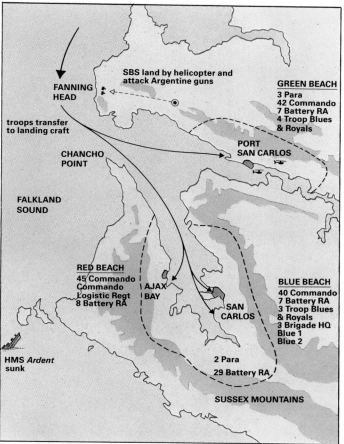

- **FANNING HEAD**
- SBS land by helicopter and attack Argentine guns
- troops transfer to landing craft
- **CHANCHO POINT**
- **FALKLAND SOUND**
- **PORT SAN CARLOS**
- **GREEN BEACH**
  - 3 Para
  - 42 Commando
  - 7 Battery RA
  - 4 Troop Blues & Royals
- **RED BEACH**
  - 45 Commando
  - Commando Logistic Regt
  - 8 Battery RA
- **AJAX BAY**
- **SAN CARLOS**
- **BLUE BEACH**
  - 40 Commando
  - 7 Battery RA
  - 3 Troop Blues & Royals
  - 3 Brigade HQ
  - Blue 1
  - Blue 2
- HMS *Ardent* sunk
- 2 Para
- 29 Battery RA
- **SUSSEX MOUNTAINS**

Left: The Argentine forces were expecting the British to land near Port Stanley, so the landings at San Carlos some 70 miles away came as a complete surprise.

Below: Royal Marines file ashore from a Royal Navy LCM9. The landings had one aim: to land a British military force on the Falklands to retake the islands.

A utility landing craft moves through San Carlos water. In the background, a North Sea ferry is typical of the many ships 'taken up from trade' which made the whole operation possible.

Commando. It's been a pleasure to have you on board,' said the tannoy as the stern gate lowered and the open sea at the mouth of San Carlos Water came flooding in. . . The four landing craft pulled away from *Fearless* and into the gentle swell. This was it; the landing was under way."

But then came more delays. There were 30 men too many in Foxtrot 1, the craft carrying the HQ company, and they had to wait for a smaller LCVP to join them from ro-ro ferry *Norland* so that they could be transferred. And there was a hold-up aboard *Norland*, where one of the men of 2 Para had fallen on the stairs in the darkness, breaking his hip and obstructing everyone behind him. But at last all the men were loaded, the jampacking aboard Foxtrot 1 was eased, and the phalanx of 40 Commando chugged expectantly up San Carlos Water in the blackness before the dawn.

"Around them a continual crashing and crumping of naval gunfire, as the warships relentlessly pounded the Argentinian positions on Fanning Head. . . Twenty yards from the beach, the man at the front of the landing craft called out, 'Brace

Below: The presence of an invasion force soon provoked a vigorous Argentine reaction. Here an Argentine air force Dagger fighter bomber makes a very low level pass just above the deck of HMS Fearless. The air attacks were pressed home with dash and courage, but were not enough to stop the landings.

Right: One of the major differences between modern amphibious operations and those of World War II is in the enormous contribution made by the helicopter. In the Falklands, helicopters operated off ships ranging from frigates and destroyers through to assault ships (seen here) and carriers.

As cargo-laden helicopters pass overhead, an LCU from HMS Fearless (identifiable from its 'tiger-stripe' camouflage) heads towards the hard-worked ferry Norland.

yourselves, we're 'ere.' And, with a sickening thud, they were. The ramp went down and the two light tanks in the bows of the craft spluttered into life. After a delay that seemed to last a lifetime, one of them lurched into the water."

The Marines followed, splashing through the icy water – but their orders had been to group beside a large white rock, and in the black hour before dawn there was no white rock to be seen. They had found the beach, but not quite the right beach. "In fairness," wrote Jeremy Hands, "after 8,000 miles, missing by 100 yards was not at all bad. But it was enough to throw the best-laid plans into some disarray."

Robert McGowan of the Daily Express went ashore in an LCU with 3 Para's 'A' Company from *Intrepid*. They were to follow 2 Para but, because of the hold-up aboard *Norland*, they were still trying to group landing craft for the assault when dawn broke.

"'Ere,' said one of the Para medics. 'Thought's just occurred to me. . . Bloody Navy took our lifejackets off us when we got into this thing. What if it sinks?' 'Then you're dipped, mate,' came the reply."

Eventually 'A' Company's LCU made the beach, only to discover that it sloped too gradually and the craft could not get close enough inshore. A smaller LCVP was brought up alongside, and by cross-decking men were able to reach shallower water. Others, impatient to get ashore, plunged into the chest-deep water and half-swam to the beach.

Then the Argentine planes arrived, but to the relief of the men on the beach they did not seem to see them, and their attack was directed solely at the ships. "Wave after wave of enemy jets screeched in, spitting cannon shells and dropping 500-lb and 1,000-lb bombs. . . Frightening fields of fire were put up in front of the warplanes as men in the ships blasted away with everything they had. Green and red tracer laced webs of fire in their path, but on they flew, often at wavetop height."

Hugh McManners described what it was like aboard *Intrepid* in 'Bomb Alley'. "The furniture would be lashed back against the walls and central pillars, and everyone not at action stations would be . . . mumbling at each other through the grubby white cotton of their anti-flash hoods. . .

We all sat there in the red glow of the emergency lighting smoking cigarettes, listening to the sitreps over the tannoy from the officer of the watch, and grimacing as the Sea Cats launched with 'bang, roar and whoosh' just outside the door. . .

"Everyone was on Zulu time, i.e. UK time, to make things easier to plan. . . All we had to do was register that sunrise was at about 11 a.m. and sunset at 10.30 p.m. The ship's watches all got up at the normal times and got breakfast eaten before going to action stations at about 10 a.m. The first air raids were generally coming soon after that and didn't stop until 10 or 11 at night. 'Action snacks' or hot dogs, soup, sandwiches and 'nutty' (that we filled our respirator bags with) kept hunger at bay until a cooked supper at midnight or a little later."

Ashore, the Task Force had met no opposition, and was dug in around San Carlos settlement and across the water on Ajax Bay. Britain's first amphibious assault since Suez in 1956 had encountered all sorts of organisational difficulties, and there were obviously lessons to be learned for the future. But it had been a success, and the liberation of the Falkland Islands was well under way.

Left: Gunsmoke stains the skies around HMS Fearless. The two 'Fearless' class assault ships were vital to the success of the San Carlos landings.

Below: In the docking well of one of the Royal Navy assault ships, medical orderlies collect a wounded Argentine pilot from the deck of a landing craft. He has been plucked from San Carlos Water after ejecting from his fighter following an unsuccessful contest with a British missile.

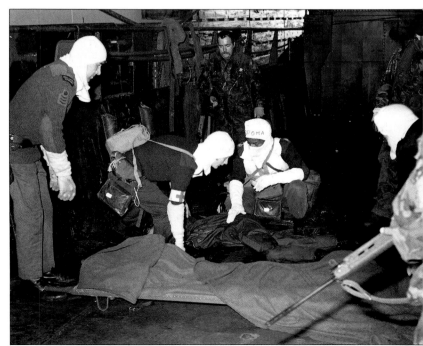

Soviets from the Sea

While the Soviet navy's amphibious forces never matched those of the US Navy, they were well trained and equipped for their more limited tasks.

The Soviets divided amphibious assaults into several categories. **Strategic landings** were to be conducted in support of theatre forces to open up a new front of operations. The Soviets did not have the resources for this kind of action, which required the amphibious units and vessels currently only available to the US Navy and the US Marine Corps. **Operational landings** were used to assist ground forces in surrounding and destroying enemy forces in a coastal area. **Tactical landings** struck at the flank or rear of enemy units along the coastline, or aim for the capture of specific objectives. These were regimental- or battalion-sized operations. Finally, **reconnais-**

sance and sabotage landings involved units ranging from battalion size down to companies and platoons. Their tasks were to gather information, to inflect significant material damage upon the enemy, or to create diversions.

Soviet amphibious assault tactics were thorough, well defined and rigorously practised by the Naval Infantry, the organic amphibious forces of the Soviet navy. Their operations fell into five parts.

1 Equipment is maintained ready for instant action, and Naval Infantry units are trained to begin operations when at sea or from their land bases. Reserve units may be called up, depending upon the size of the operation.

2 When alerted at a shore base, the amphibious assault units man their equipment and proceed to the embarkation point for loading onto naval transports. The loading is done in reverse order, so that the assault vehicles that are to make the initial attack are the last onto the vessels.

3 After loading, the ships proceed in convoy, escorted by naval vessels and aircraft. During the passage, political

Above: In a scene from before the end of the Cold War, a Soviet 'Aist' class air-cushion craft skims the Baltic accompanied by Soviet and East German Mil Mi-8 helicopters. The Soviet navy is the world's largest user of military air-cushion craft, taking advantage of their speed and their ability to travel by land and sea.

Right: A 25-man Naval Infantry reconnaissance platoon dismounts from a 'Gus'-class hovercraft of the Soviet navy.

officers address the troops to build up their fighting spirit, the men make final checks of weapons and equipment, and unit commanders review their missions, plans and orders.

4 The assault is preceded by airborne operations, air attacks and naval gunfire bombardment of enemy artillery, troop positions, and communications. The Naval Infantry then makes its assault.

5 Follow-up army units are landed, often from Soviet merchant vessels which are designed to have a secondary amphibious warfare capability, and whose commanders are usually naval reserve officers. Once the army is ashore and fighting, the Naval Infantry can be withdrawn.

1 Airborne Assault

Soviet doctrine for amphibious operations calls for air assault troops to be dropped to the rear of enemy defences before the main amphibious assault goes in. In a battalion assault, a company of paratroopers would be required. These elite troops are tasked with disrupting enemy communications, securing key features of terrain such as bridges or airfields, and blocking the approach of enemy reinforcements. The classic pre-amphibious operation airborne assault was made by the British and the Americans in World War II, when three airborne divisions were landed in Normandy the night before the Allied invasion of Europe in June 1944.

Left: Soviet airborne troopers check their equipment before boarding an Antonov An-12 'Cub' transport plane. Soviet amphibious assault doctrine calls for 'desantny' or air assault raiders to parachute or be helicoptered into action to operate in conjunction with the main landings.

Left: An Antonov An-12 can carry up to 100 fully equipped paratroops. This is enough to provide the airborne element of a battalion-sized amphibious operation.

Right: Behind the lines raiders have one task, and that is to cause as much disruption to key points such as bridges, communication centres and airfields.

2 Clearing the beach

Even as the airborne troops are going about their business, air-cushion vehicles and helicopters are approaching the beach at high speed, covered by air attacks and naval gunfire. These carry a platoon of combat engineers, highly trained men like the SEALs of the US Navy or the Special Boat Squadron of the Royal Marines. Their task is to detect mines, obstructions and barriers on the beach. The engineer platoon has to clear and mark at least three lanes through the beach defences, and is expected to take 50 per cent casualties while doing so.

Left: A 300-ton 'Aist'-class hovercraft can carry 220 naval infantrymen at speeds of up to 80 knots. However, a more usual load for the first stage of a landing might be four light tanks or APCs and 50 engineers.

3 Reconnaissance

Even as the engineers are reaching the beach to clear it, the battalion's reconnaissance unit is swimming its vehicles from an assault ship about 600 metres offshore. All Soviet light armoured vehicles are amphibious, so the BRDM scout cars and PT-76 light tanks used by the reconnaissance troop need little or no modification for beach assaults. Naval gunfire switches to engage inland targets as the reconnaissance troop comes ashore. The troop is in contact with the battalion commander, and its task is to check the terrain and report any surviving enemy positions.

Above: A PT-76 light tank moves up the beach as the other vehicles of the reconnaissance troop swim ashore.

All Soviet light armour is amphibious, so the Soviet Naval Infantry does not need special vehicles, as do the US Marines.

4 Assault

The first assault waves now begin to land. These can either swim in from assault ships standing offshore, or they can be landed direct on the beach by vessels such as the 'Polnocny' class of landing ship. If the assault swims in it is led by a company of naval infantry in BTR-70 or -80 wheeled APCs, escorted by PT-76 light tanks. As they approach the shore the vehicles will engage surviving enemy positions. Once ashore, the vehicles advance through the beach-head, while the second wave approaches.

Left: The assault wave is escorted into the beach by PT-76 light tanks, which would use their 76-mm guns to suppress beach defences.

Right: 'Polnocny'-class landing ships can land vessels directly on the beach, or launch them from a few metres offshore.

5 Expanding the beach-head

As the first wave pushes inland, the second wave lands on its left flank. This has the battalion's mortars, anti-armour weapons and anti-aircraft troops. The battalion commander accompanies this wave, as do the specialist observer teams who are tasked with directing tactical air strikes and naval gunfire. The third wave lands on the right flank, and once the whole battalion is ashore it advances in line to expand the beach-head.

Right: An amphibious assault lands in waves, with each wave coming in on the flanks of the one immediately preceding. That way they avoid interfering with each other, and they have the effect of rapidly expanding the beach-head.

6 Exploiting the landing

As the naval infantry battalion pushes forward to make contact with the airborne company, service units land to set up supply and evacuation routes. Once the battalion has cleared the routes to the interior, it waits in place until follow-up Soviet army formations can land with their heavy equipment like tanks and artillery. As the army units take up the assault, the airborne company and naval infantry battalion, or whatever is left of them, are withdrawn.

Left: It should be remembered that the purpose of a landing is not the landing itself, but to get troops ashore and fighting.

Right: The Naval Infantry are pathfinders. Their task is to clear the way for powerful Soviet army formations to come ashore.

LIGHT CARRIERS

They are called 'poor man's carriers' by the US Navy, and maybe they cannot match a supercarrier. But the modern light carrier is an economical, effective way of taking air power to sea.

When a prototype de Havilland Vampire jet touched down on the deck of HMS *Ocean* on 3 December 1945, it started a revolution in naval thinking concerning the role and design of the aircraft carrier. That revolution has today progressed to the point where most modern carriers are of one of two very distinct types: the very large 'super-carrier' carrying 80 or more aircraft, more than half of them fixed-wing strike planes; and the light carrier, deploying vertical/short take-off and landing (V/STOL) aircraft with a relatively short combat and strike range, and a wide variety of helicopters.

This divergence arose largely from the escalating cost of the large carrier, together with an extraordinary degree of vacillation in the policy of the major naval powers during the 1950s and 1960s.

At the end of World War II, the US Navy had decided that there was no longer a need for its massive Pacific carrier fleet, but the value of carrier-borne aircraft during the Korean conflict of 1950-2 persuaded it otherwise, and a number of carriers in reserve were immediately put into a re-fit pro-gramme. More importantly, the first of the supercarriers was laid-down – in the shape of the USS *Forrestal*.

British carrier strength reduced

The Royal Navy, with extensive Common-wealth commitments, was nevertheless com-pelled by financial constraints to run down its strength, a number of vessels being sold off to smaller nations, and only a few being re-fitted for fixed-wing jets. At the same time, British inventions such as the angled flight deck and the steam catapult greatly improved the jet-carrying capability of carriers, and a number of hulls already laid-down were adapted to new specifications.

The Italian light carrier **Giuseppe Garibaldi** *steams through the Mediterranean, with a flight of AV-8B Harrier IIs ranged on deck. Vertical take-off fighters have made maritime air power a practical proposition for smaller navies as rising costs have taken conventional carriers all but out of their reach.*

Aircraft from British carriers completed 99 per cent of their assigned missions in the Falklands

A new class of carrier – the CVA-01 – was planned for the Royal Navy in the 1960s, but financial considerations (together with the belief that air support of troops out of range of land-based aircraft was only likely to be necessary in a campaign in which the US Navy would also be involved) led to the cancellation of the programme. The Falklands campaign was to show that crises could arise in which the Americans could not be called upon for support, but by then it was too late. *Ark Royal, Eagle, Centaur* and *Victorious* were scrapped, and the Royal Navy now deploys only V/STOL carriers equipped with Sea Harriers and helicopters.

A number of navies now operate vessels of this sort, which fall into three groups. The largest of these vessels are the so-called 'through-deck cruisers'. Characteristically, they have a full-length flight deck set off on the port side at anything between four and 8.5 degrees. Unlike the supercarriers, they do not need to be fitted with steam catapults, leaving the foredeck free in many cases for a formidable array of missile-launchers, as well as conventional guns.

Carriers of this type ranged in size from the 13,500-ton *Giuseppe Garibaldi* of the Italian navy through the converted conven-

tional carriers *Vikrant* and *Viraat* of the Indian navy to the four 38,000-ton 'Kiev' class vessels of the Soviet navy.

The second group of vessels are the large amphibious assault ships of the US Navy. Designed to land reinforced Marine battalions, these have full flight decks, and can be used as auxiliary carriers in addition to their more typical role. As Sea Control Ships, the vessels of the 40,000-ton 'Wasp' class can carry 20 AV-8B Harrier II fighters and six SH-60 LAMPS III anti-submarine warfare (ASW)

Four Yak-38 'Forgers' line up on the flight deck of the Soviet 'Kiev' class carrier Minsk. Its limited air wing restricts the Minsk to light carrier tasks in spite of a displacement of 44,000 tons. The Soviet navy classifies the 'Kiev' class as takticheskoye avianosny kreyser, or tactical aircraft-carrying cruisers.

helicopters in place of their usual aircraft complement of 30 or 40 assault helicopters.

Finally, there are a small number of hybrid helicopter carriers in service, of cruiser size but with large flight decks at the stern. These are not really suitable for V/STOL jets, and most are used in the ASW role.

'Ski-jump' innovation

The British invention of the 'ski-jump' has been a major breakthrough in the design of aircraft-carrying ships. It is cheap and easy to construct and fit, and requires no modifications to the aircraft using it. The 'ski-jump' has already been fitted to the Royal Navy carriers *Hermes* (now the *Virat* of the Indian navy) and the three ships of the 'Invincible' class, and in the Italian *Giuseppe Garibaldi* and the Spanish *Principe de Asturias* it is an integral part of the through-deck, giving these ships strikingly unusual silhouettes.

Combined with the V/STOL capabilities of the Sea Harrier, the 'ski-jump' has led to the

---

FLASHBACK

A Hawker Hurricane perches on the catapult of a CAM ship. Although they were one-off stopgaps until escort carriers could be built, CAM ships were better than nothing.

One-shot carriers

In 1940, German long-range aircraft began to menace Britain's sea-borne lifeline. Shadowing convoys beyond the range of British air cover, they vectored U-boats in to the attack, and picked off stragglers themselves. In 1940 the aircraft alone sank 192 vessels — more than half a million tons of shipping. Catapult-armed merchantmen, or CAM ships, were a somewhat desperate countermeasure. They still carried cargos, but were equipped with a single Hurricane on a catapult. Once the fighter was launched, there was no way of landing; after (hopefully) destroying the intruder, the pilot had to crash-land or bale out near the convoy, knowing that unless he was quickly rescued, he could freeze in the icy waters. CAM ships served until the arrival of escort carriers.

LIGHT CARRIERS Reference File

323

SPAIN

Principe de Asturias

Spain's first aircraft carrier was the *Dedalo*, a World War II-vintage American light carrier which the Spanish navy acquired in the 1960s. Originally in use as a helicopter carrier, it was later equipped with British Aerospace AV-8A Matador V/STOL fighters. It was paid-off in the late 1980s, returning to the USA as a museum ship.

Although the *Dedalo* proved surprisingly useful, it really was too old for service almost half a century after its launch. Spain began planning a replacement in 1977. Based on an American design for a light helicopter carrier known as a Sea Control Ship, the ***Principe de Asturias*** is a turbine-powered vessel with a 175-

metre flight deck and a 12-degree 'ski-jump' ramp. Two aircraft lifts are fitted, one at the stern of the flight deck. The air wing comprises up to eight AV-8B Harrier IIs and a dozen SH-60 Sea Hawk and SH-3 Sea King ASW helicopters. Some of the latter are fitted with Searchwater radar for airborne early warning.

Entering service in 1987, the *Principe de Asturias* forms the heart of the Spanish navy's major ASW group. Equipped with a fully digital command and control system, the carrier can also act as a fleet flagship.

If funding permits, the Spanish navy would like a second carrier of this class, but this is unlikely in the foreseeable future.

Specification
Principe de Asturias
Type: light aircraft carrier
Displacement: 14,700 tons full load
Armament: four 12-barrel Meroka close-in weapon systems
Propulsion: two gas turbines delivering 34750 kW (46,600 shp) to

one controllable pitch propeller
Performance: maximum speed 26 knots (48 km/h; 30 mph); range 13000 km at 20 knots
Dimensions: length 196 m (642 ft 11 in); flight deck width 27 m (98 ft); draught 9.1 m (29 ft 10 in)
Crew: 790, excluding air group

HMS Invincible *was the first of the new breed of purpose-built V/STOL and helicopter carriers. Originating out of a requirement projected in the 1960s for a specialist ASW helicopter carrier to accompany the CVA-01 class strike carriers, the design evolved into a more capable vessel in the 1970s. Although still weighted towards anti-submarine warfare, the 'Invincible' first went into action in the Falklands as a strike carrier.*

development of a revolutionary concept whereby a conventional merchant ship can be converted to the aircraft-carrying role within a few days. The ship-borne containerised air defence system employs some 230 standard containers, which are mounted on the deck of a container carrier and covered with a 'ski-jump' deck. The empty containers can accommodate personnel, a command post, fuel stores, aircraft repair shops and even missile-launchers.

A further development proposed by British Aerospace is the 'Skyhook', which would do away with the flight deck altogether. A high crane mounted inboard would lift a Sea Harrier outboard, the aircraft would go into hover

---

The Professional's View:

Light carriers

"I guess if you are going to operate under land-based air power, the light carriers are good enough. But you have to prepare for the unexpected. The Brits learned that in the Falklands. Their baby flat-tops worked fine, but there were one or two problems. Mostly, they built too small. Ship steel is the least expensive element in any vessel, and they could have built a bigger ship, with a reasonable air group, for not much more money. Most of the expensive stuff, like the electronics, would have cost the same. Yet, within their limits, light carriers do a good job."

US Navy strategic analyst

324

INDIA

Vikrant/Viraat

The Indian navy has operated aircraft carriers for 30 years, since the commissioning of INS **Vikrant** in 1961. Laid-down as one of the Royal Navy's 'Majestic' class light fleet carriers, the Vikrant saw combat in the 1971 Indo-Pakistani war, with an air group of Hawker Sea Hawks and Breguet Alizés.

The Vikrant was re-fitted to operate vertical take-off fighters at the end of the 1970s, and a 'ski-jump' was added in 1983. Its air group now consists of up to 20 Sea Harriers and Sea King anti-ship/ASW helicopters.

The Vikrant has since been joined in service by the larger INS **Viraat** – the former HMS Hermes. Completed in 1959 as an 'intermediate' fleet carrier,

the Hermes was converted to a 'commando carrier' in 1977, before being modified yet again in 1980, when she became a V/STOL carrier. The flagship of the Falklands Task Force, the Hermes' aircraft complement was increased during the battle from 14 to 30, including 21 Harriers.

In May 1986, she was purchased by the Indian navy. Renamed Viraat, she received an extensive re-fit. Current plans call for both Vikrant and Viraat to be replaced by new carriers some time in the next decade, but with Vikrant out of service and Viraat over 40 years old, the Russian *Admiral Gorshkov* may be bought as an interim carrier.

Specification
Vikrant
Type: light aircraft carrier
Displacement: 19,500 tons full load
Armament: nine single 40-mm AA
Propulsion: geared steam turbines delivering 29825 kW (40,000 shp) to two propellers

Performance: maximum speed 24.5 knots (45.3 km/h; 28.2 mph); range 20000 km at 14 knots
Dimensions: length 213.4 m (714 ft); flight deck width 39 m (128 ft); draught 7.3 m (24 ft)
Crew: 1,345 (war establishment, including air group)

Right: HMS Hermes has undergone several metamorphoses in a long career: successively being a conventional carrier, a 'commando carrier', a V/STOL carrier, and now serving the Indian navy as the INS Virat.

Left: Helicopter carriers come in many shapes and sizes. The Shirane is a 5,200-ton helicopter-carrying destroyer of the Japanese Maritime Self-Defence Force, and is capable of carrying three or four large ASW helicopters.

Below: In the 1950s, carriers like HMS Centaur could carry conventional jets, but as aircraft grew larger, such light carriers proved too small to be operated effectively.

mode and, when the pilot was satisfied that everything was ready, it would be released. Recovery would require the pilot to hold the aircraft in hover while moving forward at the same speed as the crane – a manoeuvre similar to inflight refuelling. A sophisticated set of robotics in the crane mechanism would keep 'Skyhook' in the same orientation, however, the ship might roll or pitch. 'Skyhook' could be mounted in a hull

as small as 5,000 tons.

The use of the Hermes and Invincible as strike carriers in the Falklands campaign proved so successful that the three 'Invincible' class are now used in that role. In 1998 HMS 'Invincible' operated in the Gulf with 22 aircraft and helicopters including 7 RAF GR.3 Harriers for ground attack.

Small carriers are vulnerable because of their small air groups. Very large carriers,

---

325

ITALY

Vittorio Veneto

Intended to be a third cruiser of the 'Andrea Doria' class, the **Vittorio Veneto** was radically altered and enlarged while being designed, when it was realised that the earlier ships were too small to carry an effective ASW helicopter group. As a result, the new cruiser was considerably enlarged, with a raised 40 × 18.5-metre flight deck with a hangar below. The air group comprises nine AB.212 or six SH-3D or EH.101 ASW helicopters.

Forward of the flight deck, the Vittorio Veneto is a powerful guided missile cruiser. Her main armament is an American Mk 20 twin missile-launcher with 40 long-range Standard SM-1ER missiles and 20 ASROC ASW missiles. The cruiser is also fitted with

four Teseo launchers for Otomat anti-ship missiles, eight 76-mm dual-purpose guns, and three twin 40-mm turrets for close-in protection, controlled by a pair of Dardo fire control systems.

The Vittorio Veneto was commissioned in 1969, and served as the Italian navy's flagship until she was replaced by the Giuseppe Garibaldi.

Specification
Vittorio Veneto
Type: helicopter cruiser
Displacement: 8,870 tons full load
Armament: one twin Standard extended-range SAM/ASROC ASW missile-launcher; four Teseo (Otomat) anti-ship missile-launchers; eight

76-mm guns; three twin 35-mm close-in weapon systems; two triple 324-mm lightweight ASW torpedo tubes
Propulsion: geared steam turbines delivering 54435 kW (73,000 shp) to two propellers
Performance: maximum speed 31

knots (57 km/h; 35.65 mph); range 9250 km at 17 knots
Dimensions: length 179.6 m (589 ft 3 in); beam 19.3 m (63 ft 7 in); draught 6 m (19 ft 8 in)
Crew: 565

326

ITALY

Giuseppe Garibaldi

Planned as a replacement for the two 'Andrea Doria' class helicopter cruisers of the Italian navy, the **Giuseppe Garibaldi** was laid-down in 1981 and commissioned in 1985.

The design changed considerably from first conception, with the addition of features such as a six-degree 'ski-jump' to facilitate the use of V/STOL aircraft. This was a speculative venture on the part of the navy, since a law dating back to the days of Mussolini placed all fixed-wing aircraft under the control of the air force. However, a gentleman's agreement between the naval and air staffs meant that the navy could go ahead with the AV-8B Harrier II Plus.

Giuseppe Garibaldi's air wing

consists of a mix of helicopters and AV-8B Harrier II Plus STOVL fighters. Harrier II Plus STOVL fighters.

Currently in service as the flagship of the Italian navy, the carrier is designed to provide ASW protection for task forces and convoys. It can also carry up to 600 troops for short periods.

Specification
Giuseppe Garibaldi
Type: light aircraft carrier
Displacement: 13,500 tons full load
Armament: two octuple Albatros SAM systems; four Otomat 2 surface-to-surface missiles; three 40-mm twin AA gun turrets; two triple 324-mm lightweight ASW torpedo tubes
Propulsion: four gas turbines

delivering 59650 kW (80,000 shp) to two propellers
Performance: maximum speed 30 knots (55.5 km/h; 34.5 mph); range 13000 km at 20 knots

Dimensions: length 180.2 m (570 ft 8 in); flight deck width 30.4 m (99 ft 8 in); draught 6.7 m (22 ft)
Crew: 825, including air group and flag group

327

BRAZIL

Minas Gerais

Known as a *navio-aeródromo ligeiro* to the Brazilian navy, the **Minas Gerais** started life in 1945 as the Royal Navy's 'Colossus' class carrier HMS *Vengeance*. In 1948, she made an experimental cruise to the Arctic and was loaned to the Royal Australian Navy in 1953. Returned in 1955, she was purchased by Brazil in 1956, and was re-fitted in the Netherlands between 1957 and 1960, entering service in December of that year.

The *Minas Gerais* is an anti-submarine carrier. Her air group in the 1970s consisted of eight Grumman S-2 Trackers (operated by the Brazilian air force, since the Brazilian navy is forbidden fixed-wing aircraft) and four Sikorsky SH-3 Sea King ASW

helicopters, together with three Aérospatiale Ecureil and two Bell 206 JetRanger utility helicopters.

Two major refits completed in the 1980s means that the carrier will serve on into the 21st century. No decision has been made on a replacement, although the navy has considered either a nuclear-powered conventional carrier of 40,000 tons or a pair of light V/STOL carriers. Even if the money is found to build them, neither option is likely before 2010.

Specification
Minas Gerais
Type: light aircraft carrier
Displacement: 19,890 tons full load
Armament: one twin and two

quadruple 40-mm AA gun mounts
Propulsion: geared steam turbines delivering 29825 kW (40,000 shp) to two propellers
Performance: maximum speed 25.3 knots (46.8 km/h; 29 mph); range 20000 km at 14 knots

Dimensions: length 211.8 m (695 ft); flight deck width 37 m (121 ft); draught 7.5 m (24 ft 6 in)
Crew: 1,300, including air group

328

FORMER USSR

'Moskva' class

Classified by the Soviets as a *protivolodochnyy kreyser*, or anti-submarine cruiser, the **Moskva** was a hybrid helicopter carrier/missile cruiser developed to counter Western ballistic missile submarines in regional seas near the Soviet Union. She was the first Soviet attempt to produce an aviation vessel, but was not entirely successful, so the class did not stretch beyond two vessels. They were normally deployed in the Mediterranean as part of the Black Sea Fleet's Fifth Eskadra, but they occasionally made longer trips into the Atlantic, the Baltic, or the Indian Ocean as part of an ASW task force.

Forward of the steam exhaust stack, the 'Moskvas' were missile

cruisers. There was a hangar between the steam uptakes in the super-structure. The aft end of the ship was taken up by an 86 x 34-metre flight deck, with two aircraft lifts. The air group consisted of 14 Kamov 'Hormone' or 'Helix' ASW helicopters.

Specification
'Moskva' class
Type: helicopter cruiser
Displacement: 17,000 tons full load
Armament: eight twin SA-N-3 'Goblet' SAM launchers; two twin 57-mm gun turrets; one twin SUW-N-1 anti-submarine missile-launcher; two 12-barrel RBU-6000 ASW rocket-launchers
Propulsion: geared steam turbines

delivering 74500 kW (100,000 shp) to two shafts
Performance: maximum speed 30 knots (55.5 km/h; 34.5 mph); range 8300 km at 29 knots, 16600 km at 18 knots

Dimensions: length 189 m (620 ft); width 26 m (85 ft 4 in); draught 7.7 m (25 ft 3 in)
Crew: 850
Ships in class: *Moskva* and *Leningrad*

It would take all the air wings of all the light carriers of the British, Indian, Italian and Spanish navies to come close to matching the air wing of one US Navy supercarrier

The US Marine Corps is the largest user of vertical take-off fighters, operating them from shore bases and the assault ships of the US Navy. The AV-8B was developed from the British Aerospace Harrier, and is the most capable ground attack fighter of its type.

in contrast, are very tough nuts to crack. The air group can intercept missile-launching aircraft before they launch their weapons. The large hull can absorb heavy punishment, as proved during the Vietnam War, when deck and hangar explosions caused major damage.

Modern carrier armament

As a consequence of this, light carriers were fitted with missile defence systems and close-in weapon systems, such as the Phalanx. The Russian Kiev' class *taktich-eskoye avianosny kreysera* (tactical aircraft-carrying cruisers) were particularly notable

for their missile armament, being fitted with eight SS-N-12 anti ship missile launchers, two twin SA-N-3 and two twin SA-N-4 anti-aircraft missile launchers, two twin 76.2-mm guns, and eight 30-mm Gatling close-in weapon systems, as well as an array of ASW equipment and torpedoes.

With the current change in international relations, it is becoming increasingly clear that ship-based aircraft, capable of operating far from any friendly airfield, are of immense strategic importance. The argument has swung back firmly in favour of the big carrier. The US Navy is planning a new class of nuclear-powered carrier and the Royal Navy plans to build two 50,000 ships in the next decade.

An AV-8B flies off the deck of the large assault ship USS Belleau Wood. *The LHAs and LHDs have such long flight decks that a 'ski jump' is superfluous.*

Combat Comparison

329 USSR
'Kiev' class

The **Kiev** was the largest Soviet vessel ever built when commissioned in 1976. Like the 'Moskvas' the vessels of the 'Kiev' class were hybrid aviation ships/cruisers, but they were immensely more powerful. Given the stated Soviet doctrine that the task of surface vessels was to support submarine forces, the four 'Kievs' were intended to protect Soviet bastion areas and to hunt NATO SSBNs.

The air group of a 'Kiev' vessel usually consisted of about 35 aircraft, including 12 Yak-38 'Forger' VTOL fighters. The weapons and electronics fit varied from carrier to carrier, with the fourth ship being significantly different. It was made clear the *Admiral Gorshkov* had served as a trials ship when many of its systems appeared on the Soviets' first genuine aircraft carrier, the *Admiral Kuznatsov*.

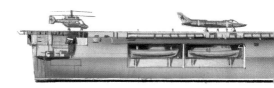

330 UNITED KINGDOM
'Invincible' class

British carrier aviation looked to be a thing of the past at the beginning of the 1970s. The carriers in service were getting on in years, and no new carriers had been planned since the demise of the revolutionary CVA-01 fleet carrier design. However, a naval staff requirement emerged in the late 1960s for a specialist anti-submarine carrier, originally called a 'through-deck cruiser' – to avoid upsetting anti-carrier politicians.

HMS **Invincible**, commissioned in 1980, was the first light STOVL carrier to enter service. The three 'Invincibles' are the largest gas turbine-powered warships in the world. Fitted with 'ski-jumps', they were designed to head ASW task groups. The normal air complement was eight Sea Harriers, nine Sea Kings or EH.101s, and three AEW Sea Kings, although in the Falklands *Invincible* carried up to a dozen Sea Harriers, and since then the air group has been enlarged.

Specification
'Invincible'class
Type: light aircraft carrier
Displacement: 19,500 tons full load
Armament: one twin Sea Dart SAM launcher, four barrel Sea Wolf SAM launchers to be fitted, three 30-mm 'Goalkeeper' close-in weapon systems, two twin 30-mm gas mountings.
Propulsion: four gas turbines delivering c 75000 kW (100,000 shp) to two propellers
Performance: maximum speed 28 knots (52 km/h, 32 mph); range 9250 km (5,750 miles) at 18 knots
Dimensions: length 207 m (678 ft); flight deck width 27.5 m (90 ft); draught 7.3 m (24 ft)
Crew: 1,320, including air group
Ships in class: *Invincible, Illustrious* and *Ark Royal*

Specification
'Kiev' class
Type: ASW carrier/heavy cruiser
Displacement: 44,000 tons full load
Armament: four twin SS-N-12 'Sandbox' surface-to-surface missiles; two twin SA-N-3 'Goblet' area-defence SAM launchers; two twin SA-N-4 'Gecko' point-defence SAM launchers; two twin 76-mm guns; eight six-barrel 30-mm close-in weapon systems; two 12-barrel MBU-600 ASW rocket-launchers; one twin SUW-N-1 anti-submarine missile launch system; two quintuple 533-mm torpedo tubes
Propulsion: four steam turbines delivering 134225 kW (180,000 shp) to four propellers
Performance: maximum speed 32 knots (59 km/h; 37 mph); range 13500 km at 18 knots
Dimensions: length 275 m (902 ft 3 in); maximum flight deck width 50 m (164 ft); draught 9.5 m (31 ft 2 in)
Crew: 1,200, excluding air group
Ships in class: *Kiev, Minsk, Novorossiysk* and *Baku*

Right: Novorossiysk *was the third of the 'Kiev' class to enter service, commissioning in August 1982. Like the others in the class, she carried a heavy cruiser armament, with surface-to-air, surface-to-surface and anti-submarine missiles being mounted on the superstructure and the foredeck.*

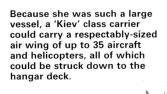

Because she was such a large vessel, a 'Kiev' class carrier could carry a respectably-sized air wing of up to 35 aircraft and helicopters, all of which could be struck down to the hangar deck.

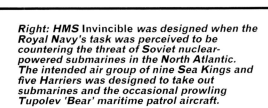

'Kiev' class carriers were designed to control ASW task groups, and to that end were equipped with extensive command, control and communications facilities.

The heavy armament of the 'Kievs' included anti-ship missiles, ASW weapons, and surface-to-air weaponry ranging from close-in Gatling guns to 50-km range missiles.

Right: HMS Invincible *was designed when the Royal Navy's task was perceived to be countering the threat of Soviet nuclear-powered submarines in the North Atlantic. The intended air group of nine Sea Kings and five Harriers was designed to take out submarines and the occasional prowling Tupolev 'Bear' maritime patrol aircraft.*

The carrier was originally intended to have an air wing of nine helicopters and five fighters, but experience in the Falklands led to the fighter complement being doubled, although the extra aircraft had to be carried on deck.

Like the 'Kiev' class, the 'Invincibles' are intended to act at the centre of anti-submarine groups, their helicopters being designed to fix on and destroy submarines discovered by the powerful sonars carried by the frigates of the task group.

'Invincible' class carriers are powered by four Rolls-Royce Olympus gas turbines, variants of the engines that power the Vulcan bomber and the Concorde airliner.

Invincible is much less heavily armed than her larger Soviet equivalent. In Falklands form, as seen here, her main defensive armament was a twin Sea Dart area-defence SAM launcher, to which has since been added close-in weapon systems and short-range missiles.

135

SMALL IS BEAUTIFUL

Light carriers have always been recognised as being less effective than larger vessels. But they have one major advantage: they are much more economical to build and to run.

The aircraft carrier has dominated war at sea since World War II. Capable of performing a wide variety of missions, projecting power over most of the globe, they are the most flexible warships ever to take to the sea.

That flexibility has been bought at a price. Aircraft carriers are expensive. They are big ships, with large crews, and are crammed with costly equipment and weaponry. Anyone wanting to make use of maritime air power has to be ready to make a huge investment, and very few nations can afford such costs. Unless, of course, they can work out some method of doing so more cheaply. Which is where light carriers come in.

In the early days, following World War I, when aircraft were smaller and of lower performance, carriers could be relatively small. Britain's HMS *Hermes* was the first vessel built as such from the start, but it was so small that it was of questionable effectiveness in battle. America's conversion of the large battlecruisers *Lexington* and *Saratoga* saw a very different kind of carrier emerge. Large, and with a considerable air wing, such vessels could take progressive upgrades and developments without any trouble, and the fleet carrier became the nucleus of the battle fleet in World War II.

But there was a serious shortage of air-capable vessels early in the war, just when the demands on maritime air power began to grow. Convoys had to be escorted, submarines had to be hunted – but what few large carriers were available were reserved for fleet use. An alternative had to be found.

Light carriers cost less than big ones. By converting cruisers on the stocks the US Navy made good some of its shortage, and the British idea of adding a flight deck to a merchant hull to produce a carrier of limited capability was to expand to a programme which saw the construction of more than 100 such vessels. Although they were nicknamed 'Woolworth carriers' or

The **Giuseppe Garibaldi is now in service as the fleet flagship of the Italian navy. This small but highly capable vessel is a good example of the latest generation of light aircraft carriers.**

'Jeep carriers', these cheap and cheerful ships made a significant contribution to the final Allied victory.

After the war, small carriers were quickly disposed of in the general run-down of fleets. Some did survive, as helicopter carriers or aircraft transports. Second-hand light carriers gave a number of smaller fleets experience in maritime air operations, but even these proved too expensive for many forces, and not until the development of vertical/short take-off and landing fighters was the light carrier to revive. Now its future seems assured, as an ever-growing number of countries become members of the light carrier club.

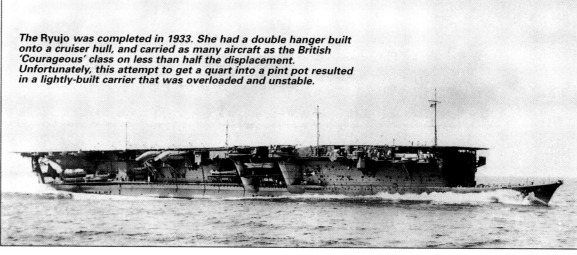

The **Ryujo** was completed in 1933. She had a double hanger built onto a cruiser hull, and carried as many aircraft as the British 'Courageous' class on less than half the displacement. Unfortunately, this attempt to get a quart into a pint pot resulted in a lightly-built carrier that was overloaded and unstable.

Left: Modern light carriers like the British 'Invincible' class are practicable propositions only because of the development of vertical take-off fighters.

Right: Light carriers had small decks, which meant that their island superstructures had to be kept to a minimum to allow maximum space for aircraft.

Below: Unlike American vessels, British light carriers were scaled-down versions of the big fleet carriers.

Light fleet carriers

The shortage of fleet carriers in the US Navy led to the development of a series of light carriers, adapted from cruisers then under construction. The 'Independence' class vessels were never very satisfactory, being too small to carry the large air groups required by the US Navy, but at least they were fast enough to keep up with the carrier task forces which swept through the Pacific in the last two years of World War II.

With the expansion of the war into the Pacific after Pearl Harbor, Britain began construction of a series of light fleet carriers in 1942. The 'Colossus' and 'Majestic' classes were scaled-down and much more .ightly-built versions of the big carriers then in service, and while they made little contribution to the war, they were to be important in the post-war years.

Japan was the other major carrier power, and deployed a number of light carriers. Some, like the *Ryujo*, were pre-war experiments in cramming the largest possible number of aircraft onto the smallest possible hull. Most, however, were pre-planned conversions of seaplane tenders and depot ships, designed to maximise the number of flight decks available in the shortest time.

Escort carriers

The conquest of Europe in 1940 gave Germany air bases, ports and submarine bases from which to strike at Britain's vital seaborne trade. The answer to most of these threats was air power, but there were too few carrier decks. The solution was to fit flight decks to merchant hulls. These could carry enough aircraft to maintain anti-submarine patrols over a convoy or to deal with long-range bombers. The first such escort carrier was HMS *Audacity*, converted in 1941 from a captured German cargo-liner. Although it was sunk by a German submarine, it proved the concept of the escort carrier, and was the first in a long line of such vessels. Nowhere was the sheer industrial power of the United States displayed to such good effect as in the production of escort carriers, with more than 100 such vessels being produced before the end of the war. At the height of production, the Henry J. Kaiser Company was completing one 'Casablanca' class carrier per week. Escort carriers were used for a variety of tasks, including convoy escort, submarine hunting, support of amphibious operations, and as transports.

Like the other two major navies, the Japanese produced escort carriers by modifying commercial hulls. But Japan, with its then ramshackle industrial organisation, completed only half a dozen vessels.

Above: As World War II progressed, escort carriers found more offensive uses. The vessels pictured are supporting the 1944 amphibious operations in the south of France.

Left: US Navy Corsairs launch from an escort carrier. They saw brief post-war service, but the new jets of the late 1940s were just too big for their tiny flight decks.

Below, left: MAC ships were converted bulk cargo vessels which retained their cargo capacity, but with a flight deck. There was no hangar, so the four aircraft were carried permanently on deck.

Below: Escort carriers gave valuable service in all oceans, braving typhoons and other storms in the Pacific and North Atlantic.

Post-war carriers

With the end of World War II, armed forces across the globe were run down. The escort carriers were hardly front-line vessels, but found a new role in the 1950s as helicopter carriers, supporting amphibious operations. Some of the larger British light fleet carriers served on into the 1960s and 1970s. Known as 'commando carriers', they were roughly equivalent to the American LPH assault ship, which was based on a World War II escort carrier design.

While the Americans pressed on with the development of the supercarrier, Britain continued to use its smaller vessels in the strike role. HMS *Triumph* was one of the first carriers to arrive off Korea in June 1950, and other 'Colossus' class vessels maintained the Royal Navy presence during the war.

British light carriers were also important in spreading maritime air power. 'Colossus' and 'Majestic' class carriers served with the Argentine, Australian, Brazilian, Canadian, Dutch, French and Indian navies. The only American carriers operating with other fleets were the 'Independence' class vessels *Cabot*, which was the Spanish *Dedalo* until the 1980s, and the *Belleau Wood* and the *Lafayette*, which were loaned to France in the 1950s.

Left: The American light fleet carrier Belleau Wood *was loaned to France in the 1950s. Seen entering Haiphong in 1954, during the first Indo-China war, the* Bois Belleau *was returned to the USA in 1960.*

Below: HMS Hermes' *varied career continues. After serving as the flagship of the Falklands Task Force, the veteran carrier was sold to India, where as the* Viraat *she will serve at least to the end of the century. Being larger than later V/STOL carriers, she had a more effective air group.*

Left: British 'Colossus' and 'Majestic' class carriers were used by a number of navies in the 1950s. HMAS Melbourne was the former Majestic, and along with HMAS Sydney she provided Australia's maritime air power into the 1970s and 1980s. The Melbourne was scheduled for replacement in the early 1980s, but in the event was laid-up without a successor.

The V/STOL revolution

Britain's revolutionary Harrier 'Jump-jet' has changed the face of warfare at sea. It can operate from small carriers without the need for expensive catapults and arrester gear, and can provide medium-sized navies with real high-performance air power. The US Marine Corps took Harriers to sea aboard its assault ships, and the Royal Navy used V/STOL carriers to keep itself in fixed-wing aviation when its last conventional carrier was paid-off in 1979. 'Harrier carriers' made their combat debut in the South Atlantic in 1982, and it is no exaggeration to say that without them, the British Task Force would not have been able to recapture the Falklands.

The Soviet Union was the other V/STOL pioneer. Although the Yak-38 'Forger' is a far more limited aircraft than the Harrier, it was housed in a highly impressive vessel. The Kiev ws the first of four powerful warships, heavily armed and equipped to operate 'Forgers' and helicopters. Since then, the Soviet navy has gone on to build its first supercarrier.

At 44,000 tons, the Soviet Kiev was larger than any fleet carrier of World War II, but as an anti-submarine vessel she was actually a descendant of the escort carrier.

A 'Kiev' class carrier passes through the Bosphorus in company with a 'Sovremenny' class destroyer. Modern Soviet vessels such as these were packed with sophisticated electronics and radar, and were more heavily armed than any Western equivalent.

Above: The 'Colossus' class carrier HMS Ocean passes the 'Essex' class carrier Oriskany in Korean waters. The 'Colossus' class bore the brunt of Britain's carrier contribution to the Korean War, with all five operational carriers doing tours. Ocean's main claim to fame, however, is that she provided the flight deck for the world's first jet carrier landing, in December 1945.

Left: Brazil's carrier Minas Gerais is the former British 'Majestic' class carrier Vengeance. In Brazilian service the vessel is used as an anti-submarine warfare vessel.

Maritime air power in the 21st century

The future of the light carrier seems assured. Easing of Cold War tensions has made the world safer from nuclear destruction, but has also opened the Pandora's box of regional conflicts. With the world now so dependent upon international trade, such local wars can also threaten the livelihood of nations on the other side of the globe; therefore that trade has to be protected. Shipping lines must be kept open, and the best way to do that is with a carrier. The supercarriers of the US Navy are often used as peacekeepers, but they can only do so much. In any case, most of the time it will be like taking a sledgehammer to crack a nut. Although smaller vessels are less capable, they can be relied upon to do the job in all but the most threatening environments. And new developments in aircraft, weapons and electronics will see the light carrier's capabilities increase dramatically over the next decades.

Above: The development of short and vertical take-off fighters is now in high gear, after years in which the Harrier and the Yak-38 were the only operational examples. Speculative platforms for such aircraft include this US Navy concept of a 'ski-jump'-equipped twin-hull light carrier.

Above: Another US Navy concept involves a different kind of vertical take-off, using tail-sitting aircraft. This is fairly impractical, since launched this way, an aircraft will never be able to carry the weapons that a similar fighter can take into action from a 'ski-jump'.

FALKLANDS

WARRIORS

Through the stormy seas of a South Atlantic autumn, the carrier battle group TG317.8 began its move south from Ascension towards the Falkland Islands on 18 April 1982. Day and night, three Sea King helicopters kept constant airborne watch over the little fleet: the carriers *Invincible* and *Hermes* (the flagship), dogged by their 'goalkeeper' frigate *Broadsword*. The destroyer *Glamorgan* and the frigates *Yarmouth* and *Alacrity* were in a broad spearhead some 30 miles in advance, acting as an anti-aircraft and anti-submarine screen, and the replenishment ships *Olmeda* and *Resource* trailed astern.

A Sea Harrier makes a dawn launch. Without its two light carriers, Britain would never have been able to retake the Falkland Islands.

Left: HMS Hermes *ploughs through the stormy South Atlantic, with the Type 22 frigate* HMS Broadsword *alongside. Although primarily ASW platforms, Type 22s are equipped with the highly effective Sea Wolf surface-to-air missile, and in the Falklands were used as 'goalkeepers', or close anti-aircraft escorts. A successful attack on the carriers would have ended Britain's chances of winning the war.*

Right: The Royal Navy Task Force steams southwards. Escorted by frigates and destroyers, and accompanied by replenishment vessels, the British light carriers were on their way to a war nobody had expected. Designed for anti-submarine or commando warfare, they had to perform as strike carriers.

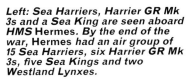

Left: Sea Harriers, Harrier GR Mk 3s and a Sea King are seen aboard HMS Hermes. *By the end of the war,* Hermes *had an air group of 15 Sea Harriers, six Harrier GR Mk 3s, five Sea Kings and two Westland Lynxes.*

Aboard *Hermes* was the commander of the Task Force, Rear Admiral J.F. Woodward, who described the scene: "The ops room on *Hermes* was about 15 feet by 15 feet, with fairly low lighting so that we could see the various radar screens and monitors. About 20 people worked in the ops room, checking the data with a group warfare officer on watch, and conducting the minute-to-minute management of the battle group.

"Normally, comparatively junior officers would have held the position, which would have meant calling the admiral every few minutes to make a decision. I thought that I was likely to be down south for a long while, and that if I was going to be called to make decisions that any captain could make, I would be running

around all the time and thus be incapable of doing the long-term thinking or planning. So I chose to change the system, and co-opted Captain Buchanan and Captain Woodhead for the job. They worked 12 hours on and 12 hours off from late April until July."

Intruder detected

All the ships were on 'defence watch' from 19 April, and two days later a high-flying aircraft was detected approaching the group. Two Sea Harriers from *Hermes'* 800 Squadron were scrambled. The intruder was identified through gaps in the

heavy cloud as an Argentine air force Boeing 707, flying at 38,000 feet on a reconnaissance mission.

Although the Sea Harriers were already armed with Sidewinder missiles, the unarmed 707 was outside the Total Exclusion Zone, and the rules of engagement did not allow it to be attacked. Instead, it was merely escorted away. This procedure was carried out on several occasions – once, the intruder turned out to be a DC-10 of the Brazilian airline, Varig, on a scheduled flight!

On 25 April the carrier group met up with the destroyers *Sheffield*, *Coventry* and *Glasgow*,

the frigate *Arrow* and the replenishment ship *Appleleaf*. On 29 April the frigates *Brilliant* and *Plymouth*, ferrying D Squadron 22 SAS and No. 2 SBS to the carriers, joined the force. The battle group was now some 500 miles east of Port Stanley. Under cover of darkness the ships refuelled, and then began their run for the Islands.

HMS *Brilliant* was the 'goalkeeper' for *Invincible*, as her captain, John Howard, described: "Whatever else I was doing, I had to flash back and fall in dead astern of *Invincible* by first light, and HMS *Broadsword* did the same for *Hermes*. Everyone was worried that an Exocet would flash out of the sky, and the Sea Wolf missile system onboard the Type 22 frigates was the only weapon available that had a chance of shooting one down."

Flight Lieutenant David Morgan of the RAF, on a tour with the Navy's 800 Squadron, flew in the first attack on the airfield at Port Stanley. "Before dawn on 1 May the Vulcans went in and dropped a bomb in the middle of the runway. We followed that up just before eight o'clock with a raid of 12 Harriers. . . When I returned to *Hermes*, I held off and let

everyone else land first because, having taken flak, I didn't know if I was going to be able to land the thing. (I later found out there was a bloody great hole in the fin.) I brought it back and rolled it onto the deck. I didn't want to do a vertical landing because the controls may have been damaged, so I rolled it on fairly slowly and stopped. That was the end of the first mission. The whole operation had taken half an hour. . .

"On the 4th, we lost Nick Taylor at Goose Green and the *Sheffield* was hit. I was on deck when I saw this great ball of smoke . . . Then the casualties started coming back onto the *Hermes*, and everyone was rather subdued and gritting their teeth and saying, 'Okay, this is it. Let's go and have those bastards.'

"At that stage, we were pulled up to sleep above the water level because of the submarine threat, which made life very uncomfortable. I was sleeping on the floor of the captain's day cabin with five other people. Most of us had camp beds but some of us were just sleeping on the cushions. There were about 40 people sleeping in the bar . . . Over the first couple of weeks we all got very, very tired and people were asleep in the cockpit on the deck."

Combat air patrols and bombing attacks continued as the weather allowed, but, as Rear Admiral Woodward explained: "For various reasons, we couldn't

actually have a landing force in before about mid-May, and we had to be finished by 1 July (when the Falklands winter would set in), so there could only be a six-week period for the land battle. It was quite a close thing as it turned out because, of course, we finished in mid-June. Fortunately, Sea Harriers were quite plentiful, which was a relief, and the carriers continued satisfactorily, with *Hermes* running for over three months and *Invincible* for more than four."

British carrier hit

D-Day finally came on 20-21 May. Harrier GR Mk 3s of RAF No. 1 Squadron joined the *Hermes* from the *Atlantic Conveyor* shortly before she was sunk on 25 May. Flight Lieutenant Morgan reflected: "We were very, very lucky . . . if they'd managed to get the helicopters off, it would've made such a difference. But had the Argentines hit 24 hours earlier, things would have been very difficult for us."

This loss deprived 3 Commando of all its air transport – three Chinooks and six Wessex HU Mk 5s – a factor that undoubtedly slowed up their advance. Rear Admiral Woodward wrote: "I would say there was one really low moment in the campaign. This was 25 May, Argentine naval day – their aircraft carrier is even named after it. I wrote in my diary: 'They will probably do something today.' Then, later in

the day, I wrote: 'Well, they don't seem to have done much; maybe we'll get away with it.' That was my mistake. . ."

However, despite these losses, the campaign was a success. The Falklands were recovered, and only three weeks after the landings at San Carlos, the Task Force saw the Union Jack flying once again over Port Stanley.

Above: **Broadsword** *keeps station close alongside the* **Hermes.** *The frigate would detach for operations at night, and then close with the carrier to protect it from daylight raids by Argentine aircraft.*

Below: **Hermes'** *hangar deck is crowded with Harriers and Marines preparing for the San Carlos landings. She had to function as both a strike carrier and 'commando carrier'.*

Above, inset: Deck crew wheel cluster bombs about the decks of the Hermes as they prepare to arm a strike. Small though they were by American standards, the 'Harrier carriers' nevertheless packed a considerable punch.

Above: HMS Invincible was more effectively armed than the Hermes, with her Sea Dart missiles able to strike at enemy aircraft from ranges of 40 km or more. However, lessons learned in battle pointed out the need for close-in weapon systems.

Below: HMS Invincible returns to Portsmouth in August 1982, two months after the rest of the Task Force. She had to remain on station until relieved by the brand-new HMS Illustrious, which had been completed in record time.

JACK OF ALL TRADES

Because light carriers are the only feasible way for smaller navies to take high-performance aircraft to sea, they will be used for tasks for which they were not designed, but which they can do better than anything but a supercarrier.

Aircraft changed warfare at sea irrevocably during World War II. The aircraft carrier became the new capital ship, the very essence of long-range power projection. After the war, the victorious US and Royal Navies continued to develop the aircraft carrier, but as aircraft grew larger and faster it became clear that carriers had to grow enormously. The supercarriers that first appeared in the 1950s were twice as big as their wartime predecessors, and the addition of nuclear power gave them almost unlimited endurance.

Unfortunately, supercarriers are phenomenally expensive. Britain, no longer an imperial power and in dire financial straits after the war, could not match American economic might, and the Royal Navy's carrier force dwindled to nothing when the decrepit *Ark Royal* was paid-off in 1979.

But fixed-wing aircraft still had a future in the Royal Navy, with the commissioning of HMS *Invincible* in 1980 pointing the way. Indeed, V/STOL aircraft operating off a light carrier is a concept that has proved attractive to several navies, which like the idea of maritime air power but cannot afford the crippling cost of conventional carriers.

They've been called 'the poor man's carrier' by the well-funded theoreticians of the US Navy. They are considered too small to

have an adequate air wing, and not flexible enough to project the power that the Pentagon's naval strategy calls for. But the modern light carrier has a number of advantages that the big-deck advocates ignore. The absence of catapults and arrester gear, which largely dictate the size of a carrier and the size of the aircraft it carries, and the much simpler launching and recovery arrangements mean that a V/STOL carrier is much cheaper to build and less challenging to operate than a conventional carrier.

Role for today's light carriers

As the Falklands war showed, the new light carriers can operate in conditions that might defeat a conventional vessel. With their smaller air group, they are not really an offensive weapon like the American giants, but for trade protection, anti-submarine operations and even amphibious assault in areas of limited threat they are perfectly acceptable.

The other argument against V/STOL carriers is that the aircraft themselves are small, carry a poor weapons load, and are of limited effectiveness. This argument was dispelled by the performance of the Harrier in the Falklands, and the latest AV-8Bs in service lose little in comparison with conventional attack aircraft, while retaining all of the earlier aircraft's versatility.

1 Power projection

Power projection is the task of the huge carriers of the US Navy. Half of each carrier's 85-strong air wing is composed of dedicated attack aircraft, which can take on the most sophisticated of land-based defences. Smaller carriers like the Royal Navy's 'Invincibles' have no such luxuries, with a single aircraft type having to fulfil a number of functions. The Sea Harrier is tasked with strike, reconnaissance and air defence, and in the Falklands war it proved

HMS Illustrious *relieves HMS* Invincible *in the South Atlantic after the Falklands war. Early lessons of the campaign are evident in the addition of Phalanx close-in anti-missile weapon systems, visible as white domes at the bow and stern of the* Illustrious *(nearest to the camera).*

2 Sea control

In the late 1960s, the US Navy looked into the possibility of producing a 'low-end' air-capable vessel designed specifically for convoy escort. Carrying helicopters with active sonars, the Sea Control Ship (SCS) was to act in concert with specialist anti-submarine frigates. In theory, the carrier's helicopters were to nail down and destroy submarines detected by the towed array sonars of the frigates. A small number of vertical take-off fighters could screen against air attack, operating just outside the range of the Standard SAMs carried by the escorts. Each SCS could free a big-deck carrier from convoy escort duties, and five or more could be obtained for the cost of a single 'Nimitz' class vessel.

Although the concept was tested successfully using the assault ship USS *Guam*, no SCSs were ordered. Nevertheless, most US Navy assault ships are capable of the sea control mission, as are the V/STOL carriers of other navies. The original SCS design was sold to Spain, and in modified form has been built as the *Principe de Asturias*.

Below: Although the US Navy is the home of the supercarrier, it does have the capacity to put light carriers to sea. The USS Guam *is normally used as a helicopter assault vessel, but in the 1970s it served as the prototype Sea Control Ship, with a mixed group of Harrier fighters and Sea King anti-submarine helicopters.*

The impressive bulk of the aviation ship Kiev *marked a new departure for the Soviet navy when it appeared in the mid-1970s. Although she was not the most potent carrier ever built, she was powerfully armed, had notable anti-submarine capacity, and had enough room to carry all the necessary equipment to serve as a flagship. Most importantly, it gave the Soviet navy valuable experience in the delicate art of operating aircraft at sea.*

highly effective in all three roles. Without the carriers *Hermes* (now the Indian *Viraat)* and Invincible, there is no way that the British Task Force could have supported the landings or retaken the Islands. In this case, the small carriers proved highly effective at projecting power, although against a more capable air threat operating closer to its air bases, the task would have undoubtedly been more difficult.

3 Anti-submarine task group

Britain's 'Invincible' class carriers were designed to challenge the latest high-technology nuclear submarines put into service by the Soviet navy. Large enough to patrol the stormy waters of the Greenland-Iceland-UK gap, equipped to operate the latest and largest ASW helicopters, and designed to lead a squadron of specialist ASW frigates, the 'Invincibles' formed the heart of the most capable ASW forces ever developed. Unlike the sea control mission, which is to defend a convoy against attacking submarines, the ASW mission involves actively hunting and destroying the enemy. On ASW missions, a flight of Sea Harriers is carried to deal with enemy bombers, although when the ships were designed they were expected to operate within range of land-based air power, or under a US Navy fighter umbrella, when providing an ASW screen to American carrier battle groups.

Spain's *Principe de Asturias* and Italy's *Giuseppe Garibaldi* are both equipped for the anti-submarine mission, the Spanish navy using LAMPS III and Sea King helicopters, while the Italians will eventually equip their carrier with the Anglo-Italian EH.101.

Above: the Soviet helicopter carrier Moskva *formed the heart of a Soviet anti-submarine task group, using her Kamov helicopters to 'sanitise' a wide area of ocean.*

Large flight decks allow the operation of large helicopters, an ability which finds its best expression in the amphibious warfare role practised by the vessels of the US Navy.

4 Amphibious assault

Light carriers gained a new lease of life after World War II with the development of the helicopter, and the US Navy used obsolescent escort carriers as helicopter platforms for amphibious assault. The British used similar 'commando carriers' well into the 1970s. HMS *Hermes* was converted into a 'Harrier carrier' in the late 1970s, in time to play a major part in the operation to retake the Falklands. Since then, the Royal Navy's 'Invincible' class vessels have been tried unsuccessfully in the amphibious assault role. To meet this requirement the Royal Navy ordered a heavily modified 'Invincible' design, the LPH HMS 'Ocean'.

The US Navy has, by far, the largest force of amphibious assault ships in the world. Most vessels can carry some Marine helicopters, but the Corps also operates the largest force of sea-going V/STOL fighters. Dedicated to the support of amphibious operations, they fly from amphibious assault ships like the 'Iwo Jima' class helicopter carriers and the giant general-purpose vessels of the 'Tarawa' and 'Wasp' classes.

BATTLESHIP!

After World War II, the battleship seemed a thing of the past in a world of nuclear submarines. Against all odds, however, it has returned.

It seemed easy, to the Lebanese gunners high in their mountain retreats. The US Marines were in a difficult position, down there by the airport, and the US Navy had already lost a couple of planes in the skies above Lebanon. Of course, there was that big new ship on the horizon, but that was 20 miles away. That could be no danger.

Well, they were wrong. One fine day, there was a huge flash on the horizon, and to the accompaniment of an unearthly howl the whole area for hundreds of yards around was obliterated in a titanic series of explosions. USS *New Jersey* was in action again. The battleship was back with a vengeance.

Awesome power

Since the time of Drake and the Spanish Armada, the big-gunned ship has ruled the seas. For five centuries, battleships grew bigger and ever more powerful, until by World War II they were titanic machines, protected by foot-thick armour plate and mounting guns with a power and destructiveness unmatched before or since. But even as the battleship reached its zenith, it was to prove a thing of the past, with little apparent place in modern war.

Thirty-two gunned capital ships were sunk during World War II. Of that total, only eight were sunk by their own kind. The rest succumbed to aircraft and submarines. Between them, these two classic 20th century weapons seemed to have put the battleship into terminal decline, to work out its remaining years as close escort to the new queen of the seas, the aircraft-carrier, or to occupy itself in shore bombardment support.

To be sure, the battleship was of great im-

The awesome blast of a 16-inch gun lights up the skies as an 'Iowa' class battleship fires a ranging shot from the centre gun of Number 2 turret.

153

portance in these roles. Their immense power made the task of amphibious landings much easier. In Normandy in 1944, the German defenders feared the salvoes of the battleships more than anything else, and all of the Pacific landings were carried to the accompaniment of battleship fire. And when the suicidal *kamikazes* fell out of the skies onto the Allied vessels off Leyte and Okinawa, the massive anti-aircraft armament of the capital ship was called into play to defend the fleets.

After World War II, the battleship went into decline. Big ships require large crews and are expensive to run, and in the financially straitened post-war years there was not much room for luxury. HMS *Vanguard*, the last British battleship, was scrapped in 1960, having spent much of the previous decade as a training ship or in reserve. The US Navy kept the four 'Iowa'-class ships, but apart from spells of duty as shore bombardment ships off

*Above: The French battleship **G**aulois was completed in 1899 and is a typical battleship of the beginning of the century. It was to be made obsolete within six years by the revolutionary British **D**readnought.*

FLASHBACK

SINK THE TIRPITZ!

Unlike the *Bismarck*, the German battleship *Tirpitz* never ventured out to challenge the power of the Royal Navy. However, its mere existence in a north Norwegian fiord and the threat to the Arctic convoys tied down huge Royal Navy assets that were needed elsewhere. *Tirpitz* had to be dealt with. Bombing and carrier-launched air attacks produced little result. Eventually the navy used X-craft, small four-man submarines, to get into Altenfiord and lay charges alongside the huge vessel. At the cost of six X-craft and 10 lives, the attack succeeded in crippling the *Tirpitz*. The battleship was eventually sunk by the Lancasters of the RAF's crack No. 617 squadron in September 1944.

*The German battleship **T**irpitz had an undistinguished war record, only venturing out of its Norwegian lair to bombard Spitzbergen (above left). Nonetheless, it had to be dealt with. It was eventually damaged by X-craft midget submarines (below left) before being sunk by the RAF.*

*Above: HMS **Q**ueen Elizabeth was the ultimate World War I Dreadnought. Powerfully armed and well armoured, the 'Queen Elizabeth' class served with distinction through two world wars.*

BATTLESHIP Reference File

29

'Iowa' Class

USA

Although battleships had been recalled to service a number of times since the end of World War II, they were regarded as little more than mobile artillery. But the need to counter the growing Soviet navy in the 1970s resulted in the re-birth of the battleship, with the recommissioning of the **'Iowa' class**. The first to see service was the *New Jersey*, beginning her first operational deployment in March 1983 in support of the Marines in Beirut. All four of the class were modernised. The electronic fit was upgraded, new weapons were mounted, and the vessels were generally prepared to operate with battle groups in high-threat areas and to provide US amphibious forces with fire-

USS New Jersey had seen action in three wars before being brought out of mothballs in the 1980s, to form the centrepiece of the US Navy's new Surface Action Groups.

support. More extensive modifications were scrapped on cost grounds, but the 'Iowa' and 'Missouri' played a major role as Tomahawk launch platforms and gunfire support ships.

Specification
Displacement: 51,000 tons standard and 57,450 tons full load

Dimensions: length 270.4 m (887 ft); beam 33 m (108 ft); draught 11.6 m (38 ft)
Machinery: geared steam turbines delivering 212,000 shp to four propellers
Speed: 33 knots
Aircraft: two or four helicopters

Armament: eight quad Tomahawk cruise missile launchers, four quad Harpoon anti-ship missile launchers, three triple 16-in (406-mm) guns, six twin 5-in (127-mm) guns, four 20-mm Phalanx Close-in Weapons
Complement: 1,537

USS Iowa fires a two-gun salvo. First becoming operational in 1943, the 'Iowas' are amongst the fastest vessels in the US fleet. Iowa was recommissioned in a hurry in 1984 to relieve New Jersey off Lebanon.

Korea they too found their way into mothballs. The USS *New Jersey* came briefly out of retirement to serve on the gunline off Vietnam, but much of her potential was wasted, and she was among the first assets to go after President Nixon began to run down US forces in South-East Asia.

But in the 1980s, the battleship gained a new lease of life as a result of two widely separated events. The US Navy recommissioned the four 'Iowas' in a new, upgraded form, and the Soviet navy launched the first of its 'Kirov'-class nuclear-powered 'battlecruisers'.

Some saw the rebirth of the 'Iowas' as a triumph of nostalgia over common sense. To others, in the days when a 600-ship navy was the Reagan administration's goal, the battleship's potential on the modern scene was so great that it would once again be amongst the most powerful ships afloat. While the battleship's nine 16-inch guns are an undoubted asset, it was the great hull's capacity for carrying modern weapons that was most attractive. And as each 'Iowa' was reactivated with improvements for the cost of one new-build frigate, it made them a bargain.

Surface-to surface weapons

Each 'Iowa' kept its main gun battery, and some of the five-inch guns. Other surface-to-surface weapons fitted were 32 Tomahawk cruise missiles in armoured box launchers and 16 Harpoon anti-ship missiles.

Even without its missiles, an 'Iowa' would find modern surface combatants easy meat once within gun range. Faster than the majority of modern warships, an 'Iowa' carried over 1,200 16-inch rounds, as compared with the four or eight missiles carried by modern cruisers and destroyers. And even if an 'Iowa' were hit, its thick armour would enable it to

---

30

'Kidd' Class

USA

The US Navy replaced many of its World War II vintage destroyers that had served through the Vietnam War with the large 'Spruance' class anti-submarine warfare destroyers. Criticised at the time for being too large and too sparsely equipped, the 'Spruances' have proved adaptable and capable of being fitted with many new weapon systems. In 1974, the Shah of Iran ordered six surface-to-air equipped versions of the 'Spruance' design. However, following the 1979 Islamic revolution, two were cancelled and the four that were under construction were taken over by the US Navy as the **'Kidd' class**. These general-purpose vessels are more powerful than standard destroyers, and have

USS Callaghan started life as the general purpose destroyer Daryush, ordered by the Iranian navy. They are the most heavily armed destroyers in American service.

significant anti-air, anti-surface, and anti-submarine capability. Unofficially known as the 'Ayatollah' class, the 'Kidds' are well suited to forming part of a Surface Action Group.

Specification

Displacement: 6,210 tons standard and 9,200 tons full load
Dimensions: length 171.6m (563ft); beam 16.8m (55ft); draught 9.1m (30ft)
Machinery: four gas-turbines delivering 80,000 shp to two propellers
Speed: 32 knots
Aircraft: two ASW helicopters
Armament: two quad Harpoon anti-

ship missile launchers, two 5-inch anti-surface/anti-aircraft guns, two twin Mk 26 missile launchers with 50 Standard SAMs and 16 ASROC anti-submarine rockets, two 20-mm Phalanx Close-in Weapons, two triple torpedo tubes
Complement: 338-346

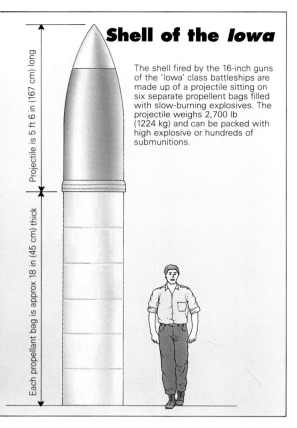

Shell of the Iowa

The shell fired by the 16-inch guns of the 'Iowa' class battleships are made up of a projectile sitting on six separate propellent bags filled with slow-burning explosives. The projectile weighs 2,700 lb (1224 kg) and can be packed with high explosive or hundreds of submunitions.

Projectile is 5 ft 6 in (167 cm) long

Each propellant bag is approx 18 in (45 cm) thick

Shore bombardment has always been a battleship task, and the amphibious operations of World War II made it even more important. Here an old US Navy battleship shells a Japanese-held island before the Marines go ashore.

shrug off a missile warhead, while a salvo of 16-inch shells would shatter modern unarmoured vehicles.

'Iowa' class ships were the leaders of surface action groups, fighting ship-versus-ship actions on the high seas. Other battleship roles include lending a new degree of versatility to carrier battle groups, bombardment support for amphibious landings, and as a highly impressive participant in peacetime 'show the flag' visits.

On her first deployment, USS *New Jersey* showed some of the flexible power projection

---

31

FORMER USSR

'Kirov' class

Kirov is the largest non-carrier warship to have been built since World War II. Very similar in conception to the abortive American Strike Cruiser proposal of the 1970s, the 'Kirov' class is large enough to fulfil a variety of functions, from serving as a fleet flagship through providing a carrier screen in high-threat areas to independent action leading a surface action group. *Kirov* has been called a battlecruiser, and in speed, size and fighting power it is not too bad a description.

The mighty Kirov is comparable in size to the battlecruisers of World War I, with less armour but nuclear powered for a vastly greater range.

Specification
Displacement: 22,000 tons standard, 28,000 tons full load
Dimensions: length 248 m (813 ft 8

in); beam 28 m (91 ft 10 in); draught 8.8 m (28 ft 11 in)
Machinery: combined nuclear/superheated steam boilers delivering 150,000 shp to two shafts
Speed: 35 knots
Aircraft: 3-5 Kamov 'Hormone' anti-submarine and missile guidance helicopters
Armament: 20 SS-N-19 vertical-launch surface-to-surface missiles, two

100-mm (3.9-in) guns (*Frunze*, the second of the class, has one twin 130-mm [5.12-in] gun turret), 12 SA-N-6 vertical launchers with 96 missiles, two twin SA-N-4 'Gecko' SAM launchers with 36 missiles (*Frunze* has in addition 16 SA-N-9 point defence missile systems with 128 missiles), eight

30-mm ADG6-30 Close-in Weapons, one twin SS-N-14 'Silex' ASW missile launcher with 16 missiles (not in *Frunze*), one 12-barrel ASW rocket launcher, two six-barrel ASW rocket launchers (not in *Frunze*), two quintuple 533-mm (21-in) torpedo tubes
Complement: 900

32

FORMER USSR

'Slava' Class

Falling midway between the massive 'Kirov' class and the 'Sovremenny' class destroyer, the **'Slava' class** cruisers make a powerful addition to the Soviet fleet. 'Slavas' are being built at the same yard that built the 'Kara' class large anti-submarine ship, and use an enlarged version of the 'Kara' hull. Unlike the 'Karas', the 'Slava' has only limited anti-submarine capability. First deployed in 1983, *Slava*, like the 'Sovremenny' class, is designed to contest vital sea areas like the Greenland-Iceland-UK Gap. The powerful anti-ship armament is centred on the 550-km (350-mile) range SS-N-12 'Sandbox' missile, which has either a nuclear or a 1000-kg high explosive warhead. Armed with such a missile, it

First of a new class of cruisers optimised for surface action, Slava's profile is dominated by the huge tubes for her SS-N-12 'Sandbox' long-range anti-ship missiles.

seems likely that the 'Slavas' are intended to mount attacks on carrier battle groups.

Specification
Displacement: 10,500 tons standard, 12,500 tons full load
Dimensions: length 187 m (613 ft 6 in); beam 20 m (65 ft 8 in); draught 7.6 m (25 ft)

Machinery: four gas turbines delivering 120,000 shp to two propellers
Speed: 35 knots
Aircraft: one missile-guidance helicopter
Armament: 16 SS-N-12 'Sandbox' anti-ship missiles, one twin 130-mm

(5.12-in) gun, eight vertical SA-N-6 SAM launchers with 64 missiles, two twin SA-N-4 'Gecko' SAM launchers with 40 missiles, six 30-mm ADG6-30 Close-in Weapons, two 12-barrel RBU 6000 anti-submarine rocket launchers, two quad 533-mm (21-in) torpedo tubes
Complement: c.600

Frunze *is the second of the 'Kirov' class, and differs in a number of minor details from the earlier vessel. One thing remains constant: most of the big cruiser's armament is hidden away in vertical launch systems below the deck.*

ability of the battleship. Cruising off the coast of Central America as a warning to the Marxist regime in Nicaragua, the battleship received orders to go to the assistance of the beleaguered US Marines of the Multinational Peacekeeping Force in the Lebanon. A high-speed run through the Panama Canal, across the Atlantic and the length of the Mediterranean saw *New Jersey* on station off Beirut. And at the end of 1983, her guns were used in anger for the first time since the Vietnam War.

The Soviet *Kirov* is a very different breed. Often called a battlecruiser in the Western press, it carries the Russian designation of *Raketnyy kreyser* or missile cruiser. As with most Russian ships, *Kirov*'s role does not exactly fit into Western practice or designation systems.

Unlike the 'Iowas', *Kirov* and her sisters carry a wide array of anti-submarine and anti-aircraft weapons in addition to their anti-surface ship missiles. Soviet naval doctrine used to consider all surface ships to be subordinate to submarine operations, and indeed *Kirov* is well suited to leading a surface force supporting friendly SSBNs and hunting out enemy submarines. But these powerful ships are equally suited to a more aggressive role, as

---

33 'Sovremenny' Class

 FORMER USSR

From the 1980s the Soviet surface fleet began to initiate problems for NATO rather than responding to Western developments. One of the new classes of warship that has changed the situation at sea was the **'Sovremenny' class.** The first Soviet destroyer designed for surface warfare since the end of World War II. *Sovremenny* and her sisters are big, robust vessels, well suited to operations in the unpleasant weather found in the north Atlantic. The powerful missile armament is made more effective by the single helicopter carried, which is not for anti-submarine warfare – the Kamov 'Hormone-B' is used primarily for over-the-horizon identification and targetting for the

The 'Sovremenny' class was the third leg of the Soviet surface action group concept. Like Kirov *and* Slava*, these big destroyers are optimised for surface action, and were built in numbers.*

destroyer's long-range anti-ship missiles. It is also equipped with powerful fully automatic guns in twin turrets.

Specification
Displacement: 6,200 tons standard and 7,800 tons full load
Dimensions: length 155.6 m (510 ft 6 in); beam 17.3 m (56 ft 9 in); draught 6.5 m (21 ft 4 in)

Machinery: geared turbo-pressurised steam turbines delivering 100,000 shp to two propellers
Speed: 36 knots
Aircraft: one missile guidance helicopter
Armament: two quadruple SS-N-22 anti-ship missile launchers, two twin

130-mm (5.12-in) guns, two SA-N-7 SAM launchers with 48 missiles, four 30-mm Close-in Weapons, two RBU-1000 anti-submarine rocket launchers, two twin 533-mm (21-in) torpedo tubes, and 30-50 mines
Complement: 350

---

34 'Niteroi' class

 BRAZIL

Most navies cannot afford to build or operate large, highly sophisticated vessels like those of the superpowers. Typically, the largest vessels they operate will be frigates, and they will often be required to carry out a number of tasks, including surface action. The Brazilian navy operates a number of **'Niteroi' class** frigates in the anti-submarine role, but two ships were completed as general-purpose vessels. Based on the British Vosper-Thornycroft Mk 10 design, the 'Niterois' are considered to be exceptionally economical and do not require large crews: another important factor in small navies. Small, but modern in conception, they were fitted with action information systems.

Most navies cannot afford large warships, making do with smaller vessels. The Brazilian 'Niteroi' is typical: basically an ASW design, but two of the class were completed with general-purpose armament.

that will allow co-ordinated ASW and surface strike operations with other units of the Brazilian navy.

Specification
Displacement: 3,200 tons standard and 3,800 tons full load
Dimensions: length 129.2 m (423 ft 11 in); beam 13.5 m (44 ft 4 in); draught 5.5 m (18 ft)

Machinery: CODOG (Combined Diesel or Gas Turbine) delivering 15,760 shp (diesels) or 56,000 shp (gas turbines) to two propellers
Speed: 22 knots (diesels) or 30.5 knots (gas turbines)
Aircraft: one Westland Lynx helicopter

Armament: four single Exocet anti-ship missiles, two 4.5-in (115-mm) guns, three 40-mm AA guns, one twin ASW rocket launcher with 54 rockets, two triple tubes for lightweight torpedoes, plus up to five depth charges
Complement: 200

It costs more than $400 million to reactivate an 'Iowa' class battleship to 1990s standards.

the nucleus of a surface action group. Unfortunately, the nuclear/steam plant proved very expensive, and the Russian Navy can no longer run these impressive ships.

Recent US defence cuts have put the battleships' future in question, however. Two out of the four 'Iowas' are to be laid up in the early 1990s. The other two are likely to remain the nucleus of a surface action force for some time to come. Meanwhile, the expansion and modernisation of the Soviet navy grows apace. With the entry into service of the first of the new 'Tbilisi'-class carriers, it may be that the US Navy's retirement of half of its battleship force is a hasty measure.

The wide open spaces of Kirov's deck belie the fact that this is one of the most heavily armed vessels built since the war. True, it only carries 20 SS-N-20 anti-ship missiles compared with more than 1,000 16-inch rounds aboard a battleship, but each of those missiles is capable of crippling a carrier.

The Rise of

Battleships grew very little in the days of sail, but the coming of steel construction and steam power changed all that. Their evolution in the 20th century was explosive. In less than 50 years, they doubled in length (as these illustrations show), doubled in speed, quadrupled in tonnage, and increased their fighting power by an incalculable amount.

1916
USS *Pennsylvania*

USS Pennsylvania's 14 inch guns were smaller than those on contemporary German and British battleships, but by using triple turrets she could carry more. Pennsylvania was severely damaged by the Japanese attack on Pearl Harbor in 1941, but was repaired and served through the latter part of the war. She ended her days as an atom-bomb target at Bikini Atoll.

1927
HMS *Nelson*

The two 'Nelson' class battleships were the first completed under the terms of the Washington Treaty, which limited displacement to 35,000 tons and gun calibre to 16 inches. This left little room for more powerful engines, so the new battleships were slow. Even so, both did sterling service throughout World War II, with the Rodney proving more than a match for the German Bismarck.

Above: Battleships were not exactly lively performers in the years after World War I. *Nelson's* 45,000 horsepower engines drove the vessel at 23.5 knots on a good day.

1941
HMS *Bismarck*

Bismarck *was the first full-scale battleship built for the German Kriegsmarine after Hitler came to power. Its design followed closely from those of the World War I 'Baden' class but with considerably increased power. Supposedly built to the Washington treaty limit of 35,000 tons it was in fact much larger, weighing in at over 50,000 tons full load. Bismarck's first (and last) operational cruise began in May 1941, when in company with the heavy cruiser Prinz Eugen the battleship attempted to break out into the Atlantic, where it could wreak havoc amongst the convoys so necessary to Britain's survival. In an epic chase, during which the full power of the Royal Navy was brought to bear on the raiders, Bismarck sank the battlecruiser HMS Hood before being brought to account by the guns of the battleships HMS Rodney and King George V.*

Below: *Bismarck* was based on a World War I battleship design. It was much larger, however, and had vastly increased power, capable of driving the 50,000-ton vessel to nearly 30 knots.

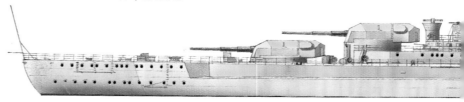

e BATTLESHIP

1892 HMS *Royal Sovereign*

In the 1890s, it was a firmly held belief that the Royal Navy should be stronger than the next two largest navies combined. As a result, for the first time battleships were built in numbers to form homogeneous squadrons. The eight 'Royal Sovereigns' contrasted strongly with French practice, which was to build ships individually.

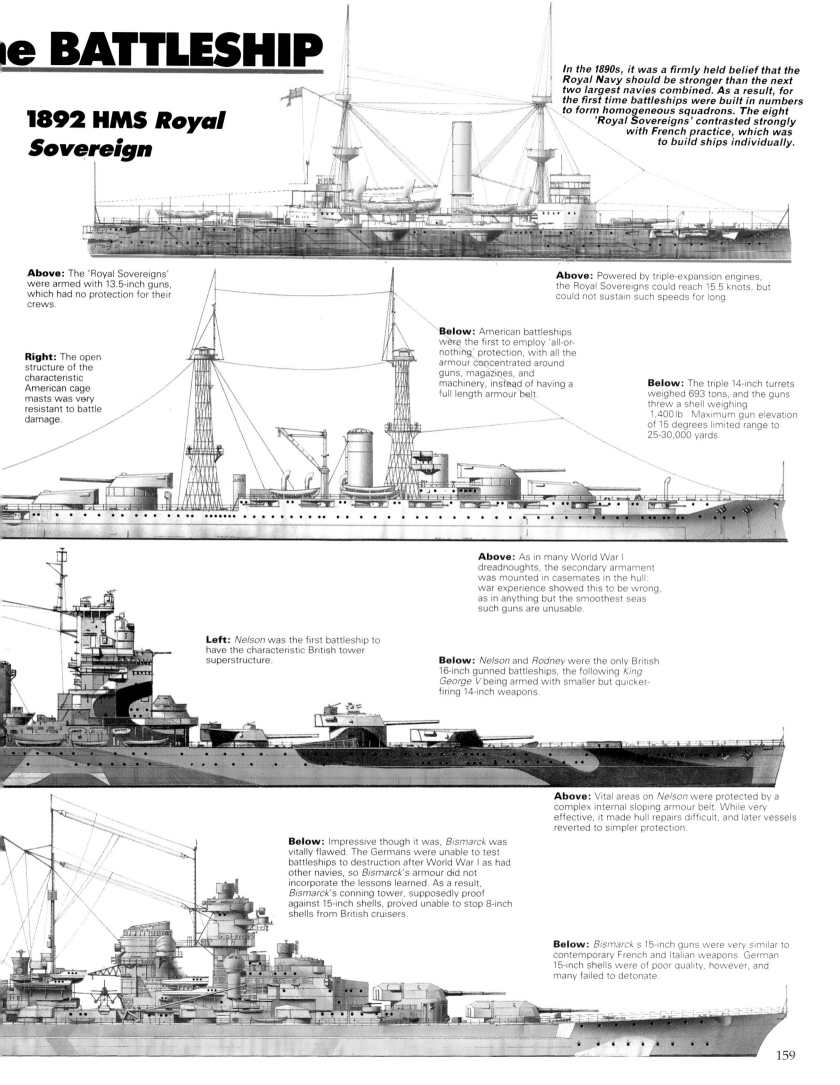

Above: The 'Royal Sovereigns' were armed with 13.5-inch guns, which had no protection for their crews.

Right: The open structure of the characteristic American cage masts was very resistant to battle damage.

Above: Powered by triple-expansion engines, the Royal Sovereigns could reach 15.5 knots, but could not sustain such speeds for long.

Below: American battleships were the first to employ 'all-or-nothing' protection, with all the armour concentrated around guns, magazines, and machinery, instead of having a full length armour belt.

Below: The triple 14-inch turrets weighed 693 tons, and the guns threw a shell weighing 1,400 lb Maximum gun elevation of 15 degrees limited range to 25-30,000 yards.

Above: As in many World War I dreadnoughts, the secondary armament was mounted in casemates in the hull: war experience showed this to be wrong, as in anything but the smoothest seas such guns are unusable.

Left: *Nelson* was the first battleship to have the characteristic British tower superstructure.

Below: *Nelson* and *Rodney* were the only British 16-inch gunned battleships, the following *King George V* being armed with smaller but quicker-firing 14-inch weapons.

Above: Vital areas on *Nelson* were protected by a complex internal sloping armour belt. While very effective, it made hull repairs difficult, and later vessels reverted to simpler protection.

Below: Impressive though it was, *Bismarck* was vitally flawed. The Germans were unable to test battleships to destruction after World War I as had other navies, so *Bismarck*'s armour did not incorporate the lessons learned. As a result, *Bismarck*'s conning tower, supposedly proof against 15-inch shells, proved unable to stop 8-inch shells from British cruisers.

Below: *Bismarck* s 15-inch guns were very similar to contemporary French and Italian weapons. German 15-inch shells were of poor quality, however, and many failed to detonate.

GUNS OF THE IOWA

Battleships are all about guns. Not the one or two medium guns thought fitting in these missile-conscious days, but nine massive 16-inch weapons that are among the most powerful artillery ever.

*Above: **USS** Iowa was first commissioned in 1943, and the ship's new seal, after recommissioning in 1984, includes that date among the emblems of the state of Iowa.*

*Right: **USS** Iowa is seen while testing her guns at the naval firing range near Vieques Island in the Caribbean in 1984. It is a full 15-gun broadside: the titanic flash of Iowa's nine 16-inch weapons obscures the smaller flash from the six guns of the starboard five-inch turrets.*

Inside th

The 16-inch gun and Mk 7 triple turret designed for the 'Iowa' class were a product of the Washington Treaty, an agreement that dealt with the size and power of battleships between the wars. The new gun and turret were the largest that could be fitted on to a battleship of 45,000 tons standard displacement, which was the treaty limit. The walls of the turret are immensely thick, both to protect from hostile shellfire and to protect the ship in the case of an accidental explosion.

Fatal a

19 April 1989. USS *Iowa* is pr coast of Puerto Rico. A mass 2 turret blasts smoke and de Obviously there has been a n of valiant firefighting and res 47 gun crew survives.

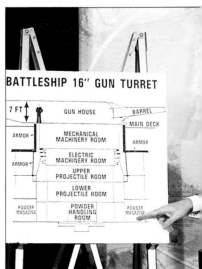

Above: A camera with a very fast shutter speed catches the instant a shell leaves the muzzle of USS Iowa's forward turret. At this point, the one-ton projectile is travelling at 825 m/sec (2,700 ft per second).

Left: There are two components to a large shell. Projectiles (seen here) can weigh up to 1225 kg. The separate propellant charge comes in 45-kg bags. A full six-bag charge can send a shell over 42,000 yards (over 38 km).

BATTLESHIP 16" GUN TURRET

7 FT | GUN HOUSE | BARREL
| | MAIN DECK
ARMOR | MECHANICAL MACHINERY ROOM | ARMOR
ARMOR | ELECTRIC MACHINERY ROOM |
| UPPER PROJECTILE ROOM |
| LOWER PROJECTILE ROOM |
POWDER MAGAZINE | POWDER HANDLING ROOM | POWDER MAGAZINE

e gun turret

4 Loading
Shells are united with six bags of propellant in the breech. Reduced charges use bags of the same thickness but of smaller diameter. The lighter charge cuts pressure in the breech on firing, reducing gun wear and increasing barrel life.

3 Handling
Shells and powder come to the turret on separate hoists. Surprisingly, the powder comes up a single-stage hoist. The doors at the top and bottom of the barbette, which can not be opened simultaneously, ensure no contact between turret and powder store in the event of an explosion.

5 Firing
The shells are propelled down the barrel by an explosion which creates 17 tons of pressure in the breech. By the time it leaves the muzzle a one-ton shell is travelling at 2,700 ft per second. Barrels need replacing after firing 300 rounds.

Below: The senior ratings in one of USS Iowa's 5-inch secondary turrets pose beside the breeches of the dual-purpose AA/surface action weapons in their charge.

2 Projectiles
Projectiles for the 16-in guns are stored behind thick armour on two levels of the barbette. Currently, the battleships are using up the stock of World War II and Korean War vintage projectiles, most of which are high capacity HE shells.

1 Powder
The most volatile part of a battleship's ammunition is the powder used to blast the shells over great distances. Powder is stored in cotton and silk bags in magazines well below the waterline for maximum safety, and is hoisted direct to the turret when required

Below: Each powder container holds three 100-lb bags of highly explosive propellant. There would have been at least 18 such bags in Number 2 turret of the Iowa at the time of the accident.

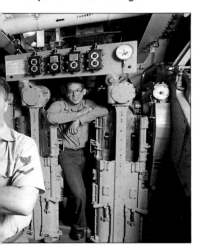

ccident

ctising gunnery off the
ve explosion within Number
ris out of the gunports.
ajor disaster and, in spite
cue attempts, none of the

Below left: In the aftermath of the fatal explosion in the gun turret aboard the USS Iowa, US Navy captain Larry Seaquist conducts a briefing for journalists at the Pentagon during which he explains the operational and safety features of the Mk 7 triple 16-in turret fielded by the 'Iowa' class.

Above: The turrets are the most highly protected areas on a battleship, which is not surprising when you consider their highly explosive contents. Armour thickness varies between 184 mm on the turret tops to 445 mm on the turret front and sides of the barbettes.

Left: The moment of the explosion in the turret of USS Iowa. The heavy armour plate of the turret is enough to contain the holocaust caused by the detonation of tons of explosive material, so there is little damage to the rest of the ship.

Right: Firefighters train hoses on the red-hot metal of Number 2 turret. The force of the explosion was contained within the turret, which saved the ship but unfortunately meant that the gun crew had no chance of survival.

SURFA

Inset: A US Navy rating plots tactical information in the CIC (Combat Information Centre) of an 'Iowa' class battleship. 'Iowas' were equipped to control the anti-ship weaponry of all the ships of a Surface Action Group from this location.

1 Control

One of the reasons for the Surface Action Group's existence was to reinforce the US Navy's hard-worked Carrier Battle Groups. The surface action group usually comprises the battleship, one or two air defence cruisers, one or two destroyers, some frigates, and a large replenishment ship. Each of the components of the group has its function, and tactical control of the group is carried out by the most suitable vessel. The battleship itself

CE ACTION

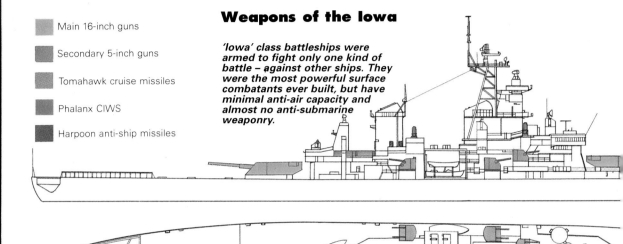

Weapons of the Iowa

- Main 16-inch guns
- Secondary 5-inch guns
- Tomahawk cruise missiles
- Phalanx CIWS
- Harpoon anti-ship missiles

'Iowa' class battleships were armed to fight only one kind of battle – against other ships. They were the most powerful surface combatants ever built, but have minimal anti-air capacity and almost no anti-submarine weaponry.

Left: USS *New Jersey cruises off the coast of Central America. The battleship forms the centre of a Surface Action Group, brought into being to relieve the US Navy's hard-worked carrier battle groups, and to add to American power-projection capability on the oceans of the world.*

2 Air Defence

The battleship has almost no defence against air attack. Anti-air warfare is the responsibility of the specialised radars and control systems of escort vessels like the 'AEGIS' class cruiser *Yorktown*. Apart from its own missiles *Yorktown* can use those of other vessels in the group to deal with an incoming airborne threat. The battleship does have a last-ditch defence in the shape of four Phalanx 20-mm CIWS Close-In Weapon Systems. These are radar-guided Gatling-type cannon that spit out a stream of shells. In a split-second encounter, the outgoing projectiles and the incoming target are tracked simultaneously, aim being adjusted until the threat is destroyed.

Below: The 'AEGIS' class cruiser USS *Yorktown fires a Standard SM-2 SAM.*

Right: A Phalanx close-in weapon system spits out 20-mm shells at incoming surface-skimming missiles.

has little anti-air capability, so air cover is handled by one of the escorting cruisers, which are designed for the task. Similarly, anti-submarine warfare is the preserve of one of the escorting destroyers which is geared to that kind of warfare. When it comes to surface warfare, all group assets are controlled from the battleship's CEC, or combat engagement centre (seen left). Most of the larger ships in the group have Tomahawk missiles, so in combat the Surface Action Group may employ a concept known as Distributed Offense. At combat ranges of several hundred miles, ships can launch missiles from widely separated locations to attack a target from a number of directions simultaneously. All the warships in the group carry Harpoon, so the same tactics can be used at shorter ranges.

Geared almost exclusively to offensive action, battleship weapons are effective from under one mile to as much as 2,500 miles. Each has its strengths and weaknesses, and the choice of weapon in each tactical situation is important.

4 Guns

Right: A Marine's-eye view of hostile gun positions outside Beirut in 1984. This time the fanatics are on the receiving end, as the USS New Jersey shells them into silence.

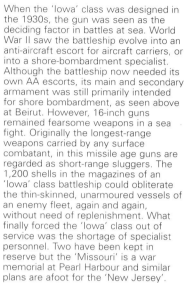

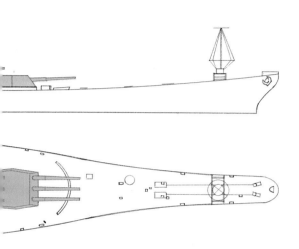

When the 'Iowa' class was designed in the 1930s, the gun was seen as the deciding factor in battles at sea. World War II saw the battleship evolve into an anti-aircraft escort for aircraft carriers, or into a shore-bombardment specialist. Although the battleship now needed its own AA escorts, its main and secondary armament was still primarily intended for shore bombardment, as seen above at Beirut. However, 16-inch guns remained fearsome weapons in a sea fight. Originally the longest-range weapons carried by any surface combatant, in this missile age guns are regarded as short-range sluggers. The 1,200 shells in the magazines of an 'Iowa' class battleship could obliterate the thin-skinned, unarmoured vessels of an enemy fleet, again and again, without need of replenishment. What finally forced the 'Iowa' class out of service was the shortage of specialist personnel. Two have been kept in reserve but the 'Missouri' is a war memorial at Pearl Harbour and similar plans are afoot for the 'New Jersey'.

Left: 16-inch muzzle flash highlights one of six 5-inch turrets. The battleship's secondary armament is equivalent to the gun armament of six modern warships.

3 Harpoon

The RGM-84 Harpoon is used in medium-range encounters out to 100 km, or against fast-moving surface targets. The battleship has 16 Harpoons, and controls the 40 or 50 missiles carried by the rest of the group. Most damage is done by Harpoon's 227-kg (500-lb) blast-penetration warhead, but any unused propellant is spread around when the missile strikes, and when it burns it does its own damage. How many missiles are fired in an encounter will depend upon the target. One missile will destroy a small target like a missile boat, or disable a destroyer or frigate. Cruisers might require three or four hits, while large targets like carriers need to be hit by four or five missiles to knock them out.

A Harpoon missile is seen in the split second before it hits a frigate, when its warhead will rip a huge hole in the target vessel.

5 Tomahawk

Long-range action calls for the use of Tomahawk. The anti-ship version of this cruise missile has a 450 kg (1,000 lb) high-explosive warhead adapted from the obsolete Bullpup missile. Tomahawk is fired in the general direction of a target indicated by a third source, which can be a maritime reconnaissance aircraft or a satellite. Once in the general area of the target the missile climbs to search altitude and begins scanning with its own onboard radar, or with other homing systems such as imaging infra-red. Once the target has been detected Tomahawk can be programmed to circle around to approach from a different direction. A nuclear warhead is also available for long-range land attack.

A battleship-fired Tomahawk sets out on a flight that will see it make a direct hit on a target (inset) over 400 miles away.

CLASH of Titans

The battleship reached the height of its power and glory during World War II, but was already being superseded by the aircraft-carrier on the world's oceans. Nevertheless, the battleship's swansong was spectacular.

Above: Few could have believed at the outbreak of the war that the aircraft was to bring about the downfall of the battleship.

EYE WITNESS

"**M**y cruiser had taken 13 bomb hits and seven torpedoes. Everywhere I looked I saw destroyers sinking or in flames. Only two seemed unharmed and they were darting protectively about the *Yamato*. As I was lifted on the crest of a wave I saw *Yamato*, six miles away. Planes swarmed around her like gnats, but she was moving: a beautiful sight. But within 10 minutes I watched in despair as the 'unsinkable' battleship rolled over and disappeared into the ocean."

Captain Tameichi Hara, IJN cruiser *Yahagi*

Above: The pall of smoke rising from the East China sea marks the grave of the Imperial Japanese Navy super-battleship Yamato. It was the most powerful battleship ever built, but even so could not fend off the hundreds of American carrier aircraft that were her doom.

The Yamato *was a 70,000-ton monster, armed with nine 18.1-inch guns able to reach out 48 km and protected by armour plate ranging from 410 mm to a massive 650 mm in thickness.*

The Japanese battleship steamed towards the huge Allied fleet off Okinawa. It was a one-way trip; those aboard knew that they were likely to die. But just let them get in amongst the American landings, and those huge 18.1-inch guns would wreak havoc. The *Yamato* was the ultimate battleship, mounting the heaviest broadside ever seen on a man-of-war, yet her downfall was brought about by a small American floatplane. It located

including two battleships. Fifteen-hundred French sailors lost their lives. Elsewhere in the Mediterranean, aggressive action by the British fleet gave it the upper hand over the Italians. In an action off Calabria, the old battleship *Warspite* scored a hit on the enemy flagship *Giulio Cesare* at a range of 26,000 yards (over 23 kilometres), which removed any aggressive notions on the part of the Italian admiral.

Germany was no more immune to the lure of the battleships than anybody else. German battleships like the *Bismarck* were intended to range the sea lanes, destroying Britain's merchant lifeline, even though U-boats were already doing that more cheaply and more effectively.

Run to ground

On her first cruise, in May 1941, *Bismarck* and the accompanying heavy cruiser *Prinz Eugen* were run to ground near Iceland by British warships, including the battlecruiser *Hood* and the brand-new battleship *Prince of Wales*. In a dawn action, *Hood*'s light armour proved a fatal liability and she blew up. *Bismarck* went on her way after suffering minor damage, occasionally exchanging long-range fire with the more seriously hurt *Prince of Wales*. Eluding their pursuers, *Bismarck* and *Prinz Eugen* separated before heading for Brest, but a massive air and sea search by the Royal Navy relocated the battleship. Slowed down by a carrier-launched aircraft's torpedo, *Bismarck* was eventually brought to bay and battered into oblivion by the battleships *King George V* and *Rodney*.

Seven months later, the battleships of the US Pacific Fleet at Pearl Harbor were to be the victims of a graphic Japanese demonstration that power at sea had moved on. Hundreds of Japanese planes, diving out of the blue, left eight battleships burning in the water, with the *Arizona* and the *Oklahoma* being completely destroyed. The surprise attack proved that carriers were the new capital ships.

Many important Pacific battles would take place without any of the main participants even seeing each other, their aircraft ranging over hundreds of miles of water.

The Italian battle fleet fires broadsides on exercise before the war. The Italians had powerful, well armed ships, and could have been a threat to the British, but the Italian navy was never able to compete with the Royal Navy.

Yamato at 11.30 in the morning, and at 12.20 the battleship's lookouts spotted hordes of US carrier aircraft in the distance. The first bomb hit *Yamato* at 12.40, and within minutes the giant battleship had been struck by at least 12 torpedoes. Burning heavily and listing to one side, the helpless ship blew up an hour later, taking most of her crew with her. It was 7 April 1945, and the battleship's reign as queen of the seas was well and truly over.

When World War II broke out, the battleship was still thought to be the ultimate expression of sea power, even in the navies which had developed their carrier forces.

After the fall of France, the French fleet fled to North Africa. However, the prospect of Germany gaining control of the ships of the French navy was unacceptable to the British, so Royal Navy battleships attacked the anchorages of their former ally and sank many French warships,

Curiously, although Japan provided conclusive proof of the importance of seaborne air power, the Imperial Japanese Navy still believed in the power of the battleship. Even the great carrier battle of Midway had been initiated with the main aim of drawing the US Fleet within range of the guns of Admiral Yamamoto's battleships.

When in 1942 the Americans started to strike back at the Japanese, the waters of the Solomon Islands became the location for a series of naval battles as fierce as any in history. Destroyers, cruisers, and aircraft-carriers all played their part, but it also was one of the few occasions when American and Japanese capital ships slugged it out face-to-face.

The battleships *Hiei* and *Kirishima* were being used to bombard the US Marines on Guadalcanal when on the night of 12/13 November they blundered into a US cruiser force. The Americans suffered greatly in a confused and vicious night action, but the *Hiei* was so badly damaged she had to be scuttled. Two nights later the *Kirishima* tried again, but this time there were two US battleships present. *Kirishima* quickly got the better of the USS *South Dakota*, whose fighting ability had been curtailed by electrical faults in her turrets, but in the confusion the Japanese failed to spot the USS *Washington* creeping to within 8,000 yards range. When *Washington* opened fire with point-blank salvoes of 16-inch shells, *Kirishima* was done for. Battered to a blazing hulk, she was scuttled the next day.

Back in Europe, action had shifted to the Arctic convoys taking supplies from the Western allies to the Soviet Union. U-boats and aircraft were the major

threats, but the Royal Navy was obsessed with the danger of the German battleship *Tirpitz* or the battlecruiser *Scharnhorst* pouncing from their lairs in northern Norway to get in amongst the convoys. In December 1943, *Scharnhorst* tried to do so.

Unwelcome shock

The weather was so bad her escorting destroyers had to turn back, and the battlecruiser failed at the first attempt to get through the British cruiser screen to the merchant ships beyond. As *Scharnhorst* moved round to make a second attempt, it sailed directly towards units of the Home Fleet, acting as distant heavy escort to the convoy. Starshells bursting

Right: The British 'King George V' class proved very effective, with the King George V herself helping to end the career of the Bismarck and the Duke of York sinking the Scharnhorst.

overhead must have been a big surprise to the crew of the *Scharnhorst*, but the distant flash of gunfire and the arrival of the first salvo of 14-inch shells from the battleship HMS *Duke of York* would have been a far more unwelcome shock. Severely outclassed, the *Scharnhorst* was sunk, and very few survivors were picked up out of the icy waters. With the surrender of the Italian fleet earlier in the year, *Tirpitz* was now the only capital ship threat to the Allies in European waters. But *Tirpitz* never ventured out to confront the Royal Navy, first being damaged by midget submarines and finally sunk by the RAF.

Even though they had lost

primacy at sea, battleships were still extremely useful weapons. In the island-hopping campaigns of the Pacific, they brought their awesome firepower down on Japanese defences before the landings and supported the Marines once they were ashore. In Normandy, battleship fire kept the Germans from concentrating any troops against the beachhead in its first days, when the Allied invasion of Europe could still have been swept into the sea. At the same time on the other side of the world, the US Navy was invading the Marianas. There, the battleships formed a gun-line capable of putting up a wall of flak between attacking Japanese carrier planes and the US Navy's

Left: HMS Nelson fires a salvo. Her broadside was the most powerful in the history of the Royal Navy, and proved a potent shore bombardment weapon.

Below: The titanic shell splashes from the guns of HMS Rodney dwarf the Bismarck just minutes before the massive German battleship is smashed to a hulk.

The battleships of the US Pacific Fleet were caught napping at Pearl Harbor. USS Pennsylvania was badly damaged in dry dock (main picture). Most of the other battleships were moored to Ford Island (far left, in a view from a Japanese plane). Within minutes the pride of the US Navy was sinking to the bottom of Pearl Harbor, including the battleships Tennessee and West Virginia (near left).

EYE WITNESS

"I was sitting at the breakfast table in the wardroom when the alarm was broadcast to all ships. 'Air raid, Pearl Harbor. This is no drill!' Assembly was sounded and the fire and rescue party was called away. As I rushed out, General Quarters was sounded. As I went up the ladder to the starboard side of the quarterdeck, I heard the word being passed by word of mouth that 'the Japs are attacking.' As I reached the quarterdeck I felt the ship being hit."

Lieutenant C.V. Ricketts, USS *West Virginia*

IN COMBAT

The old battleship USS New Mexico *pours 14-inch fire onto Japanese positions in the Marianas Islands, just before the invasion of Saipan. Pre-invasion bombardment had become a prime battleship task, and it was one that the veterans could do very well.*

EYE WITNESS

"The Japanese are coming after us. Our aircraft will first knock out the enemy aircraft-carriers, then will attack the enemy battleships and cruisers. The battleships of Admiral Lee's battle line will move from their air defence tasks and are to destroy the enemy fleet. Action against a retreating enemy must be pushed vigorously by all hands to complete the destruction of his fleet."

Admiral Raymond Spruance, Commander, Fifth Fleet, Saipan

carrier task forces, and so played a part in the 'Great Marianas Turkey Shoot' which brought an end to Japanese naval air power.

Four months later, battleships were heavily involved in the greatest sea battle in history. At Leyte Gulf, Japan's aim was to destroy the US amphibious invasion of the Philippines. To that end, a complex plan was set in motion to lure the American carriers away and make a multi-pronged attack on the invasion fleet. One force, including *Yamato* and *Musashi*, the largest battleships ever built, was intercepted by US carrier aircraft and submarines in the Sibuyan Sea. *Musashi* was sunk and the rest turned back. A second force, composed of the battleships *Fuso* and *Yamashiro*, tried to break through the Surigao Strait. Here they were met by destroyers, which managed to torpedo the *Fuso*, and by a line of old American battleships. In the last battleship-versus-battleship action in history, *Yamashiro* was sunk by the concentrated fire of USS *Tennessee, West Virginia, Mississippi, Maryland, California* and *Pennsylvania*, all but *Mississippi* being salvaged and rebuilt veterans of Pearl Harbor.

Meanwhile, the Japanese force that had been mauled in the Sibuyan Sea had reversed course once again, and penetrating the San Bernardino Strait by night had come upon the invasion fleet in the morning. The big American carriers had been decoyed north, taking with them all the modern battleships. The old battleships were in the Surigao Strait. All that stood between the Japanese and the invasion was a small force of escort carriers and lightly armed destroyer escorts.

Japanese indecision

For the first time, the Americans were at the mercy of the heavy guns of *Yamato, Nagato, Kongo* and *Haruna*. Fortunately, the escort group's plucky defence and Japanese Admiral Kurita's indecision saved the invasion, and the Japanese retired after mauling the escorts but without touching the amphibious squadrons. Japan had lost its last chance to influence the war, and apart from *Yamato's* last fateful voyage, the war was over for the big ships of the Imperial Japanese Navy, and for the battleship as a shaper of naval strategy.

Right: USS West Virginia *opens fire on the Japanese battleship* Yamashiro *in the Surigao strait. Three years after being little more than wreckage at Pearl Harbor, the old US Navy battlewagons were victorious in the last battleship versus battleship action in history.*

USS California *returns the compliment to the Japanese, firing salvoes into Okinawa only three years after being lifted from the mud at Pearl Harbor.*

The Type 42 Royal Navy destroyer HMS Manchester. This well-endowed ship is armed with missiles, guns, torpedoes and decoys.